高职高专经管类专业系列教材

GAOZHI GAOZHUAN JINGGUAN LEI ZHUANYE XILIE JIAOCAI

WAIMAO DANZHENG SHIWU

外贸单证实务

主　编　殷秀梅

副主编　刘　芳　李　敏

参　编　王　茜　向宇翔　黄　颖

　　　　彭　奇　刘莎莎

重庆大学出版社

图书在版编目（CIP）数据

外贸单证实务 / 殷秀梅主编. -- 重庆：重庆大学
出版社，2022.8
高职高专经管类专业系列教材
ISBN 978-7-5689-3378-0

Ⅰ．①外…　Ⅱ．①殷…　Ⅲ．①进出口贸易—原始凭证
—高等职业教育—教材　Ⅳ．①F740.44

中国版本图书馆 CIP 数据核字（2022）第 120808 号

高职高专经管类专业系列教材

外贸单证实务

主　编　殷秀梅
副主编　刘　芳　李　敏
策划编辑：顾丽萍
特约编辑：蒋艳松
责任编辑：杨　敬　　版式设计：顾丽萍
责任校对：关德强　　责任印制：张　策

*

重庆大学出版社出版发行
出版人：饶帮华
社址：重庆市沙坪坝区大学城西路 21 号
邮编：401331
电话：(023) 88617190　88617185(中小学)
传真：(023) 88617186　88617166
网址：http://www.cqup.com.cn
邮箱：fxk@cqup.com.cn (营销中心)
全国新华书店经销
重庆天旭印务有限责任公司印刷

*

开本：787mm×1092mm　1/16　印张：12.5　字数：300 千
2022 年 8 月第 1 版　　2022 年 8 月第 1 次印刷
印数：1—3 000
ISBN 978-7-5689-3378-0　定价：39.00 元

截至 2022 年 3 月 23 日,中国已经同 149 个国家和 32 个国际组织签署 200 余份共建"一带一路"合作文件。联合国安理会等组织的重要决议也纳入"一带一路"建设内容,"一带一路"倡议为全球经济贸易往来提供了良好的国际政商环境。

随着数字化时代的到来,服务于国际贸易的一些交易手段变得比以前快捷和便利,突出的表现是国际贸易手段的电子化。随着 EDI 和电子单据的广泛运用,高效、高品质的单证不但为外贸企业增强了竞争力,也为企业树立良好形象、建立较高的信誉起到不可估量的作用。

外贸单证工作是外贸从业人员必须掌握的基础性工作,外贸单证贯穿每笔进出口贸易的全过程,处理外贸单证业务也是整个外贸流程的核心业务环节。为国际贸易、商务英语和其他商务语言类专业开设"外贸单证实务"这门课程,旨在培养懂得外贸单证基础知识,熟悉外贸单证工作流程,熟练掌握外贸单证缮制技能和能进行外贸单证操作管理的高素质技能型人才。

本书编写具备五个特色:一是以一笔完整的出口贸易为主线,以一家虚拟公司单证员殷实在出口流程中各时段典型工作任务为工作情境,以殷实各时段工作任务所需知识和能力选取教学内容。二是在工作任务和职业能力分析的基础上,与企业和行业顾问共建外贸单证专家组共同开发课程标准。三是以课程思政为落实立德树人根本任务的重要环节,教材中的每个项目在原有知识目标和能力目标的基础上,增加了课程思政目标,供教师在挖掘课程思政元素时参考。四是书中涉及的外贸单证力求来源于外贸企业、银行和货运代理公司等一线真实材料,单证业务贴近实际;每个项目后配有实操训练,实操训练内容部分来源于单证员考试真题,部分来源于企业的真实业务,在强调实训的基础上,又兼顾单证员考试培训,内容全面、形式多样,可同时满足课堂教学、模拟实训和单证员考证培训的多项功能要求。五是本书内容力求与时事政策相一致。例如,本书在关检融合统一申报系统于 2018 年 8 月 1 日正式上线后,对海关启用新报关单进行了说明;又如,增加了新版原产地证的样本等。

本书的编写思路是以市场岗位能力需求为依据,采用情景化教学模式,以工作项目和任务驱动为导向,按照出口贸易流程中各时段单证员的典型工作任务,将其划分为 12 个工作学习项目,即外贸单证员工作基础,信用证的开立、审核与修改,发票缮制与操作,包装单据缮制与操作,商业汇票缮制与操作,运输相关单据缮制与操作,保险单据缮制与操作,报检报关单证缮制与操作,原产地证书缮制与操作,装运通知与船公司证明缮制与操作,出口商证明缮制与操作和出口结汇单证缮制与操作。每一个项目细分为若干任务模块,每一个项目下都有实操训练,供课堂实训课采用,使学生在"做"的实践中获得实践技能,为学生零距离上岗奠定基础。本书附有来自外贸企业的部分真实外贸单证,可供老师和学生参考选用。

本书由殷秀梅老师任主编,殷秀梅老师曾在湖南省金环进出口总公司先后从事外贸单证员、跟单员和外贸业务员工作,有多年的进出口实战经历;后又从事高职国际贸易专业教学工作十余年,主讲"外贸单证""外贸跟单"和"外贸业务实务"课程。刘芳、李敏老师任副主编。原湖南省金环进出口总公司经理李明和外贸业务员肖龙翔担任本书企业顾问。另外,湖南外国语职业学院的王茜、向宇翔、黄颖、彭奇、刘莎莎等老师也参与了本书的编写工作。本书在编写过程中,参阅了大量的书籍,得到了外贸从业人员的支持及多位领导和同事的无私帮助,谨在此表示衷心的感谢。由于编者水平有限,书中不足之处在所难免,恳请各位专家和读者批评、指正。

编　者

2022 年 2 月

CONTENTS 目录

项目一　外贸单证员工作基础

【项目目标】

知识目标

- 明确外贸单证工作的基本要求
- 掌握外贸单证的分类
- 了解外贸单证员的专业素质
- 掌握出口信用证常见风险的预防措施
- 明确外贸出口流程中各时段单证的种类

能力目标

- 能够画出外贸出口流程中各时段单证流转图

思政目标

- 通过对外贸单证工作要求的学习,培养学生诚实守信、团结协作、善于沟通的职业素养
- 通过对单证种类的学习,培养学生严谨细致的工作态度

【工作情景】

　　殷实从国际贸易专业毕业后,就进入了上海威尔进出口公司工作,领导分配给她的岗位是外贸单证员。上班第一天,师傅对她说:"外贸单证员就是从事进出口货物报检、报关、运输、保险、跨境收/付款、涉外收支申报等所需要的各种单证的准备、填制、申办、审核、转递工作的操作人员。国际商务通常表现为货物和货款的双向交流,货物的交付是通过单证(买卖合同和运输单据等)完成的,货款的收付虽然采用不同的支付方式,但也是通过单证(信用证和商业发票等)实现的。"由此可见,单证是进出口货物贸易的核心,抓住了这个核心,进出口货物贸易中的所有相关问题都能迎刃而解。

【工作任务】

任务一　外贸单证工作的基本要求

　　外贸单证不能随意缮制,必须符合国际商务相关惯例、法令规定和实际需要,在实际操作中,原则上应做到正确、完整、及时、简洁、清晰,以便顺利收汇。

一、正确

正确是单证工作的前提,是安全收汇的保证。"正确"至少包括以下两个方面的内容。

1. 各种单据必须做到"三相符"

各种单据必须做到"三相符"(单据与信用证相符、单据与单据相符、单据与贸易合同相符),其中"单证相符"占首要地位。"单单相符"以"单证相符"为前提,在现实操作中若单证不符,即使"单单相符",也会遭到银行的拒付。"单同相符"是指单据的内容应该与合同一致。通常从银行的角度来说,它们只控制"单证相符"和"单单相符"。而从外贸出口企业的角度来说,除以上3个"相符"外,还有一个"单货相符"也需要进行严格控制,这样单证才能真实地代表出运的货物,确保履约正常和安全收汇。

2. 各种单据必须符合有关国际惯例和进出口国的有关法令与规定

各种单据必须符合有关国际惯例《跟单信用证统一惯例》(以下简称《UCP600》)和进出口国的有关法令和规定。

二、完整

完整是构成单证合法性的重要条件之一,是单证成为有价证券的基础。"完整"包含3个方面的内容。

1. 单证种类完整

单证在通过银行议付或托收时,一般都是成套的和齐全的,遗漏一种单证,就是单证不完整。例如,在 CIF 交易中,出口商向进口商提供的单证至少应有发票、提单和保险单。出口商只有按信用证或合同规定备齐所需单证,银行(或进口商)才能履行议付或承付的责任。

2. 单证内容完整

单证内容完整,即每一种单证本身的内容(包括单证本身的格式、项目、文字、签章和背书等)必须完备齐全,否则就不能构成有效文件,也就不能被银行接受。

3. 单证份数完整

单证份数完整,即要求出口商必须要按信用证或买卖合同的要求如数交齐各种单证的份数,不能短缺,尤其是提单的份数,更应该按要求出齐。

三、及时

及时是指进出口单证工作的时间性很强,出口商必须紧紧掌握装运期、交单期和信用证的有效期。"及时"出单包括以下两个方面的内容。

1.各种单证的出单日期必须符合逻辑

各种单证都要有一个适当的出单日期,每一种单证的出单日期不能超过信用证规定的有效期或商业习惯的合理日期。如保险单和检验证书的日期应早于提单的日期,而提单的日期不应晚于信用证规定的最迟装运期限,否则,就会造成单证不符。

2.交单议付不得超过信用证规定的交单有效期

如果信用证未对交单有效期作出规定,按《UCP600》的规定:"议付银行将拒绝接受迟于运输单证出单日期21天后提交的单证。"

四、简洁

简洁是指单证的内容应力求简化。《UCP600》指出:"为了防止混淆和误解,银行应劝阻在信用证或任何修改书中加注过多细节的内容。"其目的是避免单证的复杂化,提高工作效率。

五、清晰

清晰是指单证的表面清洁、美观、大方。单证的清晰要求单证格式的设计和缮制力求标准化和规范化,单证内容的排列要行次整齐、字迹清晰、语句流畅、用词简明扼要,更改处要盖校对章或简签。如果单证涂改过多,应重新缮制单证。

任务二　外贸单证的分类

国际商务业务中涉及的单证很多,根据不同的分类标准可以产生不同的类别。

一、根据贸易双方涉及的单证划分

根据贸易双方涉及的单证可分为进口单证和出口单证。

进口单证:进口国的企业及有关部门涉及的单证,包括进口许可证、信用证、进口报关单、成交合同和保险单等。

出口单证:出口国的企业及有关部门涉及的单证,包括出口许可证、出口报关单、包装单据、出库货运单据、商业发票、保险单、汇票、检验检疫证和产地证等。

二、根据单证的性质划分

根据单证的性质可分为金融单据和商业单据。

金融单据:汇票、本票、支票或其他类似用以取得款项的凭证。

商业单据:发票、运输单据、货权凭证或其他类似单据及任何非金融单据。

三、根据单证的用途划分

根据单证的用途可分为资金单据、商业单据、货运单据、保险单据、官方单据、附属单据。

资金单据：汇票、本票、支票等信用工具。

商业单据：商业发票、形式发票、装箱单、重量单等。

货运单据：各种运输方式单据的统称。《UCP600》将运输单据分为七大类：海运提单；不可转让海运单；租船合约提单；空运单、公路、铁路、内河运输单据，专递和邮政收据；报关单；报检单；托运单。

保险单据：保险单、预保单、保险证明、投保单等。

官方单据：海关发票、领事发票、原产地证明书、检验检疫证等。

附属单据：寄单证明、寄样证明、装运通知、船舱证明等。

四、根据业务环节划分

根据进出口业务环节可分为托运单证、结汇单证、进口单证等。

任务三　外贸单证员的专业素质

一、熟练运用英语

外贸企业单证员在日常工作中需要广泛接触和使用英语，因此英语是外贸单证员的基本工作手段。注意：信用证及其他各种相关单据大都采用大写形式。

二、熟悉相关办公自动化软件

进出口贸易企业使用最多的办公自动化软件是 Word 和 Excel 等，外贸单证岗位人员必须能熟练使用这些办公自动化软件。

三、熟练使用企业 ERP 系统相关操作界面

大中型外贸企业基本上都有自己的 ERP 管理软件，单证岗位是企业 ERP 系统中的一个组成部分。因此，单证岗位人员必须熟悉相应的工作界面，并能在相应的工作界面上熟练、准确和及时地操作。

四、进出口货物贸易相关专业知识

一个优秀的外贸单证员在掌握国际贸易专业基本课程知识的基础上，还应了解我国有关进出口货物贸易的相关政策、法律、规定、出口信用保险等知识和国际惯例等，特别是必须十分了解如下国际贸易惯例。

1.《UCP600》

全称为"The Uniform Customs and Practice for Documentary Credits, 2007 revision, ICC Publication No. 600",即《跟单信用证统一惯例》,简称《UCP600》,于 2007 年 7 月 1 日生效,共有 39 条。

2.《ISBP681》

全称为"International Standard Banking Practice for the Examination of Documents and Documentary Credits, 2007 revision for UCP600, ICC Publication No. 681",即《关于审核跟单信用证项下单据的国际标准银行实务》,简称《ISBP681》,适用于《UCP600》,共有 185 条和 1 个附件。

3.《URR725》

全称为"Uniform Rules for Bank to Bank Reimbursement Under Documentary Credits, ICC Publication No. 725",即《跟单信用证项下银行间偿付统一规则》,共有 17 条,于 2008 年 10 月 1 日生效。

4.《URC522》

全称为"Uniform Rules for Collections, ICC Publication No. 522",即《托收统一规则》,简称《URC522》,1995 年修订,于 1996 年 1 月 1 日开始实施,共有 26 条。

任务四　出口信用证风险的常见预防措施

国内出口商采用信用证支付方式,只要提交相符单据("单证相符"和"单单相符"),就能得到开证行付出的即期款项或到期得到开证行付出的远期款项。货款由开证行保证承付,表面上出口货款是安全的、没有风险的,其实未必完全如此。进口商所在国家或地区,开证行规模和资信,远期信用证期限长短,信用证兑付方式,信用证规定单据种类及填制内容和出口商品特性等因素都可能导致国内出口商不能充分获得开证行的银行信用保证,国内受益人的货款风险或多或少还是存在的。因此,出口商应采取相应的货款风险预防措施。

一、选择在我国有分行的境外商业银行为开证行

国内出口商应尽量指定世界知名银行,如花旗银行、兴业银行、汇丰银行、德国商业银行、澳新银行和渣打银行等作为开证行。这些银行信誉卓著,且大都在我国有分行,只要受益人相符交单,就能取得相应的货款。国内出口商不要接受进口国的地方性小银行作为开证行。

二、采用即期信用证

采用即期信用证方式,无论是自由议付信用证,还是受益人选定指定银行付款信用证或

限制议付信用证,在受益人向指定银行交单后,指定银行一般当天或翌日就能快递寄出相关单据,开证行收到单据翌日起 5 个银行工作日内必须兑付相符交单。这样一来,受益人即使未能相符交单,也有时间妥善处理。

三、信用证内单据要求和信用证外寄单要求结合

国内受益人采用信用证方式,就是要相符交单,得到开证行付出的相应款项。显然,证内规定的单据越少越好,单据填写的内容越简单越好,这就需要说服国外进口商同意部分单据放在证内,如全套正本提单、保险单、商业发票、装箱单等,其他必需的单据则由受益人直接快递给申请人,证内可以要求提供相应的寄单证明(受益人证明和/或快递收据)。

四、海运和空运运输单据收货人栏目内容选择

在远期信用证或即期信用证规定寄 1/3 正本提单给进口商的情况下,船公司签发的指示性抬头的提单收货人栏可以选择凭开证行指定(TO THE ORDER OF THE ISSUING BANK)。进口商取得这样的提单后,提单正本必须在开证行背书后,才能用于办理提货手续。开证行一旦背书,就将卷入基础交易合同中,受益人即使不符交单,开证行也会督促申请人付款。出于同样的目的,国内受益人对空运运单的收货人栏可以选择填写开证行名称和地址。申请人凭航空公司的到货通知提货后,开证行必须付款,这对受益人信用证项下的货款安全很重要。

五、保兑信用证

对一些国别风险比较高的开证行或资产规模小的开证行开立的信用证,国内受益人不能接受远期信用证,即期信用证也须经第三国的国际性大银行加具保兑。保兑行与开证行一样承担第一性付款责任,同时受益人还要争取信用证内规定的单据少,填写的内容简单,保证相符交单。

六、特殊出口商品的"软条款"设置要合理

对欧洲等发达国家或地区出口冷冻水产品等,国外进口商往往要求货到检验检疫合格后才付款,要求在信用证内加注相应的"软条款",我国出口实务中常见的软条款有 3 种。

1. 由开证行决定的"软条款"

信用证暂不生效条款,如:"THIS CREDIT WILL BE OPERATIVE ONLY AFTER RECEIPT OF THE ISSUING BANK'S FURTHER INSTRUCTION. "

2. 由申请人决定的"软条款"

信用证内要求申请人或其代表签发品质检验证书,如:"CERTIFICATE OF QUALITY IN TRIPLICATE ISSUED BY THE APPLICANT, WHOSE SIGNATURE MUST BE IN CONFORMITY WITH THE ISSUING BANK'S FILE. "

3. 由第三方决定的"软条款"

第三方签发的检验证书,如:"AN ORIGINAL CERTIFICATE OF CARGO MATCHING IS-SUED BY THE REPRESENTATIVE OF ×××(注:独立的和公正的检验机构),WHOSE SIGNA-TURE MUST BE IN CONFORMITY WITH THE ISSUING BANK'S FILE."

不管何种软条款,从诚信角度来看,受益人都面临着难以相符交单的现实问题。国内受益人在万不得已的情况下接受单据化的"软条款"时,必须考虑必要性、公正性、公平性和合理性。不必要、不公平和不合理的"软条款"绝不能接受。

任务五 出口流程中各时段单证的种类

根据外贸单证的广义分类,外贸单证员应熟悉和掌握的出口流程中各时段单证的种类如下。

一、交易磋商阶段的相关单证

交易磋商阶段的相关单证包括买方询盘、卖方报盘、买方还盘、卖方接受函、外销合同等。

二、落实信用证阶段的相关单证

落实信用证阶段的相关单证包括形式发票、催证函电、信用证通知书、信用证、要求改证的函电、信用证修改通知书等。

三、出口备货阶段的相关单证

出口备货阶段的相关单证包括内销合同、品质控制文件等。

四、租船订舱阶段的相关单证

租船订舱阶段的相关单证包括出口货物明细单、配船及费用确认单据等。

五、出口报检阶段的相关单证

出口报检阶段的相关单证包括报检委托书、外销合同、信用证、商业发票、装箱单、健康证明等。

六、出口报关阶段的相关单证

出口报关阶段的相关单证包括报关委托书、商业发票、装箱单、出口货物报关单等。

七、装船出运阶段的相关单证

装船出运阶段的相关单证包括出口货物明细单、装货单、场站收据副本、装运通知等。

八、出口结汇阶段的相关单证

出口结汇阶段的相关单证包括商业发票、海运提单、装箱单、健康证明、受益人证明、汇票、一般原产地证、普惠制原产地证、船公司证明等。

九、收汇核销阶段的相关单证

收汇核销阶段的相关单证包括收汇水单、出口收汇核销单、报关单、商业发票、核销单送审登记表等。

【实操训练】

1. 外贸单证制作有哪些原则？

2. 学生上网浏览"全国国际商务单证考试中心"网站，查询有关外贸单证员考试的相关信息。

3. 2021 年年初，某出口公司向尼日利亚客户出口一批汽车配件，信用证规定要一家检验机构检验，并在发票上贴上检验标签。信用证上有这样的规定"ON INVOICE ENDORSED BY COIN LABEL"。在出货时，货代公司代为检验，结果把标签贴在了发票的正面。该出口公司将所有单据交到银行议付，单据到了开证行，遭到了拒付。实际上是因为最终客户对价格不满意，进口商要求降价 5%。经出口公司多次交涉，进口商才同意付款，结汇延迟了两个月。请问，从这个案例中应吸取什么教训？

（提示：信用证上的规定"ON INVOICE ENDORSED BY COIN LABEL"意思是在发票的背面贴上圆形标签。）

4. 上机操作及情景模拟。

学生在计算机上用 Word 文档制作一份个人求职简历。要求以外贸单证员为目标岗位，然后组成小组，进行角色分工，模拟公司求职面试场景，深入了解企业对单证员的岗位要求。

（1）学生分组，按角色分饰面试官和应聘者，完成递交简历和互为问答的过程，相互打分。

（2）为学生制作的简历评分，作为平时成绩记录在案。

项目二　信用证的开立、审核与修改

【项目目标】
知识目标
- 掌握外贸合同的主要内容
- 了解外贸合同与开证申请书的关系
- 掌握开证申请书的缮制方法
- 掌握申请开立信用证的业务流程
- 掌握信用证的主要内容
- 掌握信用证的审证要点
- 掌握信用证修改申请书的缮制方法

能力目标
- 能根据外贸合同审核信用证并提出修改意见

思政目标
- 通过对信用证开立、审核过程的学习,引导学生关注行业发展,了解行业规则
- 通过对信用证的修改相关内容的学习,培养学生认真负责、严谨细致和精益求精的职业素养

【工作情景】

　　上海威尔进出口公司与国外客户 NU BONNETERIE DE GROOTE 签订了 5000 条短裤的外销合同,对方按期开来了信用证,单证员殷实根据外销合同和《UCP600》开始审核信用证。

【工作任务】

任务一　信用证开立操作

　　信用证是买方[开证申请人(Applicant)]向买方所在地或其他地方的银行[开证行(Issuing Bank)]申请,由开证行开给卖方[受益人(Benificiary)]的有条件的书面付款保证。买方在向银行申请开立信用证时,要先按照买卖合同填写开证申请书,然后开证行按照开证申请书的指示开立信用证。

一、开证申请书的概念

开证申请书(Irrevocable Documentary Credit Application)是开证申请人(合同的买方)和开证行之间的契约。它是开证申请人根据买卖合同填写的,向开证行申请开立信用证时提交给开证行的开立信用证的依据。开证申请人应根据银行规定的开证申请书格式,一般填写一式三份,一份银行结算部门留存,一份银行信贷部门留存,一份开证申请人留存。填写开证申请书必须按合同规定写明对信用证的各项要求,内容要明确、完整。

二、开立信用证的程序

1. 填写开证申请书

开证申请人按照合同内容,将开证行固定格式的开证申请书填写好。

2. 在承诺书上签字

开证申请书的背面是开证申请人承诺书,开证申请人需要在上面签字盖章,以明确开证行和开证申请人双方的责任。

3. 提交有关合同的副本和附件

为了规避风险,除了开证申请书外,银行还要求开证申请人提供合同及其工商注册等资料。

4. 支付开证保证金

为了保证资金的安全,开证银行一般要求开证申请人缴纳开证保证金,金额为开证金额的0%~100%。提交保证金的多少,主要取决于开证行给予开证申请人的授信额度。

5. 支付开证手续费

开证申请人向开证行缴纳一定比例的手续费。

三、认识开证申请书

开证申请书见表2.1。

表2.1　开证申请书

IRREVOCABLE DOCUMENTARY CREDIT APPLICATION

To: BANK OF CHINA BEIJING BRANCH　(1)	Date:　(2)
☐Issue by airmail　　☐With brief advice by teletransmission ☐Issue by express delivery ☐Issue by teletransmission(which shall be the operative instrument)　(3)	Credit No.　(4) Date and place of expiry　(5)

续表

Applicant （6）	Beneficiary （Full name and address） （7）

Advising Bank （8）	Amount （9）

Partial shipments （10） ☐allowed ☐not allowed	Transshipment （11） ☐allowed ☐not allowed	Credit available with （16） By ☐sight payment ☐acceptance ☐negotiation ☐deferred payment at
Loading on board/dispatch/taking in charge at/from （12） not later than （13） For transportation to：（14）		against the documents detailed herein （17） ☐and beneficiary's draft(s) for _____ % of invoice value
☐FOB ☐CFR ☐CIF ☐or other terms （15）		at_____ sight drawn on _____ .

Documents required：（marked with ×） （18）

1. （ ） Signed commercial invoice in _____ copies indicating L/C No. and Contract No.

2. （ ） Full set of clean on board Bills of Lading made out to order and blank endorsed, marked "freight ［ ］ to collect ∕［ ］prepaid ［ ］ showing freight amount" notifying _____ _____ .

 （ ） Airway bills/cargo receipt/copy of railway bills issued by _____ showing "freight ［ ］ to collect∕［ ］ prepaid ［ ］ indicating freight amount" and consigned to_____ _____ .

3. （ ） Insurance Policy/Certificate in _____ copies for _____ % of the invoice value showing claims payable in _____ in currency of the draft, blank endorsed, covering All Risks, War Risks and _____ .

4. （ ） Packing List/Weight Memo in _____ copies indicating quantity, gross and weights of each package.

5. （ ） Certificate of Quantity/Weight in _____ copies issued by _____ .

6. （ ） Certificate of Quality in _____ copies issued by ［ ］ manufacturer/［ ］ public recognized surveyor _____ .

续表

7. (　　) Certificate of Origin in _____ copies.

8. (　　) Beneficiary's certified copy of fax/telex dispatched to the applicant within _____ days after shipment advising L/C No., name of vessel, date of shipment, name, quantity, weight and value of goods.

Other documents, if any _____.

Description of goods：　（19）

Additional instructions：　（20）

1. (　　) All banking charges outside the opening bank are for beneficiary's account.

2. (　　) Documents must be presented within _____ days after date of issuance of the transport documents but within the validity of this credit.

3. (　　) Third party as shipper is not acceptable, Short Form/Blank back B/L is not acceptable.

4. (　　) Both quantity and credit amount _____ % more or less are allowed.

5. (　　) All documents must be sent to issuing bank by courier/speed post in one lot.

　(　　) Other terms, if any _____.

Signature and Stamp：　（21）

四、开证申请书的缮制方法与操作注意事项

1. 开证申请书的缮制方法

①"To"后填写开证行名称。

②"Date"后填写申请开证日期。

③信用证的传递方式：用"×"选择信用证的传递方式。

④信用证号：由开证行填写。

⑤信用证有效期和到期地点：按买卖合同的支付条款填写。

⑥开证申请人：填写买卖合同的买方全称、地址、联系方式。

⑦受益人：填写买卖合同的卖方全称、地址、联系方式。

⑧通知行：由开证行填写。

⑨信用证金额：按买卖合同规定填写大、小写金额，如果有一定比率的上下浮动幅度，也应表示清楚。

⑩分批装运：按买卖合同规定用"×"选择"允许"或"不允许"。

⑪转运：按买卖合同规定用"×"选择"允许"或"不允许"。

⑫装运港（地）：按买卖合同规定填写装运港（地）。

⑬最迟装运期：按买卖合同规定填写最迟装运期。

⑭目的港（地）：按买卖合同规定填写目的港（地）。

⑮按买卖合同规定用"×"选择"FOB""CFR""CIF"或"其他术语"。

⑯付款方式:在"Credit available with"后填写银行名称,在"By"后用"×"选择"即期付款""承兑""议付""延期付款"。

⑰汇票要求:在"beneficiary's draft(s) for"后按规定填写信用证项下支付发票金额的百分比;在"at ＿＿ sight"之间按国际贸易合同规定填写汇票的付款期限,如"30 days""60 days""90 days"等;在"drawn on"后填写汇票的受票人(即付款人),按《UCP600》规定,信用证项下汇票的付款人必须是银行。

⑱所需单据:用"×"选择所需单据,并填上对单据份数和内容的要求。在"Other documents, if any"后补填上面没有列出的所需单据。

⑲货物描述:按买卖合同规定填写品名、规格、数量、包装、单价、唛头等。

⑳附加条款:用"×"选择附加条件,在"Other terms, if any"后补填上面没有列出的条件。

㉑开证申请人签字盖章。

2. 开证申请书的操作注意事项

①开证申请人必须严格按照买卖合同规定的开证时间按时向银行申请开立信用证。

②开证申请人必须严格按照买卖合同的内容填写开证申请书。

③若买卖合同为远期付款,要明确汇票的付款期限。

④价格条款中使用的贸易术语必须与相应的单据要求及费用负担等相吻合。

⑤为使货物质量等符合合同规定,买方可在合同中并相应地在信用证中要求卖方提供商品检验检疫机构出具的装船前检验检疫证明,并明确规定货物的品质规格,指定检验检疫机构。这样,若卖方交单与信用证规定不一致,可拒付货款。

⑥开证申请书内容必须正确无误,应明确规定各种单据的出单人(商业发票、运输单据、保险单据除外)及各种单据应表述的内容。

⑦由于信用证的特点是单据买卖,买方应将有关规定转化为单据,以此约束卖方。

⑧通知行由开证行指定,如果卖方在合同中坚持指定通知行,买方可在开证申请书上注明,供开证行在选择通知行时参考。

任务二　信用证审核与修改

各国银行开过来的信用证内容不完全一样,但是基本内容和格式相似。现在进出口业务中使用的信用证多为电开信用证,其中以 SWIFT(Society for Worldwide Interbank Financial Telecommunications)信用证居多。

一、信用证标准格式

SWIFT 意为环球同业银行金融电信协会,它是一个国际银行间非营利性的国际合作组织,总部设在比利时的布鲁塞尔,同时在荷兰阿姆斯特丹和美国纽约分别设立交换中心

(Swifting Center),并为各参加国开设集线中心(National Concentration),为国际金融业务提供快捷、准确、优良的服务。SWIFT 运营着世界级的金融电文网络,银行和其他金融机构通过它与同业交换电文(Message)来完成金融交易。SWIFT 的使用,为银行的结算提供了安全、可靠、快捷、标准化、自动化的通信业务,从而大大提高了银行的结算速度。由于 SWIFT 的格式具有标准化,因此目前信用证的格式主要是用 SWIFT 电文,SWIFT 电文由开证行发送给通知行,用于说明由发报方(开证行)发出的跟单信用证的条款和状态。

表 2.2 是 SWIFT 信用证标准化格式。

表 2.2　SWIFT 信用证标准化格式

状态	标号	栏位名称
M	27	Sequence of Total 合计次序
M	40A	Form of Documentary Credit 跟单信用证类别
M	20	Documentary Credit Number 跟单信用证号
O	23	Reference to Pre-advice 预告的编号
O	31C	Date of Issue 开证日期
O	40E	Applicable Rules 适用的惯例
M	31D	Date and Place of Expiry 有效期及到期地点
O	51A	Applicant Bank 申请人银行
M	50	Applicant 申请人
M	59	Beneficiary 受益人
M	32B	Currency Code, Amount 货币代号、金额
O	39A	Percentage Credit Amount Tolerance 信用证金额加减百分率
O	39B	Maximum Credit Amount 最高信用证金额
O	39C	Additional Amounts Covered 相关附加金额
M	41A	Available with… by…向……银行押汇,押汇方式为……
O	42C	Draft at 汇票期限
O	42A	Drawee 受票人
O	42M	Mixed Payment Details 混合付款指示
O	42P	Deferred Payment Details 延期付款指示
O	43P	Partial Shipments 分批装运
O	43T	Transshipment 转运
O	44A	Loading on Board/Dispatch/Taking in Charge at/from 由……装船/发运/接管
O	44B	Place of Final Destination/of Delivery 运至地
O	44C	Latest Date of Shipment 最迟装运日期

状态	标号	栏位名称
O	44D	Shipment Period 装运期限
O	45A	Description of Goods and/or Services 货物或服务描述
O	46A	Documents Required 所需单据
O	47A	Additional Conditions 附加条件
O	71B	Charges 费用
O	48	Period for Presentation 提示期限
M	49	Confirmation Instructions 保兑指示
O	53A	Reimbursing Bank 偿付行
O	78	Instructions to the Paying/Accepting/Negotiating Bank 对付款/承兑/议付行的指示
O	57A	Advise Through Bank 收讯银行以外的通知银行
O	72	Sender to Receiver Information 附言(发报方给收报方)

注:M=必选　O=可选

二、信用证的主要内容

各个银行开来的信用证内容不尽相同,基本内容如下。

1.关于信用证本身的说明

这部分内容包括信用证的性质和种类、开证日期、信用证编号、信用证有关当事人、金额、有效期和到期地点等。

2.汇票条款

根据具体情况,这一内容可以有,也可以没有。

3.对货物的描述

这部分内容主要包括货物品名、品质、数量、包装和单价等。

4.对运输的要求

这部分内容主要包括运输方式、装运港(地)、目的港(地)、最迟装运期等。

5.对单据的要求

根据业务需要,每份信用证要求的单据不尽相同。信用证通常要求的单据有商业发票、装箱单、海运提单、保险单、产地证/普惠制产地证、受益人证明、装船通知等。

6. 特殊要求

根据业务需要,每份信用证的特殊要求也不一样。通常的要求是单据用英文制作,提交的单据若有不符点,不符点费用将被征收等。

7. 开证行对议付行/付款行/承兑行的指示

这部分主要包括以下内容。
①议付金额背书条款。
②寄单方法。
③偿付方法。

8. 根据国际商会《UCP600》开立的信用证文句

一般规定为本信用证适用于 UCP 最新的版本。
信用证样例见表2.3。

表2.3 信用证样例

2021 MAY 20 09：23：46	Logical Terminal SH87
MT S700 Issue of a Documentary Credit	Page 00001
	Fune SHQP7××

MSGACK DWS7651 Auth OK, Key B206011564111EE2, BKCHCNBJ BERUBEEB record

Basic Header   F01BKCHCNBJA530 1377 777377

Application Header   0 700 1420 060327 BERUBEBBA900 7696 949021 060327 N

           * ING BELGIUM NV/SV(FORMERLY BANK

           * BRUSSELS LAMBERT SA), GENT

           * GENT

User Header	Service Code	103：
Bank Priority		113：
Msg. User Ref.		108： IRM0001042814301
Info. from CI		115：
Sequence of Total		*27：1/ 1
Form of Doc. Credit		*40 A：IRREVACABLE
Doc. Credit Number		*20：DTBEGM705014
Date of Issue		31C：210520
Expiry		*31D：Date 210805 Place CHINA
Applicant		*50：NU BONNETERIE DE GROOTE
		AUTOSTRADEWEG 69090 MEUE BELGIUM
Beneficiary		*59：SHANGHAI WILL TRADING CO., LTD
		NO. 2021 CHENGNAN ROAD, PUDONG, SHANGHAI, CHINA
Amount *32B：		Currency HKD Amount 63250. 00

Max. Credit Amount	39B：NOT EXCEEDING
Available with/by	41D：ANY BANK
	BY NEGOTIATION
Drafts at	42C：30 DAYS AFTER SIGHT
Drawee	42A：BBRUBEBBA900
	*ING BELGIUM NV/SA（FORMERLY BANK
	*BRUSSELS LAMBERT SA），GENT
	*GENT
Partial Shipment	43P：IS NOT ALLOWED
Transshipment	43T：IS ALLOWED
Loading in Charge	44A：SHANGHAI PORT/AIRPORT
For Transport to	44B：
	ANTWERP PORT/BRUSSELS AIRPORT
Latest Date of Ship.	44C：210710
Descript. of Goods	45A：
	BY SEA FROM SHANGHAI, CHINA TO ANTWERP,
	AT LATEST ON 10/07/2021 FOR ORDER D0900326，D0900327
	COVERING FOLLOWING GOODS：
	+2000 PCS SHORT TROUSERS 100PCT COTTON TWILL AT USD 12.65/PC AS PER ORDER D2100326 AND SALES CONTRACT NUMBER 2021SW326，ART. REF. 53.06.06243. K
	+ 3000 PCS SHORT TROUSERS 100PCT COTTON TWILL AT USD 12.65/PC AS PER ORDER D2100327 AND SALES CONTRACT NUMBER 2021SW326，ART. REF. 53.06.06243. K
	SALES CONDITIONS：CIF ANTWERP PORT（IN CASE OF SEA SHIPMENT）
	CIP BRUSSELS AIRPORT（IN CASE OF AIR SHIPMENT）
Documents required 46A：	1. SIGNED COMMERCIAL INVOICES IN 4 ORIGINAL AND 4 COPIES
	2. A FULL SET OF CLEAN ON BOARD OCEAN BILLS OF LADING, MADE OUT TO ORDER, BLANK ENDORSED AND ISSUED BY ENSIGN FREIGHT（CHINA）LTD.
	ROOM 603-605，SHANGHAI XINGTENG MANSION
	NO.1，SOUTH HENAN ROAD
	SHANGHAI CHINA
	TEL. ：+86 21 6373 8393
	FAX：+86 21 6535 6767
	WEBSITE：SHANGHAIATTENSION. COM. CN
	CONTACT PERSON：MISS DELIA LAN

续表

AND MARKED FREIGHT PREPAID

NOTIFY: NU BONNETERIE DE GROOTE

AUTOSTRADEWEG

69090 MEUE

BELGIUM

IN CASE OF AIR SHIPMENT AT SUPPLIER'S EXPENSE:

AIRWAY BILL (ORIGINAL 3 FOR SHIPPER) EVIDENCING DISPATCH OF GOODS (ACTUAL FLIGHT NO. AND DATE MUST BE SHOWN) TO THE ADDRESS OF APPLICANT, MARKED FREIGHT PREPAID

NOTIFY: NU BONNETERIE DE GROOTE BELGIUM

AUTOSTRADEWEG

69090 MEUE

BELGIUM

3. BENEFICIARY'S CERTIFICATE STATING THAT, FOR EACH ORDER NUMBER COVERED BY THIS L/C, THE ORIGINAL CERTIFICATE OF ORIGIN GSP FORM A ISSUED BY THE COMPETENT AUTHORITY CONFIRMING THAT GOODS ARE OF CHINA ORIGIN WAS SENT DIRECTLY TO APPLICANT BY ANY COURIER SERVICE (COPY OF COURIER RECEIPT, CLEARLY INDICATING THE ORDER NUMBER, TO ACCOMPANY THIS CERTIFICATE).

4. PHOTOCOPY OF CERTIFICATE OF ORIGIN AND/OR GSP FORM A ISSUED BY THE COMPETENT AUTHORITY CONFIRMING THAT GOODS ARE OF CHINA ORIGIN.

5. PACKING LIST IN QUADRUPLICATE STATING CONTENTS OF EACH PACKAGE SEPRATELY.

6. INSURANCE POLICY/CERTIFICATE ISSUED IN DUPLICATE IN NEGOTIABLE FORM, COVERING ALL RISKS AND WAR RISK, FROM WAREHOUSE TO WAREHOUSE FOR 120 PCT OF INVOICE VALUE. INSURANCE POLICY/CERTIFICATE MUST CLEARLY STATE IN THE BODY CLAIMS, IF ANY, ARE PAYABLE IN BELGIUM IRRESPECTIVE OF PERCENTAGE.

7. SHIPPING ADVICE BY TELEX OR FAX STATING EXACT SHIPMENT DATE AND B/L OR AWB NUMBER TO BE SENT DIRECTLY TO APPLICANT.

8. QUALITY CERTIFICATE ISSUED BY COMPETENT AUTHORITY.

Additional Cond. 47 A:

1. ALL DOCUMENTS PRESENTED UNDER THIS L/C MUST BE ISSUED IN ENGLISH.

续表

2. THE NEGOTIATING BANK, IF DIFFERENT FROM ADVISING BANK, MUST CERTIFY ON THEIR REMITTANCE LETTER THAT ALL CHARGES AND COMMISSION OF ADVISING BANK(S) ARE PAID OR WILL BE DEDUCTED FROM PROCEEDS.

3. ON RECEIPT OF THE DOCUMENTS, WE WILL PAY AS REQUESTED, PROVIDED ALL THE TERMS AND CONDITIONS OF THIS CREDIT HAVE BEEN COMPLIED WITH.

4. DRAFT(S) MUST INDICATE NUMBER, DATE AND NAME OF ISSUING BANK OF THIS CREDIT.

5. THE AMOUNT OF EACH DRAFT NEGOTIATED UNDER THIS CREDIT MUST BE ENDORSED ON THIS CREDIT BY THE NEGOTIATING BANK, AND THE PRESENTATION OF ANY SUCH DRAFT FOR SETTLEMENT SHALL BE A WARRANTY BY THE NEGOTIATING BANK THAT SUCH ENDORSEMENT HAS BEEN MADE.

6. IF GOODS ARE NOT SHIPPED IN DUE TIME, GOODS MUST BE SENT BY AIR TO BRUSSELS AIRPORT AT SUPPLIER'S EXPENSE.

7. IN CASE THE DOCUMENTS CONTAIN DISCREPANCIES, WE RESERVE THE RIGHT TO CHARGE DISCREPANCY FEES AMOUNTING TO EUR 75 OR EQUIVALENT.

8. DOCUMENTS MUST BE FORWARDED TO US IN ONE SET BY COURIER SERVICE
To: ING BELGIUM NV, W. WILSONPLEIN 5B, 9000 GENT, BELGIUM.

9. L/C WILL BECOME OPERATIONAL UPON BUYER'S APPROVAL OF SAMPLES SENT AS REQUIRED ON ORDER SHEETS.

10. THIS CREDIT IS FREELY NEGOTIABLE BY ANY BANK IN CHINA.

Details of Charges	71 B: ALL COMMISSIONS AND CHARGES ARE FOR BENEFICIARY'S ACCOUNT.
Presentation Period	48: DOCUMENTS MUST BE PRESENTED WITHIN 5 DAYS AFTER ISSUANCE OF THE TRANSPORT DOCUMENT BUT WITHIN THE VALIDITY OF THIS CREDIT.
Confirmation	*49: WITHOUT
Trailer	MAC: 768965EB
	CHK: ZAC18EA8F08E

三、信用证审证要点与操作注意事项

1. 信用证审证要点

信用证依据国际贸易合同开立,因而信用证内容应该与国际贸易合同条款相一致。然而在实际业务中,信用证内容与买卖合同不符的情况时有发生。产生这种情况的原因各不相同,有的是买方或银行工作上的疏忽和差错,有的是某些进口国家或地区的习惯做法或另有特殊规定,有的是买方对我国政策不了解,也有的是买方故意在信用证内加列一些额外的要求。因此,为了保障安全收汇和合同的顺利执行,审核信用证必须十分谨慎、仔细,稍有疏忽就有可能影响履约,甚至造成重大损失。按照我国信用证业务的做法,凡是国外银行开来的信用证,由银行和外贸企业共同审查,银行重点审查开证行的政治背景、资讯、付款责任和索汇路线及鉴别信用证的真伪等。如经银行审查无问题，即将信用证转交给外贸企业进行审查，外贸企业则依据买卖合同和《UCP600》对信用证进行全面、细致的审核，外贸企业审核信用证的要点如下。

（1）31C 开证时间

外贸企业要对照买卖合同的支付条款审核信用证的开证日期是否符合规定，如果信用证的开证日期晚于合同规定则会影响卖方的交货时间，对卖方不利。

（2）31D 信用证的有效期和到期地点

外贸企业要对照买卖合同的支付条款，审核信用证的有效期和到期地点是否符合规定。信用证的有效期是指信用证约束卖方（受益人）向银行交单的时间，如果信用证的有效期规定早于合同规定，则会缩短卖方向银行交单的时间，对卖方不利。到期地点是指卖方向银行交单的地点，一般卖方只接受在其所在国到期的信用证，否则，卖方不好掌握交单的时间。

（3）50/59 信用证开证申请人/受益人

外贸企业要审核开证申请人和受益人的名称、地址是否与合同相符，如不相符，应要求对方修改信用证。

（4）32B 信用证金额

外贸出口企业要仔细审核信用证金额条款中的货币和金额是否符合合同规定，如果信用证规定的货币和金额与合同不符，就会对卖方或者买方不利。

（5）42C 汇票的付款期限

汇票的付款期限须与外贸合同的支付条款相符，否则，需要修改信用证。

（6）42A 受票人

信用证付款方式下的汇票受票人应为银行，如果信用证规定的受票人是开证申请人，则与信用证的特点相违背，需要修改信用证。

（7）43P/43T 分批装运/转运

如果买卖合同规定允许分批装运和转运，信用证应作相同的规定；否则，应该修改信用证。

（8）44A/44B 信用证的装运港/目的港

装运港应与合同规定一致，如果信用证规定的装运港与合同不符，应根据具体情况来判断此项是否需要修改。目的港必须与合同规定一致，如果信用证规定的目的港与合同不符，必须进行修改，因为各港口费用差别很大。

（9）44C 装运期

信用证的装运期须与合同规定相符，否则，应该修改。信用证的装运期与有效期一般应有一定的间隔，如果信用证只规定有效期而未规定装运期，可视为装运期和有效期同一天到期，即"双到期"。"双到期"对卖方不利，一般应请对方修改有效期。如果信用证只规定装运期而没有规定有效期，则应立即请对方明确有效期，因为有效期是信用证必不可少的内容。

（10）45A 货物的描述

来证中对有关品名、规格、数量或重量、包装和单价等项内容的描述，均须与合同规定相符,如有不符,应要求对方修改。

(11)46A 需要提交的单据

对信用证中规定的要求受益人提交的单据,要重点审核,如发现有与合同不符或无法提交的单据,应及时要求对方修改信用证。

(12)71B 费用

按惯例,信用证的费用负担应该是开证行所在国的费用由开证行负担,开证行所在国以外的费用由受益人负担。如果信用证规定所有的费用均由受益人负担,则不合理,应该修改信用证。

(13)48 交单期

外贸企业要认真审核信用证的交单期与合同规定是否相符,如果不符,需要修改信用证。如果信用证中没有规定交单期,按照《UCP600》的规定,理解为交单期为装运日期后 21 天。

2. 信用证的审证操作注意事项

①注意信用证是否为有条件生效。

②信用证有无保证付款的文句。

③信用证中有无加列受《UCP600》最新版本约束的条款。

④开证申请人和受益人名称、地址是否有误。

⑤货物描述、单价、总值、合同号等是否与合同规定相符。

⑥装运港、目的港、分批和转运,以及保险金额、保险险别等是否与合同规定相符。

⑦信用证装运期、有效期、交单期等是否与合同规定相符。

⑧各种单据的规定是否与合同规定相符,且相互之间不矛盾。

⑨银行费用的规定是否符合惯例的规定。

⑩有无对卖方不利的软条款。

四、信用证修改申请书的概念与缮制方法

1. 信用证修改申请书的概念

信用证修改申请书是指信用证开立后,受益人审核信用证发现有些内容与买卖合同规定不符,要求开证申请人请开证行对不符之处进行修改的申请文件。

信用证修改申请书样例见表2.4。

表2.4　信用证修改申请书样例

<table>
<tr><td colspan="2" align="center">中国银行
BANK OF CHINA
信用证修改申请书
APPLICATION FOR AMENDMENT</td></tr>
<tr><td>Date of Amendment： （1）</td><td>No. of Amendment： （2）</td></tr>
<tr><td colspan="2">Amendment to Our Documentary Credit No. （3）</td></tr>
<tr><td colspan="2">To： （4）</td></tr>
</table>

续表

Applicant (5)	Advising Bank (6)
Beneficiary (Before this amendment) (7)	Amount (8)

The above amendment credit is amended as follows：(9)

☐Shipment date extended to _____

☐Expiry date extended to _____

☐Amount increased/decreased by _____ to _____

☐Other terms：

☐Banking charges：(10)

All other terms and conditions remain unchanged.

Authorized Signature(s) (11)

This amendment is subject to Uniform Customs and Practice for Documentary Credits（UCP600）(12)

2. 信用证修改申请书的缮制方法

①修改日期(Date of Amendment)：填写申请修改信用证的日期。

②修改书号码(No. of Amendment):由开证行填写。

③修改的信用证号码(Amendment to Our Documentary Credit No.):填写拟修改的信用证号码。

④致(To):填写向其申请修改信用证的开证行名称。

⑤开证申请人(Applicant):填写信用证开证申请人全称、地址等。

⑥通知行(Advising Bank):由开证行填写。

⑦受益人(Beneficiary):填写修改信用证前买卖合同的卖方全称、地址、联系方式。

⑧信用证金额(Amount):按买卖合同规定填写大、小写金额,如果有一定比率的上下浮动幅度,也应表示清楚。

⑨上述修改的信用证修改如下(The above amendment credit is amended as follows):

A. 装运期延至(Shipment date extended to)_____。

B. 有效期延至(Expiry date extended to)_____。

C. 金额由_____增加到_____/减少到(Amount increased/decreased by)_____ (to)_____。

D. 其他需要修改的条款(Other terms)_____。

⑩银行费用(Banking charge):按《UCP600》规定,信用证方式下的银行费用由发出指示一方负担。

⑪开证申请人签字盖章(Authorized Signature)。

⑫本修改书以《跟单信用证统一惯例》国际商会第 600 号出版物为准[This amendment is subject to Uniform Customs and Practice for Documentary Credits (UCP600)]。

五、信用证修改书

信用证修改书是指开证行应开证申请人的要求和指示对原信用证进行修改的文件。按照《UCP600》规定,信用证修改书须经同一家银行转交给受益人方为有效。受益人收到信用证修改书,对其中的内容只能全部接受或拒绝,不能只接受一部分,而拒绝另一部分。

SWIFT 信用证格式中 MT S707 为信用证修改书。

信用证修改书样例见表2.5。

表2.5 信用证修改书样例

2021 MAY 28　　　　　　09∶37∶36
Logical Terminal　　　　　SH87
MT S707　　　Amendment to a Documentary Credit　　　　Page 00001
Pune　SHHQP7××
MSGACK DWS7651 Auth OK, Key B206011564111EE2, BKCHCNBJ BERUBEEB record
Basic Header　　　　　　　　F01　BKCHCNBJA530 1383 998183
Application Header 0 707 1410 060420 BERUBEBBA900 8038 199203 060420 N
* ING BELGIUM NV/SV (FORMERLY BANK
* BRUSSELS　LAMBERT　SA), GENT
* GENT

续表

User Header	Service Code	103：
	Bank Priority	113：
	Info. from CI	115：
Sender's Ref.	*20： DTBEGM705014	
Receiver's Ref.	*21： NONREF	
Date of Issue	31C： 210520	
Date of Amendment	30： 210528	
Number of Amendment	26E： 1	
Beneficiary	*59： SHANGHAI WILL TRADING CO., LTD	
	NO. 2021 CHENGNAN ROAD, PUDONG, SHANGHAI, CHINA	
New Date of Expiry	31E： 210813	
Amount	32B： Currency USD Amount 63250. 00	
Max. Credit Amount	39B： NOT EXCEEDING	
Latest Date of Ship.	44C： 210720	
Narrative	79： + PLEASE CHANGE：	
	-UNDER FIELD 32B：	
	CURRENCY CODE HAS TO BE USD INSTEAD OF HKD	
	-UNDER FIELD 42C：	
	THE TENOR OF DRAFT SHOULD BE AT SIGHT	
	-UNDER FIELD 43P：	
	PARTIAL SHIPMENT HAS TO BE ALLOWED	
	-UNDER FIELD 44C：	
	THE LATEST SHIPMENT HAS TO BE 170720	
	-UNDER FIELD 46A：	
	THE AMOUNT INSURED HAS TO BE 110 PCT OF INVOICE VALUE	
	INSTEAD OF 120 PCT OF INVOICE VALUE.	
	-UNDER FIELD 71B：	
	THE CHARGE CLAUSE SHOULD BE ALL COMMISSIONS AND	
	CHARGES OUTSIDE BELGIUM ARE FOR ACCOUNT OF	
	BENEFICIARY	
	-UNDER FIELD 48：	
	TI-IE PERIOD OF PRESENTATION SHOULD BE 15 DAYS	
	AFTER ISSUANCE OF THE TRANSPORT DOCUMENT BUT	
	WITHIN THE VALIDITY OF THIS CREDIT.	
Trailer	MAC： 4078015A	
	CHK： 95EFBB09DB17	

【实操训练】

1. 根据销售合同填写开证申请书。

销售合同

SALES CONTRACT

SELLERS: TAKAMRA IMP. & EXP. TRADE CORP.　　CONTRACT NO. TA20210601

　　324, OTOLIMACH TOKYO, JAPAN　　DATE: 2021-06-01

　　TEL: 028-54872456

BUYERS:　GREAT WALL TRADING CO., LTD.

　　RM201 HUASHENG BUILDING

　　TIANJIN P. R. CHINA

THIS SALES CONTRACT IS MADE BY AND BETWEEN THE SELLER AND THE BUYER, WHEREBY THE SELLER AGREES TO SELL AND THE BUYER AGREES TO BUY THE UNDER-MENTIONED GOODS ACCORDING TO THE TERMS AND CONDITIONS STIPULATED BELOW:

品名及规格 (COMMODITY AND SPECIFICATIONS)	数量 (QUANTITY)	单价 (UNIT PRICE)	金额 (AMOUNT)
48″ COLOUR TV SETS	100 SETS	CIF TIANJIN USD1000.00/SET	USD100000.00
TOTAL	100 SETS		USD100000.00

PACKING: IN CARTONS OF ONE SET EACH

SHIPPING MARK: GWTCL/TOKYO/NOS. 1-100

SHIPMENT FROM TOKYO, JAPAN TO TIANJIN, CHINA

TIME OF SHIPMENT: NOT LATER THAN AUG. 31, 2021.

PARTIAL SHIPMENT AND TRANSSHIPMENT ARE NOT ALLOWED.

TERMS OF PAYMENT: BY 100% IRREVOCABLE LETTER OF CREDIT IN FAVOR OF THE SELLERS.

TO BE AVAILABLE BY SIGHT DRAFT TO BE OPENED AND TO REACH THE SELLERS BEFORE JULY 1, 2021 AND TO REMAIN VALID FOR NEGOTIATION IN JAPAN UNTIL 15 DAYS AFTER TIME OF SHIPMENT.

INSURANCE: TO BE EFFECTED BY SELLERS FOR 110% OF FULL INVOICE VALUE COVERING ALL RISKS AND WAR RISK AS PER CIC OF PICC.

DOCUMENTS REQUIRED:

+COMMERCIAL INVOICE IN TRIPLICATE SHOWING L/C NO. AND S/C NO.

+PACKING LIST IN TRIPLICATE.

+FULL SET OF CLEAN ON BOARD OCEAN BILLS OF LADING MADE OUT TO ORDER AND ENDORSED IN BLANK MARKED "FREIGHT PREPAID" AND NOTIFY APPLICANT.

+INSPECTION CERTIFICATE ONE COPY ISSUED BY THE GOVERNMENT.

　　　　THE SELLER　　　　　　　　　THE BUYER

　TAKAMRA IMP. & EXP. TRADE CORP.　　GREAT WALL TRADING CO., LTD.

　　　　高田一郎　　　　　　　　　　　李立

附加资料:

(1)开证行:BANK OF CHINA, TIANJIAN BRANCH.

(2)通知行:ABC BANK, TOKYO.

(3)申请开证日期:JUNE 20, 2021.

IRREVOCABLE DOCUMENTARY CREDIT APPLICATION

To: (1)	Date: (2)
☐Issue by airmail　　☐With brief advice by teletransmission ☐Issue by express delivery	Credit No.　(4)

续表

□Issue by teletransmission（which shall be the operative instrument）（3）	Date and place of expiry （5）
Applicant （6）	Beneficiary □Full name and address （7）
Advising Bank （8）	Amount （9）

Partial shipments （10） □allowed □not allowed	Transshipment （11） □allowed □not allowed	Credit available with （16） By
Loading on board/dispatch/taking in charge at/from （12） not later than （13） For transportation to：（14）		□sight payment □acceptance □negotiation against the documents detailed herein （17） □and beneficiary's draft(s) for _____ % of invoice value
□FOB □CFR □CIF □or other terms （15）		at _____ sight drawn on

Documents required：（marked with ×）（18）

1.（ ） Signed commercial invoice in _____ copies indicating L/C No. and Contract No.

2.（ ） Full set of clean on board Bills of Lading made out to order and blank endorsed，marked "freight [ ] to collect / [ ] prepaid [ ] showing freight amount" notifying _____

_____.

   （ ） Airway bills/cargo receipt/copy of railway bills issued by _____ showing "freight [ ] to collect/[ ] prepaid [ ] indicating freight amount" and consigned to _____

_____.

3.（ ） Insurance Policy/Certificate in _____ copies for _____ % of the invoice value showing claims payable in _____ in currency of the draft, blank endorsed, covering All Risks, War Risks and _____.

4.（ ） Packing List/Weight Memo in _____ copies indicating quantity, gross and weights of each package.

5.（ ） Certificate of Quantity/Weight in _____ copies issued by _____.

6.（ ） Certificate of Quality in _____ copies issued by [ ] manufacturer/[ ] public recognized surveyor_____.

7.（ ） Certificate of Origin in _____ copies.

8.（　　）Beneficiary's certified copy of fax /telex dispatched to the applicant within ＿＿＿＿＿＿ days after shipment advising L/C No. , name of vessel, date of shipment, name, quantity, weight and value of goods.

Other documents, if any ＿＿＿＿＿＿＿＿＿＿＿＿＿＿＿＿＿＿＿＿＿＿＿＿＿＿＿＿＿＿＿＿.

Description of goods：（19）

Additional instructions：（20）

1.（　　）All banking charges outside the opening bank are for beneficiary's account.

2.（　　）Documents must be presented within ＿＿＿＿＿＿ days after date of issuance of the transport documents but within the validity of this credit.

3.（　　）Third party as shipper is not acceptable, Short Form/Blank back B/L is not acceptable.

4.（　　）Both quantity and credit amount ＿＿＿＿＿＿＿＿＿＿＿＿ % more or less are allowed.

5.（　　）All documents must be sent to issuing bank by courier/speed post in one lot.

（　　）Other terms, if any ＿＿＿＿＿＿＿＿＿＿＿＿＿＿＿＿＿＿＿＿＿＿＿＿＿＿＿.

2.根据下述合同的内容审核信用证,指出不符之处,并提出修改意见。

（1）合同。

SALES CONFIRMATION

Contract No. YM0806009

Date：June 05, 2021

The Seller：TIANJIN YIMEI INTERNATIONAL CORP.

Address：58 DONGLI ROAD TIANJIN, CHINA

The Buyer：VALUE TRADING ENTERPRISE LLC

Address：RM. 1008 GREEN BUILDING KUWAIT

This Sales Contract is made by and between the Seller and the Buyer, whereby the Seller agrees to sell and the Buyer agrees to buy the under-mentioned goods according to the terms and conditions stipulated below：

Specification of Goods	Quantity	Unit Price	Amount
MAN'S WIND BREAKER			
STYLE NO. YM082		CIFC5 KUWAIT	
COLOUR：BLACK	2500 PCS	USD15. 10/PC	USD37750. 00
KHAKI	2500 PCS	USD15. 10/PC	USD37750. 00
TOTAL	5000 PCS		USD75500. 00
TOTAL AMOUNT：SAY U. S. DOLLARS SEVENTY FIVE THOUSAND FIVE HUNDRED ONLY.			

Packing：　20PCS ARE PACKED IN ONE EXPORT STANDARD CARTON.

Shipping Marks：VALUE

ORDER NO. A01

KUWAIT

C/No. 1-UP

Time of Shipment: Before AUG. 10, 2021

Loading Port and Destination: From Tianjin, China to Kuwait

Partial shipment: Not allowed

Transshipment: Allowed

Insurance: To be effected by the seller for 110% invoice value covering All Risks and War Risk as per CIC of PICC dated 01/01/1981

Terms of Payment: By L / C at 60 days after sight, reaching the seller before June 15, 2021, and remaining valid for negotiation in China for further 15 days after the effected shipment. L / C must mention this contract number. L / C advised by BANK OF CHINA. All banking charges outside China (the mainland of China) are for account of the Drawee.

Documents:

+ Signed commercial invoice in triplicate.

+ Full set (3/3) of clean on board ocean Bill of Lading marked Freight Prepaid made out to order blank endorsed notifying the applicant.

+ Insurance Policy in duplicate endorsed in blank.

+ Packing List in triplicate.

+ Certificate of Origin issued by China Chamber of Commerce.

Signed by:

THE SELLER:	THE BUYER:
TIANJIN YIMEI INTERNATIONAL CORP.	VALUE TRADING ENTERPRISE, LLC
Jack	Julia

（2）信用证。

```
27:  SEQUENCE OF TOTAL:1/1
40A: FORM OF DOC. CREDIT: IRREVOCABLE
20:   DOC. CREDIT NUMBER:  KR369/03
31C: DATE OF ISSUE: 210619
40E: APPLICABLE RULES: UCP LATEST VERSION
31D: DATE AND PLCAE OF EXPIRY: 210825 KUWAIT
51D: APPLICANT BANK: VALUE TRADING ENTERPRISE CORP.
             RM1008 GREEN BUILDING KUWAIT
50:  APPLICANT:   AORE SPECIALTIES MATERIAL CORP.
                YARIMCA, KOCAELI 41740, IZMIT, TURKEY
59:  BENEFICIARY: TIANJIN YIMEI INTERNATIONAL CORP.
             58 DONGLI ROAD TIANJIN, CHINA
32B: CURRENCY CODE, AMOUNT: USD71500.00
41A: AVAILABLE WITH ... BY: BANK OF CHINA
                     BY NEGOTIATION
42C: DRAFTS AT ...: 90 DAYS AFTER SIGHT
```

42A：DRAWEE：VALUE TRADING ENTERPRISE, LLC

43P：PARTIAL SHIPMENTS：NOT ALLOWED

43T：TRANSSHIPMENT：NOT ALLOWED

44E：PORT OF LOADING/AIRPORT OF DEPARTURE：ANY CHINESE PORT

44F：PORT OF DISCHARGE / AIRPORT OF DESTINATION：KUWAIT BY SEA FREIGHT

44C：LATEST DATE OF SHIPMENT：210710

45A：DESCRIPTION OF GOODS AND / OR SERVICES：5000 PCS WIND BREAKER
STYLE NO. YM085
AS PER ORDER NO. A01 AND S/C NO. YM009
AT USD15.10/PC CIF KUWAIT
PACKED IN CARTON OF 20 PCS EACH

46A：DOCUMENTS REQUIRED

+ SIGNED COMMERCIAL INVOICE IN TRIPLICATE INDICATING L/C NO. AND
CONTRACT NO.

+ FULL SET (3/3) OF CLEAN ON BOARD OCEAN BILL OF LADING MADE OUT TO
APPLICANT AND BLANK ENDOSED MARKED "FREIGHT TO COLLECT"
NOTIFY THE APPLICANT

+ SIGNED PACKING LIST IN TRIPLICATE SHOWING THE FOLLOWING DETAILS：
TOTAL NUMBER OF PACKAGES SHIPPED,CONTENT(S) OF PACKAGE(S), GROSS
WEIGHT, NET WEIGHT AND MEASUREMENT.

+ CERTIFICATE OF ORIGIN ISSUED AND SIGNED OR AUTHENTICATED BY A
LOCAL CHAMBER OF COMMERCE LOCATED IN THE EXPORTING COUNTRY.

+ INSURANCE POLICY/CERTIFICATE IN DUPLICATE ENDORSED IN BLANK FOR 120%
INVOICE VALUE, COVERING ALL RISKS AND WAR RISK OF CIC OF PICC(1/1/1981)

71B：CHARGES：ALL CHARGES AND COMMISSIONS ARE FOR ACCOUNT OF
BENEFICIARY INCLUDING REIMBURSING CHARGES

经审核,信用证存在的问题及修改意见如下：

_____

_____

_____

3. 根据下面合同和相关资料,指出下列开证申请书中错误的地方。

2021 年 6 月 20 日,上海华联皮革制品有限公司（SHANGHAI HUALIAN LEATHER
GOODS CO., LTD. 156 CHANGXING ROAD, SHANGHAI, P. R. CHINA）向 SVS DESIGN
PLUS CO., LTD. 1-509 HANNAMDONG YOUNGSAN-KU, SEOUL,KOREA 就出口 DOUBLE
FACE SHEEP SKIN 一批,达成以下主要合同条款：

1. COMMODITY：DOUBLE FACE SHEEP SKIN
COLOUR CHESTNUT

2. QUANTITY：3175.25 SQFT(平方英尺)

3. PACKING：IN CARTONS

4. UNIT PRICE：USD7.40/SQFT CIF SEOUL

5. AMOUNT：USD23496.85

6. TIME OF SHIPMENT： DURING NOV.2021

    PORT OF LOADING： SHANGHAI, CHINA

    PORT OF DESTINATION：SEOUL,KOREA

    PARTIAL SHIPMENT： ALLOWED

    TRANSSHIPMENT： PROHIBITED

7. INSURANCE：TO BE COVERED BY THE SELLER FOR 110% INVOICE VALUE COVERING ALL RISK AND WAR RISK AS PER CIC OF THE PICC DATED 01/01/1981.

8. PAYMENT：BY IRREVOCABLE LETTER OF CREDIT AT 45 DAYS SIGHT TO REACH THE SELLER NOT LATER THAN JUNE 24, 2021, VALID FOR NEGOTIATION IN CHINA UNTIL THE 15TH DAY AFTER TIME OF SHIPMENT.

9. DOCUMENT：(1) SIGNED COMMERCIAL INVOICE IN 3 FOLD.

    (2) SIGNED PACKING LIST IN 3 FOLD.

    (3) FULL SET OF CLEAN ON BOARD OCEAN B/L IN 3/3 ORIGINALS ISSUED TO OR-DER AND BLANK ENDORSED MARKED "FREIGHT PREPAID" AND NOTIFY THE AP-PLICANT.

    (4) CERTIFICATE OF ORIGIN IN 1 ORIGINAL AND 1 COPY ISSUED BY THE CHAMBER OF COMMERCE IN CHINA.

    (5) INSURANCE POLICY/CERTIFICATE IN DUPLICATE ENDORSED IN BLANK FOR 110% INVOICE VALUE COVERING ALL RISKS AND WAR RISKS OF CIC OF PICC (01/01/1981). SHOWING THE CLAIMING CURRENCY IS THE SAME AS THE CURRENCY OF CREDIT.

相关资料：

①信用证号码：MO722111057。

②合同号码：HL20210315。

SVS DESIGN PLUS CO.，LTD 外贸单证员金浩于 2021 年 6 月 23 日向 KOOKMIN BANK，SEOUL,KOREA 办理申请电开信用证手续,通知行是 BANK OF CHINA, SHANGHAI BRANCH。

IRREVOCABLE DOCUMENTARY CREDIT APPLICATION

To：BANK OF CHINA   Date：JUNE 25, 2021

Beneficiary (full name and address)		L/C No. MO722111059
SVS DESIGN PLUS CO.，LTD.		Contract No. HL20210315
1-509 HANNAMDONG YOUNGSAN-KU,		Date and place of expiry of the credit
SEOUL,KOREA		NOV. 15, 2021 in CHINA
Partial shipment NOT ALLOWED	Transshipment ALLOWED	Issued by teletransmission (which shall be the operative instrument)
Loading on board/dispatch/taking in charge at/from		Amount (both in figures and words)

SEOUL,KOREA Not later than OCT. 31, 2021 For transportation to SHANGHAI, CHINA	EUR23496.85 SAY EURO TWENTY THREE THOUSAND FOUR HUNDRED NINETY SIX POINT EIGHTY FIVE ON- LY
Description of goods: DOUBLE FACE SHEEP SKIN COLOUR CHESTNUT 3175.25 PCS Packing: IN GUNNY BAGS	Credit available with ANY BANK IN CHINA by negotiation against the documents detailed herein and beneficiary's draft for 100% of the invoice value AT SIGHT drawn on U.S.
	CFR

Documents required: (marked with ×)

1. (×) Signed Commercial invoice in 5 copies indicating invoice No., contract No.

2. (×) Full set of clean on board ocean Bill of Lading made out to order of issuing bank and blank endorsed, marked "freight" (×) to collect / (   ) prepaid showing freight amount notify the applicant.

3. (×) Insurance Policy / Certificate in 2 copies for 120% of the invoice value showing claims payable in China in currency of the draft, blank endorsed, covering (×) Ocean Marine Transportation / (   ) Air Transportation / (   ) Over Land transportation All risks.

4. (×) Packing List / Weight Memo in 5 copies indication quantity / gross and net weights for each package and packing conditions as called for by the L/C.

5. (   ) Certificate of Quantity / Weight in _____ copies issued by an independent surveyor at the loading port, indicating the actual surveyed quantity / weight of shipped goods as well as the packing condition.

6. (   ) Certificate of Quality in _____ copies issued by (   ) manufacturer / (   ) public recognized surveyor / (   ).

7. (   ) Beneficiary's Certified copy of FAX dispatched to the accountee within _____ after shipment advising (   ) name of vessel / (   ) date, quantity, weight and value of shipment.

8. (   ) Beneficiary's Certificate certifying that extra copies of the documents have been dispatched according to the contract terms.

9. (   ) Shipping Company's Certificate attesting that the carrying vessel is chartered or booked by accountee or their shipping agents.

10. (×) Other documents, if any: _____.

11. Certificate of Origin in 3 copies issued by authorized institution.

Additional Instructions: _____.

...

Advising bank:
KOOKMIN BANK, SEOUL, KOREA

项目三　发票缮制与操作

【项目目标】

知识目标

- 熟悉商业发票和形式发票的概念与作用
- 掌握商业发票和形式发票的格式与缮制方法

能力目标

- 能够熟练缮制商业发票和形式发票

思政目标

- 通过对商业发票的缮制方法的学习,培养学生实事求是,不虚报、瞒报的职业素养
- 通过对商业发票的作用的学习,激发学生的家国情怀、担当意识,做一个自觉纳税和遵纪守法的好公民

【工作情景】

　　上海威尔进出口公司业务员在落实国外客户开来的信用证同时,即应着手出口货物的准备工作。一方面,应与国内产品供货厂商联系,按照出口合同和信用证规定准备货物;另一方面,要求单证员殷实缮制商业发票等单证,同时要求跟单员着手办理订舱、报检、报关、投保、出运工作。单证员殷实备好出口流程中各时段所需的商业发票,根据业务管理需要将发票号码确定为"WT980",根据项目二任务二中的信用证样例和信用证修改书样例确定发票日期为2021年7月1日。请以上海威尔进出口公司单证员殷实的身份制作商业发票。

【工作任务】

任务一　商业发票缮制与操作

　　发票是指在买卖商品、提供或接受劳务、服务以及从事其他经营活动中,卖方或供方提供给买方或受方的收付款凭证。它是财务收支、会计核算的原始依据,也是审计机关、税务机关执法检查的重要依据。

　　发票是卖方签发的中心单据。我国进出口贸易中使用的发票主要有商业发票（Commercial Invoice）、海关发票（Customs Invoice）、形式发票（Proforma Invoice）、领事发票

（Consular Invoice）及厂商发票（Manufacturer's Invoice）等。

一、商业发票的概念

商业发票是卖方向买方开列的发货价目清单,是买卖双方记账的依据,也是进出口报关、纳税的依据。商业发票代表一笔业务的全貌,内容包括品名、品质、数量、价格、金额、包装等内容,同时也是买方办理进口报关不可缺少的文件。因此,商业发票是全套出口单据的核心,在单据制作过程中,其余单据均需参照商业发票缮制。

二、商业发票的作用

1. 核对卖方履约情况是否符合合同规定

商业发票是对一笔交易的全面叙述,表明了以价格为中心的合同主体内容,将商业发票内容与合同条款逐条核对,可了解卖方交货情况。

2. 买卖双方记账及核算的依据

商业发票作为卖方交付货物、卖方结算货款的凭证,是卖方核算经济效益及买卖双方结算记账的基本依据。

3. 报关、纳税的依据

商业发票载明的价值和有关货物的说明是海关凭以核定税款的依据,也是进出口国海关验关放行、清关提货的依据。

4. 替代汇票作为付款的依据

在不使用汇票的业务中,商业发票可以替代汇票作为付款的依据。

此外,商业发票还可以作为海关统计、保险索赔的依据。

目前,我国外贸企业使用的商业发票无统一格式,一般都由卖方自行设计。

商业发票样例见表3.1。

表3.1　商业发票样例

商业发票

COMMERCIAL INVOICE

1. Exporter 　（1）	4. Invoice date and No. 　（4）	
	5. S/C No. 　（5）	6. L/C No. 　（6）

续表

2. Importer （2）		7. Country/Region of origin （7）		
		8. Trade mode （8）		
3. Transport details （3）		9. Terms of delivery and payment （9）		

10. Shipping marks;
    Container No.
 	
（10）
	11. Number and kind of package;
	    Description of goods
	
	（11）
		12. Quantity
		
		（12）
			13. Unit price
			
			（13）
				14. Amount
				
				（14）

Total				
15. Total amount（in figure and word）（15）				
				16. Exporter's stamp and signature　（16）

三、商业发票缮制方法和操作注意事项

1. 商业发票缮制方法

商业发票上应明确标明"INVOICE"（发票）或"COMMERCIAL INVOICE"（商业发票）字样。在信用证项下,为防止单、证不符,发票名称应与信用证一致。

（1）出口商（Exporter）

此处填写出口商名称、地址及电话、传真等,此栏必须同买卖合同的卖方或信用证的受益人的描述一致。

（2）进口商（Importer）

除信用证有其他要求之外,此栏一般缮制为信用证的开证申请人（Applicant）或买卖合同的买方名称、地址,以及电话、传真等。

（3）运输事项（Transport details）

此处填写装运港（地）、目的港（地）及运输方式,例如"From Shanghai,China to Hamburg,Germany by sea"。

（4）发票日期和发票号（Invoice date and No.）

发票日期最好不要晚于提单的出具日期,而且要在信用证规定的议付期之前。此外,卖方经常签订合同后即开立发票,出具日期也就早于信用证开立日期,根据《UCP600》的规定,这是允许的,但必须在信用证规定的期限内提交,发票号由出口商自行编写,一般是根据出口商名称缩写字母和年份数字编写。

（5）合同号（S/C No.）

由于发票是证明卖方履行合同情况的文件，因此必须要注明具体的合同号。一笔交易若有多个合同号，应分别列出。

（6）信用证号（L/C No.）

在采用信用证支付条件下，还要注明具体的信用证号。

（7）原产地国/地区（Country/Region of origin）

此栏注明该批货物的原产地国家或地区的名称。

（8）贸易方式（Trade mode）

注明该笔业务的贸易方式，如"一般贸易""加工贸易"等。

（9）交货和付款条款（Terms of delivery and payment）

填写该笔业务采用的贸易术语和支付方式，如"CIF、L/C"。

（10）运输标志和集装箱号（Shipping marks；Container No.）

填写运输标志（唛头）和集装箱号。

（11）包装类型及件数和商品描述（Number and kind of package；Description of goods）

填写包装的件数和种类、商品的描述（包括品名、品质）。内容必须与信用证规定的货描（Description of Goods）完全一致，必要时要照信用证原样打印，不得随意减少内容，否则有可能被银行视为不符点。但有时信用证货描非常简单，此时按信用证打印完毕后，再按合同要求列明货物具体内容。若信用证对此部分有开错的，应将错就错，或用括号注明正确的描述。

（12）数量（Quantity）

填写成交的数量，与合同和信用证保持一致。

（13）单价（Unit price）

国际贸易中的单价必须包括计价货币、单位价格金额、计量单位和贸易术语4个组成部分，要与合同和信用证保持一致。对应不同货物标明相应单价，注意货币单位及数量单位要与合同和信用证一致。

（14）金额（Amount）

小写金额，为单价和数量相乘的结果。

（15）总值（用数字和文字表示）[Total amount（in figure and word）]

与小写金额保持一致，并标明大写金额。

（16）出口商签章（Exporter's stamp and signature）

若信用证要求Signed invoice，就要求卖方签字、盖章，签字的方式有手签、盖章签字和打孔签字等。按《UCP600》的规定，除非信用证另有规定，商业发票无须签章。

2. 商业发票操作注意事项

①《UCP600》规定：除非信用证另有规定，商业发票无须签字。

②除非信用证另有规定，商业发票的出具人与汇票的出具人应相同，大多数情况下为信用证的受益人，即合同的卖方；抬头人为开证申请人，即合同的买方。

③货物描述与信用证和合同的描述相同。

④发票上包括信用证和合同提及的其他资料,如唛头、运输细节等须与其他单据保持一致。

⑤发票上的货币与信用证一致,发票金额与汇票金额一致,且不能超过信用证金额。

⑥注意上下浮动的幅度,如信用证的金额、单价、数量前有"约(about)"字样,则有关金额、单价、数量有10%上下增减幅度。《UCP600》规定,除非信用证规定货物数量不得增减,在所支取的金额不超过信用证金额的条件下,货物的数量准许有5%的增减,但当信用证规定数量以包装单位或个数计量的,此项浮动则不适用。

⑦如果信用证规定商业发票注明基本内容以外的其他内容,应填制在(11)栏货物描述的下边。

⑧公司名称和地址要分两行打,名称一般一行打完,不能换行,地址则可合理分行。

殷实根据项目二中的信用证样例和信用证修改书样例缮制完成的商业发票如下(表3.2)。

表3.2 商业发票

WILL SHANGHAI TRADING CO. ,LTD.

NO. 2009 CHENGNAN ROAD, PUDONG, SHANGHAI, P. R. CHINA

COMMERCIAL INVOICE

To: NU BONNETERIE DE GROOTE   Invoice No. :   WT980

AUTOSTRADEWEG 69090 MELLE, BELGIUM   Invoice Date: JULY 1 ,2021

From: SHANGHAI, CHINA   To: ANTWERP

Marks and Numbers	Number and Kind of Package; Description of Goods	Quantity	Unit Price	Amount
				CIF ANTWERP
N/M	SHORT TROUSERS-100PCT COTTON TWILL AS PER ORDER D1700326 AND SALES CONTRACT NUMBER 2021SW326, ART. REF. 53. 06. 06243. K	2000 PCS	USD12. 65/PC	USD25300. 00
	SHORT TROUSERS-100 PCT COTTON TWILL AS PER ORDER D1700327 AND SALES CONTRACT NUMBER 2021SW326, ART. REF. 53. 06. 06243. K	3000 PCS	USD12. 65/PC	USD37950. 00
	TOTAL	5000 PCS	—	USD63250. 00

SAY TOTAL: U. S. DOLLARS SIXTY THREE THOUSAND TWO HUNDRED AND FIFTY ONLY.

WILL SHANGHAI TRADING CO. ,LTD.

殷实

任务二　形式发票缮制与操作

一、形式发票的概念

形式发票是一种非正式发票,是卖方对潜在的买方报价的一种形式,买方常常需要形式发票,以作为申请进口许可证和批准外汇之用。

形式发票是在没有正式合同之前,经双方签字或盖章之后产生法律效力的充当合同的文件,它包括产品描述、单价、数量、总金额、付款方式、包装、交货期、卖方开户银行名称及账号等。形式发票本来只是在客户确认了价格并下订单之后卖方所做的供对方再次确认的发票,但在没有正式合同之前,形式发票即合同。

二、形式发票的作用

形式发票是买方安排开立信用证的依据,是买方安排预付货款的依据,更是买方申请进口许可证的依据。

形式发票样例见表3.3。

表3.3　形式发票样例

宏达国际贸易有限公司

HONGDA TRADING CO. , LTD.

No. 29 , Wuyi Road , Changsha 410001 , **P. R. CHINA**

TEL: 0731-4715004 , 0731-4715619　　　**FAX**: 0731-4691619

PROFORMA INVOICE

To:

INVOICE NO. :　_____

INVOICE DATE:　_____

S/C NO. :　_____

S/C DATE:　_____

TERM OF PAYMENT:　_____

PORT OF LOADING:　_____

PORT OF DESTINATION:　_____

TIME OF DELIVERY:　_____

INSURANCE:　_____

VALIDITY:　_____

续表

MARKS AND NUMBERS	NUMBER AND KIND OF PACKAGE DESCRIPTION OF GOODS	QUANTITY	UNIT PRICE	AMOUNT

TOTAL AMOUNT:

SAY TOTAL:

BENEFICIARY:

ADVISING BANK:

NEGOTIATING BANK:

三、形式发票缮制方法与操作注意事项

1. 形式发票缮制方法

形式发票无统一的格式,其内容与商业发票相似,只是发票名称为"Proforma Invoice"。另外,形式发票需要标明出口商的银行账号等详细信息,以便于进口商预付款项。

2. 形式发票操作注意事项

①形式发票的内容与商业发票一致,单据名称必须显示"形式发票"。

②形式发票不要漏打出口商的银行账号等详细信息。

【实操训练】

1. 根据买卖合同缮制商业发票。

SALES CONFIRMATION

NO.：ZC2021017

DATE：FEB 06，2021

The seller：

Zhong cheng International Trade Co.， Ltd

20，HangZhou RD.，Nanjing，P. R. China

The buyer：

Green Trade Co.

22 Mark Street，Oslo，Norway

The undersigned Seller and Buyer have agreed to close the following transactions according to the terms and conditions stipulated below：

Commodity and Specification	Quantity	Unit Price	Amount
Hand Tools		CIF OSLO	
Art No. :1018	5000 SETS	USD4.00/SET	USD20000.00
Art No. :1019	5000 SETS	USD3.00/SET	USD15000.00
Goods are Chinese origin			
Total	10000 SETS		USD35000.00

Total Amount：Say US Dollars Thirty Five Thousand Only.

Time of Shipment：Not later than April 30，2021

Partial Shipment and Transshipment are Allowed.

Port of Shipment：Shanghai,P. R. China

Port of Discharge：Oslo,Norway

Payment：By D/P at 30 days after B/L date

Insurance：To be effected by the seller for 110% of the invoice value covering all risk and war risk as per PICC clause.

The buyer：

Green Trade Co.

Mary

The seller：

ZhongCheng International Trade Co.,Ltd

Li Ling

附加资料：

①发票号码自编

②100 sets packed in a carton

③唛头:标准化唛头

④包装:100 set/carton

商业发票
COMMERCIAL INVOICE

Exporter	Invoice Date and No.	
Importer	S/C NO.	L /C NO.
Transport Details	Terms of Payment	

Shipping Marks; Container No.	Number and Kind of Package; Description of Goods	Quantity	Unit Price	Amount
	Total			
Total Amount（in words）				
			Signature：	

2. 根据信用证缮制商业发票。

FROM：NATIONAL COMMERCIAL BANK, JEDDAH

To：BANK OF CHINA, JIANGSU BR.

DATE OF ISSUE：JAN. 3, 2021

L/C NO.：LTC6688

L/C AMOUNT：USD28820.00

APPLICANT：ABC COMPANY, JEDDAH

BENEFICIARY：XYZ COMPANY, NANJING

TIME OF SHIPMENT：APR. 30, 2021

DATE OF EXPIRY：JULY 2, 2021

DRAFTS TO BE DRAWN ON US AT SIGHT FOR 90PCT OF INVOICE VALUE

PARTIAL SHIPMENT：NOT ALLOWED

MERCHANDISE：ABT 48000 CANS OF MEILING BRAND CANNED ORANGE JAM, 250 GRAM/CARTON, 12 CANS IN A CARTON

UNIT PRICE：USD6.55/CARTON CIF JEDDAH

COUNTRY OF ORIGIN：P. R. CHINA

DOCUMENTS REQUIRED：

+COMMERCIAL INVOICE 3 COPIES DATED THE SAME DATE AS THAT OF L/C ISSUANCE DATE INDICATING COUNTRY OF THE GOODS AND CERTIFIED TO BE TRUE AND CORRECT INDICATING CONTRACT NO. SUM356/05 AND L/C NO.

+FULL SET OF CLEAN SHIPPED ON BOARD OCEAN BILL OF LADING MADE OUT TO ORDER OF ISSUING BANK, NOTIFYING APPLICANT AND MARKED FREIGHT PREPAID.

+PACKING LIST INDICATING QUANTITY, G. W, N. W. PACKAGE AS REQUIRED BY L/C.

+FULL SET OF INSURANCE POLICY IN DUPLICATE IN NEGOTIABLE FORM BLANK ENDORSED FOR 110PCT OF INVOICE VALUE COVERING ALL RISKS, STRIKES OF PICC, INCLUDING WAREHOUSE TO WAREHOUSE, I. O. P. CLAIMS PAYABLE AT DESTINATION IN THE CURRENCY OF L/C.

ADDITIONAL CONDITIONS：ALL DOCUMENTS MUST INDICATE SHIPPING MARKS AS JAM IN DIAMOND JEDDAH

附加信息：

①发票号码：XY22073017

②受益人的有权签字人为吴仁

③出仓单显示货物：52800 CANS OF MEILING BRAND CANNED ORANGE JAM

④提单显示货物从上海运往吉达

⑤船名：LINDA V. 123

⑥POLICY NO：789654

⑦G. W：18 KGS/CTN　　　N. W: 25 KGS/CTN　　　MEA: 30 CM×25 CM×45 CM/CTN

商业发票

COMMERCIAL INVOICE

Exporter		Invoice Date and No.		
Importer		S/C No.		L/C No.
Transport Details		Terms of Payment		
Shipping Marks；Container No.	Number and Kind of Package；Description of Goods	Quantity	Unit Price	Amount
	Total			
Total Amount(in words)				
			Signature	

3. 根据买卖合同、信用证通知书、信用证和附加信息缮制商业发票。

（1）合同。

SHANGHAI IMPORT&EXPORT TRADE CORPORATION

1321 ZHONGSHAN ROAD SHANGHAI, CHINA

TEL: 021-65788877   FAX:021-65788876

S/C NO. : HX050264

DATE: JAN. 01, 2021

To: TKAMLA CORPORATION

6-7,KAWARA MACH OSAKA, JAPAN

DEAR SIRS:

WE HEREBY CONFIRM HAVING SOLD TO YOU THE FOLLOWING GOODS ON TERMS AND CONDITIONS AS SPECIFIED BELOW:

MARKS & NO	DESCRIPTION OF GOODS	QUANTITY	UNIT PRICE	AMOUNT
T. C	COTTON BLANKET		CIF OSAKA	
OSAKA				
C/NO. 1—250	ART NO. H666	500 PCS	USD5.50/PC	USD2750.00
	ART NO. HX88	500 PCS	USD4.50/PC	USD2250.00
	ART NO. HE21	500 PCS	USD4.80/PC	USD2400.00
	ART NO. HA56	500 PCS	USD5.20/PC	USD2600.00
	ART NO. HH46	500 PCS	USD5.00/PC	USD2500.00
	PACKED IN 250 CTNS			
	TOTAL	2500 PCS		USD12500.00

LOADING PORT: SHANGHAI

DESTINATION: OSAKA PORT

PARTIAL SHIPMENT: PROHIBITED

PAYMENT: L/C AT SIGHT

INSURANCE: FOR 110% OF THE INVOICE VALUE COVERING ALL RISKS AND WAR RISK.

TIME OF SHIPMENT: LATEST DATE OF SHIPMENT MAR. 10, 2021

THE BUYER   THE SELLER

TKAMLA CORPORATION   SHANGHAI IMPORT & EXPORT TRADE CORPORATION

高田一郎   童莉

（2）信用证通知书。

BANK OF CHINA SHANGHAI BRANCH
NOTIFICATION OF DOCUMENTARY CREDIT

TO： SHANGHAI IMPORT & EXPORT TRADE CORPORATION 1321 ZHONGSHAN ROAD SHANGHAI, CHINA	WHEN CORRESPONDING PLEASE QUOTE OUR REF NO.：W556678
	JAN. 12,2021
ISSUING BANK： FUJI BANK LTD 1013，SAKULA OTOLIKINGZA MACHI TOKYO, JAPAN	TRANSMITTED TO US THROUGH 转递行/转让行
L/C NO.：33416852	AMOUNT：USD12500
DATED：20210112	

DEAR SIRS,

WE ADVISE YOU THAT WE HAVE RECEIVED FROM THE A/M BANK A LETTER OF CREDIT, CONTENTS OF WHICH ARE AS PER ATTACHED SHEET(S).

THIS ADVICE AND THE ATTACHED SHEET MUST ACCOMPANY THE RELATIVE DOCUMENTS WHEN PRESENTED FOR NEGOTIATION.

PLEASE NOTE THAT THIS ADVICE DOES NOT CONSTITUTE OUR CONFIRMATION OF ABOVE L/C NOR DOES IT CONVEY ANY ENGAGEMENT OR OBLIGATION ON OUR PART.

IF YOU FIND ANY TERMS AND CONDITIONS IN THE L/C WHICH YOU ARE UNABLE TO COMPLY WITH AND /OR ANY ERROR(S), IT IS SUGGESTED THAT YOU CONTACT APPLICANT DIRECTLY FOR NECESSARY AMENDMENT(S) SO AS TO AVOID ANY DIFFICULTIES WHICH MAY ARISE WHEN DOCUMENTS ARE PRESENTED.

THIS L/C ADVICE IS SUBJECT TO ICC UCP PUBLICATION NO. 600.

THIS L/C CONSISTS OF SHEET, INCLUDING THE COVERING LETTER AND ATTACHMENT.

REMARKS：

YOURS FAITHFULLY

FOR BANK OF CHINA

（3）信用证。

SEQUENCE OF TOTAL	*27:	1/1
FORM OF DOC CREDIT	*40A:	IRREVOCABLE
DOC CREDIT NUMBER	*20:	33416852
DATE OF ISSUE	31C:	210112
DATE AND PLACE OF EXPIRY	*31D:	DATE 210326 PLACE IN THE COUNTRY OF BENEFICIARY
APPLICANT	*50:	TKAMLA CORPORATION
		6-7,KAWARA MACH OSAKA, JAPAN
ISSUING BANK	52A:	FUJI BANK LTD
		1013 SAKULA OTOLIKINGZA MACHI TOKYO, JAPAN
BENEFICIARY	*59:	SHANGHAI IMPORT & EXPORT TRADE CORPORATION
		1321 ZHONGSHAN ROAD SHANGHAI, CHINA
AMOUNT	*32B:	CURRENCY USD AMOUNT 12500
AVAILABLE WITH/BY	*41D:	ANY BANK IN CHINA BY NEGOTIATION
DRAFTS AT	42C:	DRAFTS AT SIGHT FOR FULL INVOICE COST
DRAWEE	42A:	FUJI BANK LTD
PARTIAL SHIPMENT	43P:	PROHIBITED
TRANSSHIPMENT	43T:	PROHIBITED
LOADING ON BOARD	44A:	SHANGHAI
FOR TRANSPORATION TO	44B:	OSAKA PORT
LATEST DATE OF SHIPMENT	44C:	210316
DESCRIPTION OF GOODS	45A:	COTTON BLANKET
		ART NO. H666 500 PCS USD5.50/PC
		ART NO. HX88 500 PCS USD4.50/PC
		ART NO. HE21 500 PCS USD4.80/PC
		ART NO. HA56 500 PCS USD5.20/PC
		ART NO. HH46 500 PCS USD5.00/PC
		CIF OSAKA
DOCUMENTS REQUIRED	46A:	+SIGNED COMMERCIAL INVOICE IN TRIPLICATE CERTIFYING THAT THE CONTENTS OF THE INVOICE ARE TRUE AND CORRECT.
		+PACKING LIST IN TRIPLICATE
		+CERTIFICATE OF ORIGIN, ISSUED BY THE CHAMBER OF COMMERCE OR OTHER AUTHORITY DULY ENTITLED FOR THIS PURPOSE.
		+FULL SET OF CLEAN ON BOARD OCEAN BILL OF LADING MADE OUT TO ORDER OF SHIPPER AND BLANK ENDORSED AND MARKED "FREIGHT PREPAID" AND NOTIFY APPLICANT.
		+FULL SET OF NEGOTIABLE INSURANCE POLICY OR CERTIFICATE BLANK ENDORSED FOR 110 PCT OF INVOICE VALUE COVERING ALL RISKS AND WAR RISK.
CHARGES	71B:	
PERIOD FOR PRESENTATION	48:	ALL BANKING CHARGES OUTSIDE JAPAN ARE FOR ACCOUNT OF BENEFICIARY.
		DOCUMENTS MUST BE PRESENTED WITHIN 15 DAYS AFTER THE DATE OF SHIPMENT BUT WITHIN THE VALIDITY OF THE CREDIT.

（4）补充资料。

①INVOICE NO：XH056671

②INVOICE DATE：FEB.01，2021

③G.W：20.5 KGS/CTN

④N.W：20 KGS/CTN

⑤MEAS：0.2 CBM/CTN

⑥PACKED IN 250 CARTONS，10 PCS/CTN

⑦PACKED IN TWO 20' CONTAINER（集装箱号：TEXU2263999，TEXU2264000）

⑧H.S.CODE：58023090.00

COMMERCIAL INVOICE

SHANGHAI IMPORT & EXPORT TRADE CORPORATION

1321 ZHONGSHAN ROAD SHANGHAI，P.R.CHINA

COMMERCIAL INVOICE

TEL：   INVOICE NO：

FAX：   DATE：

　TO：   S/C NO：

                                               L/C NO：

FROM：   TO：

MARKS & NO.	DESCRIPTION OF GOODS	QUANTITY	UNIT PRICE	AMOUNT
TOTAL				

TOTAL AMOUNT：

项目四　包装单据缮制与操作

【工作情景】

在上海威尔进出口公司与 NU BONNETERIE DE GROOTE 公司达成的出口 5000 条短裤的交易中,上海威尔进出口公司单证员殷实在缮制商业发票的同时也应缮制包装单据。在制作装箱单证时,单证员应知晓每个纸箱的短裤装箱件数、种类、颜色、尺码、净重、毛重和体积等。请以单证员殷实的身份制作装箱单。

【工作任务】

任务一　装箱单缮制与操作

包装单据(Packing Documents)是指一切记载商品包装情况的单据,是对商业发票的补充说明,也是货运单据中的一项重要单据。除散装货交易外,包装单据是外贸单证中不可缺少的单据。进口国海关验关放行、进口商核对货物,也都离不开包装单据。

包装单据主要有装箱单(Packing List)、重量单、尺码单、花色搭配单(Assortment List)、包装说明(Packing Specification)、详细装箱单(Detailed Packing List)、包装提要(Packing Summary)、重量证书(Weight Certificate/Certificate of Weight)、磅码单(Weight Memo)等。目前,外贸企业使用的主要是装箱单、重量单、尺码单,货物内容一般也包括在装箱单中。

一、装箱单的概念

装箱单又称包装单,重点说明每件商品包装的详细情况,表明货物名称、规格、数量、唛头、箱号、件数、重量及包装情况,尤其对不定量包装的商品,要逐件列出每件包装的详细情况。对定量箱装,每件商品都是统一的重量,则只需说明总件数多少、每箱多少重量、合计重量多少,如果信用证来证条款要求提供详细包装单,则必须提供尽可能详细的装箱内容,描述每件包装的细节,包括商品的货号、色号、尺寸搭配、毛净重及包装的尺寸等内容。

二、装箱单的作用

装箱单是卖方缮制商业发票及其他单据时计量、计价的基础资料,是买卖双方交接货物、对照单货是否相符的依据之一,是进出口国海关查验货物的凭证之一,也是公证或商检机构查验货物的参考资料。

目前,我国外贸企业使用的装箱单无统一格式,一般都由卖方自行设计。

装箱单样例见表4.1。

表4.1　装箱单样例

装箱单

PACKING LIST

1. Exporter （1）		3. Packing List Date （3）	
2. Importer （2）		4. Contract No. （4）	
		5. Invoice No. and Date （5）	
6. Shipping Marks; Container No.	7. Number and Kind of Package; Commodity Name	8. N. W；G. W	9. Measurement
（6）	（7）	（8）	（9）
10. Exporter's Stamp and Signature（10）			

三、装箱单的缮制方法与操作注意事项

1.装箱单的缮制方法

（1）出口商（Exporter）

此处填写合同卖方的名称、地址。信用证方式填写受益人的名称和地址。

（2）进口商（Importer）

此处填写合同买方的名称和地址。信用证方式填写开证申请人的名称和地址。

（3）装箱单日期（Packing List Date）

此处可填写与发票相同的日期，但不得早于发票日期。

（4）合同号（Contract No.）

此处填写买卖双方订立的国际货物买卖合同号码。

（5）发票号和日期（Invoice No. and Date）

此处按商业发票填写。

（6）唛头和集装箱号码（Shipping Marks、Container No.）

此处按商业发票的唛头填写，集装箱号码按实际情况填写。

（7）包装类型及件数、商品名称（Number and Kind of Package、Commodity Name）

此处按实际商品名称、包装及件数填写，并与发票和其他单据保持一致。

（8）净重和毛重（N.W and G.W）

此处按实际毛净重情况填写，并与其他单据保持一致。

（9）体积（Measurement）

此处按实际体积情况填写，并与其他单据保持一致。

（10）出口商签章（Exporter's Stamp and Signature）

此处由卖方签字盖章，与发票保持一致。

2.装箱单的操作注意事项

①单据名称和份数必须符合信用证规定。

②货物的名称、规格、数量、唛头等须与其他相关单据保持一致。

③数量、毛重、净重、尺码须与其他相关单据保持一致。

④装箱单的内容应与货物实际包装相符，并与商业发票、提单等所列内容一致。

殷实根据项目二中的信用证样例和信用证修改书样例缮制完成的装箱单见表4.2。

（100PCS/CTN，N.W：8KGS/CTN，G.W：9KGS/CTN，MEAS：0.5M³/CARTON）

表 4.2 完成的装箱单

WILL SHANGHAI TRADING CO. ,LTD.

JZNO. 2009 CHENGNAN ROAD, PUDONG, SHANGHAI, P. R. CHINA

装箱单

PACKING LIST

ISSUER： WILL SHANGHAI TRADING CO. ,LTD. NO. 2021 CHENGNAN ROAD, PUDONG, SHANGHAI, P. R. CHINA		INVOICE NO. : WT980				
		S/C NO. : 2021SW326				
TO： NU BONNETERIE DE GROOTE AUTOSTRADEWEG 69090 MELLE, BELGIUM		DATE：JULY 1ST, 2021				
TRANSPORT DETAILS：FROM SHANGHAI TO ANTWERP						
MARKS AND NOS.	DESCRIPTION	QUANTITY	PACKAGES	N. W	G. W	MEAS
N/M	SHORT TROUSERS-100PCT COTTON TWILL AS PER ORDER D2100326 AND SALES CONTRACT NUMBER 2021SW326, ART. REF. 53. 06. 06243. K	2000 PCS	20 CARTONS	160 KGS	180 KGS	10 CBM
	SHORT TROUSERS-100PCT COTTON TWILL AS PER ORDER D2100327 AND SALES CONTRACT NUMBER 2021SW326, ART. REF. 53. 06. 06243. K 100PCS OF EACH CARTON	3000 PCS	30 CARTONS	240 KGS	270 KGS	15 CBM
TOTAL		5000 PCS	50 CARTONS	400 KGS	450 KGS	25 CBM

任务二 复杂的装箱单缮制与操作

一、复杂的装箱单的概念

有些公司出口的商品属于细、小、杂的商品,种类、规格比较多,每一种商品的包装件数、毛净重、尺码都不一样。这种情况就需要卖方提供详细的装箱单,以便对商业发票进行很好的说明,也供买方和买方所在国海关等部门核查货物,办理清关手续等。

二、复杂的装箱单的缮制方法和操作注意事项

1.缮制方法

复杂的装箱单和一般装箱单的作用和缮制方法相同,就是烦琐一些。因为货物的种类,规格,数量,包装,毛、净重,尺码等过多,所以要求制单人员一定要细致。

2.操作注意事项

①复杂的装箱单缮制一定要仔细再仔细,把每一种货物的型号,规格,数量,包装,毛、净重,尺码等一一横行对齐。

②数量,包装,毛、净重,尺码等小计和总数要对得上。

③相关内容需与合同和信用证保持一致。

【实操训练】

1.根据买卖合同及相关资料缮制装箱单。

SALES CONFIRMATION

NO.:ZC2021017

DATE:FEB. 06, 2021

The seller:

ZhongCheng International Trade Co., Ltd.

20, HangZhou RD., Nanjing, P. R. China

The buyer:

Green Trade Co.

22 Mark Street, Oslo, Norway

The undersigned Seller and Buyer have agreed to close the following transactions; according to the terms and conditions stipulated below:

Commodity and Specification	Quantity	Unit Price	Amount
Hand Tools		CIF OSLO	
Art No.:1018	5000 SETS	USD4.00/SET	USD20000.00
Art No.:1019	5000 SETS	USD3.00/SET	USD15000.00
Goods are Chinese origin			
Total	10000 SETS		USD35000.00

Total Amount: Say US Dollars Thirty Five Thousand Only.

Time of Shipment: Not later than April 30, 2021

Partial Shipment and Transshipment are Allowed.

Port of Shipment:Shanghai,P. R China　　　　Port of Discharge:Oslo,Norway

Payment: By D/P at 30 days after B/L date

Insurance: To be effected by the seller for 110% of the invoice value covering all risks and war risk as per PICC clause.

The buyer	The seller
Green Trade Co.	ZhongCheng International Trade Co.，Ltd.
Mary	Li Ling

补充资料：

①发票号码自编

②唛头：标准化唛头

③B/L DATE：APR. 25，2021 B/L NO：CUSC052765   VESSEL：LINDA V.123

G. W：20 KGS/CTN   N. W：15 KGS/CTN   MEA：30 CM×75 CM×45 CM/CTN

100SETS PACKED IN A CARTON

装箱单

PACKING LIST

ISSUER：			INVOICE NO.：			
			S/C NO.：			
TO：			DATE：			
TRANSPORT DETAILS：						
MARKS AND NOS.	DESCRIPTION	QUANTITY	PACKAGES	N. W	G. W	MEAS
	TOTAL					

2.根据信用证及相关资料缮制装箱单。

FROM：NATIONAL COMMERCIAL BANK, JEDDAH

TO：BANK OF CHINA, JIANGSU BR.

DATE：JAN. 3，2021

L/C NO.：LTC6688

L/C AMOUNT：USD28820.00

APPLICANT：ABC COMPANY, JEDDAH

BENEFICIARY：XYZ COMPANY, NANJING

TIME OF SHIPMENT：APR. 30，2021

DRAFTS TO BE DRAWN ON US AT SIGHT FOR 90PCT OF INVOICE VALUE

PARTIAL SHIPMENT：NOT ALLOWED

MERCHANDISE：ABT 48000 CANS OF MEILING BRAND CANNED ORANGE JAM, 250 GRAM/CAN, 12 CANS IN A CTN

UNIT PRICE：USD6.55/CTN CIF JEDDAH

COUNTRY OF ORIGIN：P. R. CHINA

DOCUMENTS REQUIRED：

+COMMERCIAL INVOICE 3 COPIES DATED THE SAME DATE AS THAT OF L/C ISSUANCE DATE INDI-CATING COUNTRY OF THE GOODS AND CERTIFIED TO BE TRUE AND CORRECT INDICATING CONTRACT NO. SUM356/05 AND L/C NO.

+FULL SET OF CLEAN SHIPPED ON BOARD OCEAN BILL OF LADING MADE OUT TO ORDER OF ISSU-ING BANK, NOTIFYING APPLICANT AND MARKED FREIGHT PREPAID.

+PACKING LIST INDICATING QUANTITY, G. W, N. W. PACKAGE AS REQUIRED BY L/C.

+FULL SET OF INSURANCE POLICY IN DUPLICATE IN NEGOTIABLE FORM BLANK ENDORSED FOR 110PCT OF INVOICE VALUE COVERING ALL RISKS, STRIKES OF PICC, INCLUDING WAREHOUSE TO WAREHOUSE, I. O. P. CLAIMS PAYABLE AT DESTINATION IN THE CURRENCY OF L/C.

ADDITIONAL CONDITIONS：ALL DOCUMENTS MUST INDICATE SHIPPING MARKS AS JAM IN DIAMOND JEDDAH

附加信息：

①发票号码：XY22013015

②受益人的有权签字人为吴仁

③出仓单显示货物：52800 CANS OF MEILING BRAND CANNED ORANGE JAM

④提单显示货物从上海运往吉达

⑤G. W：18 KGS/CTN　　N. W：25 KGS　　MEA：30 CM×25 CM×45 CM/CTN

装箱单
PACKING LIST

ISSUER：			INVOICE NO. ：		
			S/C NO. ：		
TO：			DATE：		
TRANSPORT DETAILS：					
MARKS AND NOS.	DESCRIPTION	QUANTITY	PACKAGES	N. W	G. W	MEAS
	TOTAL					

3. 根据买卖合同、信用证及附加资料缮制装箱单。

（1）合同。

SHANGHAI IMPORT & EXPORT TRADE CORPORATION

1321 ZHONGSHAN ROAD SHANGHAI, CHINA

SALES CONTRACT

TEL：021-65788877　　　　　　　　　　　　S/C NO. ：　HX050264

FAX：021-65788876　　　　　　　　　　　　DATE：JAN. 1, 2021

TO：TKAMLA CORPORATION

　　　6-7，KAWARA MACH OSAKA，JAPAN

DEAR SIRS：

WE HEREBY CONFIRM HAVING SOLD TO YOU THE FOLLOWING GOODS ON TERMS AND CONDITIONS AS SPECIFIED BELOW：

MARKS & NO.	DESCRIPTION OF GOODS	QUANTITY	UNIT PRICE	AMOUNT
T. C	COTTON BLANKET		CIF OSLO	
OSAKA	ART NO. H666	500 PCS	USD5.50/PC	USD2750.00
C/NO. 1-250	ART NO. HX88	500 PCS	USD4.50/PC	USD2250.00
	ART NO. HE21	500 PCS	USD4.80/PC	USD2400.00
	ART NO. HA56	500 PCS	USD5.20/PC	USD2600.00
	ART NO. HH46	500 PCS	USD5.00/PC	USD2500.00
	PACKED IN 250 CTNS			
TOTAL		2500 PCS		USD12500.00

LOADING PORT：SHANGHAI

DESTINATION：OSAKA PORT

PARTIAL SHIPMENT：PROHIBITED

PAYMENT：L/C AT SIGHT

INSURANCE：FOR 110% OF THE INVOICE VALUE COVERING ALL RISKS AND WAR RISK

TIME OF SHIPMENT：LATEST DATE OF SHIPMENT MAR. 10，2021

THE BUYER	THE SELLER
TKAMLA CORPORATION	SHANGHAI IMPORT & EXPORT TRADE CORPORATION
高田一郎	童莉

（2）信用证通知书。

BANK OF CHINA SHANGHAI BRANCH

NOTIFICATION OF DOCUMENTARY CREDIT

TO： SHANGHAI IMPORT & EXPORT TRADE CORPORATION 1321 ZHONGSHAN ROAD SHANGHAI, CHINA	WHEN CORRESPONDING PLEASE QUOTE OUR REF NO：W556678
	JAN. 12,2021
ISSUING BANK： FUJI BANK LTD 1013，SAKULA OTOLIKINGZA MACHI TOKYO，JAPAN	TRANSMITTED TO US THROUGH 转递行/转让行
L/C NO.：33416852	AMOUNT：USD12500
DATED：20210112	

续表

DEAR SIRS,

WE ADVISE YOU THAT WE HAVE RECEIVED FROM THE A/M BANK A LETTER OF CREDIT, CONTENTS OF WHICH ARE AS PER ATTACHED SHEET(s).

THIS ADVICE AND THE ATTACHED SHEET MUST ACCOMPANY THE RELATIVE DOCUMENTS WHEN PRESENTED FOR NEGOTIATION.

THIS ADVICE DOES NOT CONVEY ANY ENGAGEMENT OR OBLIGATION ON OUR PART UNLESS WE HAVE ADED OUR CONFIRMATION.

IF YOU FIND ANY TERMS AND CONDITIONS IN THE L/C WHICH YOU ARE UNABLE TO COMPLY WITH AND/OR ANY ERROR, IT IS SUGGESTED THAT YOU CONTACT APPLICANT DIRECTLY FOR NECESSARY AMENDMENT SO AS TO AVOID ANY DIFFICULTIES WHICH MAY ARISE WHEN DOCUMENTS ARE PRESENTED.

THIS L/C ADVICE IS SUBJECT TO ICC UCP PUBLICATION NO. 600.

THIS L/C CONSISTS OF SHEET, INCLUDING THE COVERING LETTER AND ATTACHMENT.

REMARKS:

YOURS FAITHFULLY

FOR BANK OF CHINA

（3）信用证。

SEQUENCE OF TOTAL	*27:	1/1
FORM OF DOC CREDIT	*40A:	IRREVOCABLE
DOC CREDIT NUMBER	*20:	33416852
DATE OF ISSUE	31C:	210112
DATE AND PLACE OF EXPIRY	*31D:	DATE 210321 PLACE IN THE COUNTRY OF BENEFICIARY
APPLICANT	*50:	TKAMLA CORPORATION
		6-7, KAWARA MACH OSAKA, JAPAN
ISSUING BANK	52A:	FUJI BANK LTD
		1013 SAKULA OTOLIKINGZA MACHI TOKYO, JAPAN
BENEFICIARY	*59:	SHANGHAI IMPORT & EXPORT TRADE CORPORATION
		1321 ZHONGSHAN ROAD SHANGHAI, CHINA
AMOUNT	*32B:	CURRENCY USD AMOUNT 12500
AVAILABLE WITH/BY	*41D:	ANY BANK IN CHINA BY NEGOTIATION
DRAFTS AT	42C:	DRAFTS AT SIGHT FOR FULL INVOICE COST
DRAWEE	42A:	FUJI BANK LTD.

PARTIAL SHIPMENT	43P：	PROHIBITED
TRANSSHIPMENT	43T：	PROHIBITED
LOADING ON BOARD	44A：	SHANGHAI
FOR TRANSPORATION TO	44B：	OSAKA PORT
LATEST DATE OF SHIPMENT	44C：	210316
DESCRIPTION OF GOODS	45A：	COTTON BLANKET
		ART NO. H666 500 PCS USD5. 50/PC
		ART NO. HX88 500 PCS USD4. 50/PC
		ART NO. HE21 500 PCS USD4. 80/PC
		ART NO. HA56 500 PCS USD5. 20/PC
		ART NO. HH46 500 PCS USD5. 00/PC
		CIF OSAKA
DOCUMENTS REQUIRED	46A：	+SIGNED COMMERCIAL INVOICE IN TRIPLICATE
		+PACKING LIST IN TRIPLICATE
		+CERTIFICATE OF ORIGIN, ISSUED BY THE CHAMBER OF COMMERCE OR OTHER AUTHORITY DULY ENTITLED FOR THIS PURPOSE.
		+FULL SET OF CLEAN ON BOARD OCEAN BILL OF LADING MADE OUT TO ORDER OF SHIPPER AND BLANK ENDORSED AND MARKED "FREIGHT PREPAID" AND NOTIFY APPLICANT.
		+FULL SET OF NEGOTIABLE INSURANCE POLICY OR CERTIFICATE BLANK ENDORSED FOR 110 PCT OF INVOICE VALUE COVERING ALL RISKS AND WAR RISK.
CHARGES	71B：	ALL BANKING CHARGES OUTSIDE JAPAN ARE FOR ACCOUNT OF BENEFICIARY.
PERIOD FOR PRESENTATION	48：	DOCUMENTS MUST BE PRESENTED WITHIN 15 DAYS AFTER THE DATE OF SHIPMENT BUT WITHIN THE VALIDITY OF THE CREDIT.

补充资料：

①INVOICE　NO.：XH056671

②INVOICE DATE：FEB. 01, 2021

③PACKING：PACKED IN 250 CTNS

④G. W：20. 5 KGS/CTN N. W：20 KGS/CTN　MEAS：0. 2 CBM/CTN　PACKED IN 250 CARTONS, 10 PCS/CTN　PACKED IN TWO 20' CONTAINER(集装箱号：TEXU2263999, TEXU2264000) H. S. CODE：58023090. 00

⑤唛头：N/M

SHANGHAI IMPORT & EXPORT TRADE CORPORATION

1321 ZHONGSHAN ROAD SHANGHAI, P. R. CHINA
PACKING LIST

ISSUER				INVOICE NO.			
				S/C NO.			
TO				DATE			
TRANSPORT DETAILS							
MARKS AND NOS.	DESCRIPTION	QUANTITY	PACKAGES	N. W	G. W	MEAS	
	TOTAL						

项目五　商业汇票缮制与操作

【项目目标】

知识目标

- 掌握汇票的概念
- 掌握信用证和托收方式下汇票的含义
- 掌握汇票的格式与内容
- 掌握信用证项下汇票的缮制方法
- 掌握托收项下汇票的缮制方法

能力目标

- 能够准确缮制汇票

思政目标

- 通过对商业汇票概念的学习,引导学生关注国际国内相关法律法规,培养学生遵纪守法、严谨细致的职业素养
- 通过对汇票缮制方法的学习,让学生明确信用是票据的灵魂和基石,积极发展票据信用,有利于更好地服务实体经济,从而培养学生的爱国精神和担当意识

【工作情景】

上海威尔进出口公司外贸单证员殷实在缮制商业发票、装箱单等单据时,可同时准备好汇票(Bill of Exchange),为交单议付作准备。单证员应熟知汇票当事人、汇票金额、出票时间地点、付款期限等信息。请以单证员殷实的身份填制汇票。

【工作任务】

任务一　信用证方式下汇票缮制与操作

一、信用证方式下汇票的含义

汇票是国际贸易中常用的支付工具。按照英国相关票据法律所下定义,汇票是指"由一人签发给另一人的无条件书面支付命令,要求受票人见票时或于未来某一规定的或可以确定的时间,将一定金额的款项支付给某一特定的人或者其指定的人或持票人"。

信用证方式下汇票是指出票人(受益人)开给受票人(开证银行或其指定银行)的无条件

支付命令,命令其见票或在将来可以确定的时间付款给收款人(受益人或其往来银行)。

信用证方式下商业汇票样例见表5.1。

表5.1 信用证方式下商业汇票样例

二、信用证方式下汇票缮制方法与操作注意事项

1.信用证方式下汇票缮制方法

(1)出票根据(Drawn under)

信用证项下,出票根据一栏注明开证行完整的名称。

出票根据条款是说明开证行在一定的期限内对汇票的金额履行保证付款责任的法律依据,是信用证项下的汇票不可缺少的重要内容之一。

(2)信用证号码(L/C No.)

此处填写信用证编码,这一栏目的内容要求填写准确无误。

(3)开证日期(Date)

此处填写信用证的开证日期。

(4)年息(Payable with interest@ …%)

此处填写信用证规定的利息率。

(5)号码(No.)

此处填写此项交易的商业发票号码,以便用来核对商业发票与汇票中相关内容,也使整套单据有机联系起来。

(6)汇票金额(the sum of …)

汇票金额用数字小写(Amount in figures)和文字大写(Amount in words)分别表明。在Exchange for栏填小写金额,小写金额栏由货币名称缩写和用阿拉伯数字小写的货币金额构成。缮制时应先填货币名称缩写,再填阿拉伯数字,并保留到小数点后两位,如"USD3478.00"。

在 the sum of 栏填大写金额。大小写要完全一致,包括货币名称和用文字大写的货币金额。缮制时先填货币全称,再填金额的数目文字。习惯上在句首加一个"SAY"意指"计",在句尾打一个"ONLY"意为"整",如"SAY U. S. DOLLARS THREE THOUSAND FOUR HUNDRED AND SEVENTY EIGHT ONLY"。

(7)出票日期

出票日期一般在提单日期之后、信用证到期日之前。

(8)付款期限(At...sight)

付款期限在各国票据中都被认为是票据的重要项目,一张汇票没有确定的期限,这张汇票将是无效的。在缮制汇票付款期限时,应按照信用证的规定填写。如为即期汇票需在"At...sight"中间打上"＊＊＊＊＊＊＊";如为远期汇票,可视情况填写"At ××× days after sight"(见票后×××天)、"At ××× days after date"(出票后×××天)和"At ××× days after B/L date"(提单日后×××天)或直接在横线上填上未来某个具体日期,表示定日付款,如"At 28 June""2021 fixed"并将汇票上的"sight"画去。

(9)收款人(Pay to the order of)

收款人即汇票的抬头人。按国际惯例,信用证和托收项下的汇票一般做成指示性抬头,汇票上写明"付给×××的指定人(Pay to the order of ×××)",×××是该汇票的记名收款人,通过他的背书,汇票可以转让。这是目前出口业务中使用最广泛的类型,汇票的格式也基本上印妥"Pay to the order of..."。

信用证项下汇票的收款人,如果信用证没有特别规定,应以议付行为收款人。托收项下的汇票,一般应以托收行(出口地银行)为收款人。

(10)付款人(To ...)

付款人,又称受票人,一般位于汇票左下角,即"To ..."栏,信用证项下,汇票的付款人应是开证行或信用证指定的银行。

信用证项下汇票的付款人和合同的付款人不完全相同,从信用证的角度来看,汇票的付款人应是提供这笔交易的信用的一方,即开证行或其指定付款行的付款人。但从合同的角度来看,信用证只是一种支付方式,交易中最终的付款人都是进口方,即信用证的开证申请人。根据《UCP600》的规定,"信用证不应要求开立以申请人为付款人的汇票",否则该汇票就成为附加单据,而不能成为支付工具。

(11)出票人及出票地点

出票人即签发汇票的人,在进出口业务中,通常是卖方(信用证的受益人)。按照我国的习惯,出票人一栏通常打上出口公司的全称,并由公司经理签署,也可以盖上出口公司包括有经理章字模的印章。

必须注意,汇票出票人应该是信用证指定的受益人。如果信用证内的受益人不是出具汇票的公司,应修改信用证。如未作修改,汇票的出票人应该是信用证指定的受益人名称,按来证照打,否则,银行将当作出单不符而拒收。同时,汇票的出票人也应同其他单据的签署人名称相符。

汇票上必须注明出票地点,这是因为汇票如在一个国家出票、在另一个国家付款时,需要确定以哪个国家的法律为依据,来判断汇票所具备的必要项目是否齐全,从而使之有效。对此,各国采用出票地法律或行为地法律的原则,即以出票行为的当地法律认为汇票已具备必要项目而生效时,付款地点也同样认为有效。

2. 信用证方式下汇票的操作注意事项

①信用证方式下汇票的受票人(即付款人)应为银行,不能是开证申请人。

②汇票金额大小写须一致,并与信用证规定相符。

③汇票期限须一致,并与信用证规定相符。

④汇票的出票时间和交单时间须符合信用证规定。

殷实根据项目二中的信用证样例和信用证修改书样例缮制完成的信用证方式下的汇票见表5.2。

表5.2 信用证方式下汇票

BILL OF EXCHANGE

| 凭 Drawn under | ING BELGIUM NV/SA(FORMERLY BANK BRUSSELS LAMBERT SA), GENT | | 不可撤销信用证 Irrevocable L/C No. DTBEGM705014 |

日期 Date　　MAY 20, 2021　　支取 Payable with interest @ 　% 按 息 付款

号码 No.　WT980　汇票金额 Exchange for　　USD63250.00　　上海 Shanghai　2021年 7 月 21 日

见票 日后(本汇票之副本未付)付交

at　　*****　　sight of this FIRST of exchange (Second of exchange

Being unpaid) Pay to the order of　BANK OF CHINA , SHANGHAI BRANCH

金额 the sum of　U.S. DOLLARS SIXTY THREE THOUSAND TWO HUNDRED AND FIFTY ONLY.

此致 To　ING BELGIUM NV/SA(FORMERLY BANK BRUSSELS LAMBERT SA), GENT

WILL SHANGHAI TRADING CO., LTD.

殷实
(Authorized Signature)

任务二　托收方式下汇票缮制与操作

一、托收方式下汇票的含义

托收方式下汇票是指出票人(买卖合同的卖方)开给受票人(买卖合同的买方)的无条件支付命令,命令其见票或将来可以确定的时间付款给收款人(卖方或其往来银行)。

二、托收方式下汇票的缮制方法

在以托收方式托收票款时,使用的汇票与信用证支付条件的汇票相似,但在填写方法上

有以下区别:在出票依据"Drawn under"后面填写发运货物的名称、数量,有的还加起运港和目的港以及合同号等,如:"Covering 800 cartons of non-woven bags shipped from Shanghai to Toronto under Contract No. EG200810"(清偿第 EG200810 合同项下自上海装运至多伦多的无纺布袋800 箱)。在"付款期限"栏目内,填写"D/P at sight"(即期付款交单)或"D/P ××××days"(×××天远期付款交单),"D/A×××days"(×××天承兑交单),在"受款人"栏内填写托收行名称。在"付款人"栏内应为买方的名称和地址,在"出票地点"栏内应为委托人(卖方)向托收银行办理托收手续的地点。

【实操训练】

1.根据所给资料缮制汇票。

BENEFICIARY:ABC LEATHER GOODS CO.,LTD.

        123 HUANGHE ROAD,TIANJIN CHINA

APPLICANT:XYZ TRADING COMPANY

        456 SPAGNOLI ROAD,NEW YORK 11747 USA

DRAFTS TO BE DRAWN AT 30 DAYS AFTER SIGHT ON ISSUING BANK FOR 90% OF INVOICE VALUE.

YOU ARE AUTHORIZED TO DRAWN ON ROYAL BANK OF NEW YORK FOR DOCUMENTARY IRREVO-CABLE CREDIT NO.98765 DATED APR. 15, 2021,EXPRITY DATE MAY 31, 2021 FOR NEGOTIATION.

AVAILABLE WITH ANY BANK IN CHINA BY NEGOTIATION

附加资料:

①发票号:1234567

②发票金额:USD108000 CIF NEW YORK

③授权签字人:李炎

BILL OF EXCHANGE		
凭 Drawn under		不可撤销信用证 Irrevocable L/C No.
日期 Date	支取 Payable with interest @ % 按 息 付款	天津 年 月 日 Tianjin
号码 No.	汇票金额 Exchange for	
	见票 at	日后(本汇票之副本未付)付交 sight of this FIRST of exchange (Second of exchange
Being unpaid) Pay to the order of		
金额 the sum of		
此致 To		
		(Authorized Signature)

2. 根据买卖合同缮制汇票。

SALES CONFIRMATION

NO. :ZC2021017

DATE：FEB. 6, 2021

The seller：

ZhongCheng International Trade Co. , Ltd.

20, HangZhou RD. , Nanjing, P. R. China

The buyer：

Green Trade Co.

22 Mark Street, Oslo, Norway

The undersigned Seller and Buyer have agreed to close the following transactions according to the terms and conditions stipulated below：

Commodity and Specification	Quantity	Unit Price	Amount
Hand Tools		CIF OSLO	
Art No. : 1018	5000 SETS	USD4. 00/SET	USD20000. 00
Art No. : 1019	5000 SETS	USD3. 00/SET	USD15000. 00
Goods are Chinese origin			
Total	10000 SETS		USD35000. 00

Total Amount：Say US Dollars Thirty Five Thousand Only.

Time of Shipment：Not later than April 30, 2021.

Partial shipment and transshipment are allowed.

Port of Shipment：Shanghai,P. R. China   Port of Discharge：Oslo,Norway

Payment：By D/P at 30 days after B/L Date

Insurance：To be effected by the sellers for 110% of the invoice value covering all risks and war risk as per PICC clause.

The buyer：

Green Trade Co.

MARY

The seller：

ZhongCheng International Trade Co. , Ltd.

LI LING

BILL OF EXCHANGE

凭
Drawn under

日期
Date

号码
No.

汇票金额
Exchange for

见票
at

合同
S/C.

第   号
No.

支取 Payable with interest @   %   按   息   付款

南京   年   月   日
Nanjing

日后（本汇票之副本未付）付交
sight of this FIRST of exchange （Second of exchange

Being unpaid) Pay to the order of

金额
the sum of

此致
To

(Authorized Signature)

3. 根据信用证及相关信息缮制汇票。

FROM：NATIONAL COMMERCIAL BANK，JEDDAH

TO：BANK OF CHINA，JIANGSU BR.

DATE：JAN. 3, 2021

L/C NO.：LTC6688

L/C AMOUNT：USD28820.00

APPLICANT：ABC COMPANY，JEDDAH

BENEFICIARY：XYZ COMPANY，NANJING

TIME OF SHIPMENT：APR 30, 2021

DRAFTS TO BE DRAWN ON US AT SIGHT FOR 90PCT OF INVOICE VALUE

PARTIAL SHIPMENT：NOT ALLOWED

MERCHANDISE：ABOUT 48000 CANS OF MEILING BRAND CANNED ORANGE JAM，250 GRAM/CAN，12 CANS IN A CARTON

UNIT PRICE：USD6.55/CARTON CIF JEDDAH

COUNTRY OF ORIGIN：P. R. CHINA

DOCUMENTS REQUIRED：

+COMMERCIAL INVOICE 3 COPIES DATED THE SAME DATE AS THAT OF L/C ISSUANCE DATE INDICATING COUNTRY OF THE GOODS AND CERTIFIED TO BE TRUE AND CORRECT INDICATING CONTRACT NO. SUM356/05 AND L/C NO.

+FULL SET OF CLEAN SHIPPED ON BOARD OCEAN BILL OF LADING MADE OUT TO ORDER OF ISSUING BANK，NOTIFYING APPLICANT AND MARKED FREIGHT PREPAID.

+PACKING LIST INDICATING QUANTITY，G. W，N. W. PACKAGE AS REQUIRED BY L/C.

+FULL SET OF INSURANCE POLICY IN DUPLICATE IN NEGOTIABLE FORM BLANK ENDORSED FOR 110PCT OF INVOICE VALUE COVERING ALL RISKS，STRIKES OF PICC，INCLUDING WAREHOUSE TO WAREHOUSE，I. O. P. CLAIMS PAYABLE AT DESTINATION IN THE CURRENCY OF L/C.

ADDITIONAL CONDITIONS：ALL DOCUMENTS MUST INDICATE SHIPPING MARKS AS JAM IN DIAMOND JEDDAH

附加信息：

①发票号码：XY22073017

②受益人的有权签字人为吴仁

③出仓单显示货物：52800 CANS OF MEILING BRAND CANNED ORANGE JAM

④提单显示货物从上海运往吉达

G. W:18 KGS/CTN   N. W:25 KGS   MEA：30 CM×25 CM×45 CM/CTN

```
BILL OF EXCHANGE

凭                                        不可撤销信用证
Drawn under                              Irrevocable    L/C No.
日期
Date                支取 Payable with interest @      %      按      息      付款
号码          汇票金额                        南京          年    月    日
No.          Exchange for                Nanjing
            见票                          日 后(本 汇 票 之 副 本 未 付)付 交
            at                          sight of this FIRST of exchange (Second of exchange
Being unpaid) Pay to the order of
金额
the sum of


此致
To




                                                        (Authorized Signature)
```

4. 根据买卖合同、信用证及附加资料缮制汇票。

（1）合同。

SHANGHAI IMPORT & EXPORT TRADE CORPORATION
1321 ZHONGSHAN ROAD SHANGHAI, CHINA
SALES CONTRACT

TEL：021-65788877   S/C NO.： HX050264

FAX：021-65788876   DATE： JAN. 01，2021

To：TKAMLA CORPORATION

　　6-7,KAWARA MACH OSAKA，JAPAN

DEAR SIRS：

WE HEREBY CONFIRM HAVING SOLD TO YOU THE FOLLOWING GOODS ON TERMS AND CONDITIONS AS SPECIFIED BELOW：

MARKS & NO.	DESCRIPTION OF GOODS	QUANTITY	UNIT PRICE	AMOUNT
T. C	COTTON BLANKET		CIF OSLO	
OSAKA	ART NO. H666	500 PCS	USD5.50/PC	USD2750.00
C/NO.1-250	ART NO. HX88	500 PCS	USD4.50/PC	USD2250.00
	ART NO. HE21	500 PCS	USD4.80/PC	USD2400.00
	ART NO. HA56	500 PCS	USD5.20/PC	USD2600.00
	ART NO. HH46	500 PCS	USD5.00/PC	USD2500.00
	PACKED IN 250 CTNS			

LOADING PORT：SHANGHAI

DESTINATION：OSAKA PORT

PARTIAL SHIPMENT：PROHIBITED

PAYMENT：L/C AT SIGHT

INSURANCE：FOR 110% OF THE INVOICE VALUE COVERING ALL RISKS AND WAR RISK

TIME OF SHIPMENT：LATEST DATE OF SHIPMENT MAR 10，2021

THE BUYER	THE SELLER
TKAMLA CORPORATION	SHANGHAI IMPORT & EXPORT TRADE CORPORATION
高田一郎	童莉

（2）信用证通知书。

BANK OF CHINA SHANGHAI BRANCH
NOTIFICATION OF DOCUMENTARY CREDIT

TO： SHANGHAI IMPORT & EXPORT TRADE CORPORATION 1321 ZHONGSHAN ROAD SHANGHAI, CHINA	WHEN CORRESPONDING PLEASE QUOTE OUR REF NO. ：W556678
	JAN. 12，2021
ISSUING BANK： FUJI BANK LTD. 1013，SAKULA OTOLIKINGZA MACHI TOKYO，JAPAN	TRANSMITTED TO US THROUGH 转递行/转让行
L/C NO. ：33416852	AMOUNT：USD12500
DATED：20210112	

DEAR SIRS，

　　WE ADVISE YOU THAT WE HAVE RECEIVED FROM THE A/M BANK A LETTER OF CREDIT，CONTENTS OF WHICH ARE AS PER ATTACHED SHEET(s).

　　THIS ADVICE AND THE ATTACHED SHEET MUST ACCOMPANY THE RELATIVE DOCUMENTS WHEN PRESENTED FOR NEGOTIATION.

　　THIS ADVICE DOES NOT CONVEY ANY ENGAGEMENT OR OBLIGATION ON OUR PART UNLESS WE HAVE ADED OUR CONFIRMATION.

　　IF YOU FIND ANY TERMS AND CONDITIONS IN THE L/C WHICH YOU ARE UNABLE TO COMPLY WITH AND/OR ANY ERROR，IT IS SUGGESTED THAT YOU CONTACT APPLICANT DIRECTLY FOR NECESSARY AMENDMENT SO AS TO AVOID ANY DIFFICULTIES WHICH MAY ARISE WHEN DOCUMENTS ARE PRESENTED.

　　THIS L/C ADVICE IS SUBJECT TO ICC UCP PUBLICATION NO. 600.

　　THIS L/C CONSISTS OF SHEET，INCLUDING THE COVERING LETTER AND ATTACHMENT.

　　REMARKS：

YOURS FAITHFULLY

FOR BANK OF CHINA

（3）信用证。

SEQUENCE OF TOTAL	*27：	1/1
FORM OF DOC CREDIT	*40A：	IRREVOCABLE
DOC CREDIT NUMBER	*20：	33416852
DATE OF ISSUE	31C：	210112
DATE AND PLACE OF EXPIRY	*31D：	DATE 210317 PLACE IN THE COUNTRY OF BENEFICIARY
APPLICANT	*50：	TKAMLA CORPORATION
		6-7, KAWARA MACH OSAKA, JAPAN
ISSUING BANK	52A：	FUJI BANK LTD
		1013 SAKULA OTOLIKINGZA MACHI TOKYO, JAPAN
BENEFICIARY	*59：	SHANGHAI IMPORT & EXPORT TRADE CORPORATION
		1321 ZHONGSHAN ROAD SHANGHAI, CHINA
AMOUNT	*32B：	CURRENCY USD AMOUNT 12500
AVAILABLE WITH/BY	*41D：	ANY BANK IN CHINA BY NEGOTIATION
DRAFTS AT	42C：	DRAFTS AT SIGHT FOR FULL INVOICE COST
DRAWEE	42A：	FUJI BANK LTD
PARTIAL SHIPMENT	43P：	PROHIBITED
TRANSSHIPMENT	43T：	PROHIBITED
LOADING ON BOARD	44A：	SHANGHAI
FOR TRANSPORATION TO	44B：	OSAKA PORT
LATEST DATE OF SHIPMENT	44C：	210316
DESCRIPTION OF GOODS	45A：	COTTON BLANKET
		ART NO. H666 500PCS USD5.50/PC
		ART NO. HX88 500PCS USD4.50/PC
		ART NO. HE21 500PCS USD4.80/PC
		ART NO. HA56 500PCS USD5.20/PC
		ART NO. HH46 500PCS USD5.00/PC
		CIF OSAKA
DOCUMENTS REQUIRED	46A：	+SIGNED COMMERCIAL INVOICE IN TRIPLICATE
		+PACKING LIST IN TRIPLICATE
		+CERTIFICATE OF ORIGIN, ISSUED BY THE CHAMBER OF COMMERCE OR OTHER AUTHORITY DULY ENTITLED FOR THIS PURPOSE.
		+FULL SET OF CLEAN ON BOARD OCEAN BILL OF LADING MADE OUT TO ORDER OF SHIPPER AND BLANK ENDORSED AND MARKED "FREIGHT PREPAID" AND NOTIFY APPLICANT.
		+FULL SET OF NEGOTIABLE INSURANCE POLICY OR CERTIFICATE BLANK ENDORSED FOR 110 PCT OF INVOICE VALUE COVERING ALL RISKS AND WAR RISK.
CHARGES	71B：	ALL BANKING CHARGES OUTSIDE JAPAN ARE FOR ACCOUNT OF BENEFICIARY.
PERIOD FOR PRESENTATION	48：	DOCUMENTS MUST BE PRESENTED WITHIN 15 DAYS AFTER THE DATE OF SHIPMENT BUT WITHIN THE VALIDITY OF THE CREDIT.

（4）补充资料。

①INVOICE　NO：XH056671

②INVOICE DATE：FEB.01，2021

③PACKING

④G.W：20.5 KGS/CTN

⑤N.W：20 KGS/CTN

⑥MEAS：0.2 CBM/CTN

⑦PACKED IN 250 CARTONS，10 PCS/CTN

⑧PACKED IN TWO 20' CONTAINER（集装箱号：TEXU2263999，TEXU2264000）

⑨H.S.CODE：58023090.00

BILL OF EXCHANGE

凭
Drawn under

日期
Date

号码
No.

凭票
Exchange for

见票
at

Being unpaid) Pay to the order of

金额
the sum of

此致
To

不可撤销信用证
Irrevocable　　L/C　No.

支取 Payable with interest @　　　%　　按　　息　　付款
上海　　　年　　月　　日
Shanghai

日后（本汇票之副本未付）付交
sight of this FIRST of exchange (Second of exchange

(Authorized Signature)

项目六　运输相关单据缮制与操作

【项目目标】

知识目标

- 掌握订舱委托书的概念、内容和缮制方法
- 掌握海运提单的概念、性质和作用
- 掌握海运提单的内容和缮制方法
- 掌握进口换单和提货单的概念

能力目标

- 能够缮制订舱委托书
- 能够缮制海运提单
- 能够进行进口换单操作

思政目标

- 通过对海运提单具有物权特征作用的教学,告诫学生伪造提单骗取货款的事件屡屡发生,阻碍了国际贸易的发展;帮助学生树立廉洁自律、诚实守信、遵规守纪的责任意识

【工作情景】

　　上海威尔进出口公司按照与外商签订的合同和信用证要求,已准备好货物。临近交货期,出口商开始着手安排货物运输事宜,单证员应熟知订舱委托书的内容和填写要求,熟悉海运提单的内容及操作流程。请以上海威尔进出口公司单证员殷实的身份填制货物订舱委托书,并及时取得满足信用证要求的提单。

【工作任务】

任务一　订舱委托书

　　国际贸易中,买卖双方交接货物要通过运输来实现,买卖双方及各有关当事人处理运输事宜时需要以运输单据为依据。与运输有关的单据有订舱委托书(Booking Note)、海运提单、装船通知、装船指示等。

一、订舱委托书的概念

　　订舱委托书是进出口商为了买卖商品,通过货代公司向船公司进行订舱的申请书。

订舱委托书样例见表6.1。

表6.1 海运订舱委托书样例

海运订舱委托书

委托编号 （Entrusting Serial）（1）	提单号 （B/L No.）（2）	合同号 （Contract No.）（3）	委托日期 （Entrusting Date）（4）
发货人名称地址（Shipper's Full Name and Address） （5）			
收货人名称地址（Consignee's Full Name and Address） （6）			
通知方名称地址（Notify Party's Full Name and Address） （7）			
装货港（Port of Loading） （8）	目的港（Port of Destination） （9）		船名（Vessel）航次（Voy.） （10）

唛头标记 （Marks & No.）	包装件数及种类 （No. & Kind of Package）	货物说明 （Description of Goods）	毛重 （Gross Weight in KGS）	体积 （Measurement in CBM）
（11）	（12）	（13）	（14）	（15）

装船日期（Loading Date）（16）	可否转船（Transshipment）（17）	可否分批（Partial Shipment）（18）
信用证有效期 （L/C Expiry Date）（19）	提单份数 （20） （Copies of B/L）	正本 Original　　副本 Copy

运费及支付地点（Freight Payable at）（21）

备注（Remarks）：

委托人签字（Entrusting Party Signature）：（22）
地址（Address）：
电话（Telephone）：

二、订舱委托书缮制方法和操作注意事项

1.订舱委托书缮制方法

（1）委托编号（Entrusting Serial）
填写发票号。
（2）提单号（B/L No.）
留空不填。

（3）合同号（Contract No.）

按照实际合同号填写。

（4）委托日期（Entrusting Date）

填写委托办理租船订舱的日期。

（5）发货人名称地址（Shipper's Full Name and Address）

填出口企业的名称和地址,若由货代公司代理货主租船订舱的,则填该货代公司的名称。

（6）收货人名称地址（Consignee's Full Name and Address）

信用证方式下,一般信用证提单条款都会予以规定,应按规定填写;托收方式下,一般填"To Order"或空白不填。收货人的写法有以下 3 种。

①记名抬头。在收货人（Consignee）栏内填写"×××Co."一般是合同的买方。此种提单只能由提单上规定的收货人提货,不能转让。

②指示抬头。在收货人（Consignee）栏内填写"to order"（凭指示）或"to order of ×××"（凭×××指示）。此种提单可以经过背书转让,广泛使用在国际贸易中。

③不记名抬头。在收货人（Consignee）栏内留空或填写"Bearer"（来人）,此种提单对收货人的权利没有保障,很少使用。

（7）通知方名称地址（Notify Party's Full Name and Address）

一般由买方或其代理人指定,其职责是及时接受船方发出的到货通知并将之转告真实收货人,故要求填写详细名称和地址。

信用证方式下按规定填写;其他方式下填写买方名称和地址。

（8）装货港（Port of Loading）

装运港即船方收货的港口,一般按信用证的规定填写,注意不能用国名或地名代替,若遇重名港口,应加注国名或地名。

（9）目的港（Port of Destination）

目的港即船方卸货的港口,一般按信用证的规定填写,注意不能用国名或地名代替,若遇重名港口,应加注国名或地名。

（10）船名（Vessel）航次（Voy.）

填写订舱的船名和航次,注意准确无误。

（11）唛头标记（Marks & No.）

若信用证有规定,则按规定填写;若信用证未规定,一般由卖方自行设计;若无唛头,则应注明"N/M"。

（12）包装件数及种类（No. & Kind of Package）

此处填写包装的件数和包装的种类。按最大包装的实际件数填写,如 10 万码花布,分别用粗坯布捆成 100 捆,则填"100 捆"。若出口货物有多件,包装方式和材料都不同,则填每种货物的最大包装件数,如 20 个托盘、10 个集装袋、25 个捆包布匹,合计 55 件。

（13）货物说明（Description of Goods）

货物的大类名称或统称,若同时出口不同的商品,则应分别填写。

（14）毛重（Gross Weight）

按货物实际毛重填写，计量单位为千克。若一次装运的货物有几种不同的包装材料或是完全不同的货物，则应分别填写，然后合计。

（15）体积（Measurement）

按货物实际体积填写，计量单位为立方米。重量和尺码是船公司计算运费的基础，应如实填写。

（16）装船日期（Loading Date）

按合同和信用证规定的装运期填写。

（17）可否转船（Transshipment）

严格按合同和信用证的规定，填写"允许"或"不允许"。

（18）可否分批（Partial Shipment）

严格按合同和信用证的规定，填写"允许"或"不允许"。

（19）信用证有效期（L/C Expiry Date）

按信用证规定的有效期填写。

（20）提单份数（Copies of B/L）

用大写英文数字表示，正本提单份数一般填写为"Three"，副本提单份数根据买方需要份数填写。

（21）运费及支付地点（Freight Payable at）

根据买卖合同中的贸易术语填写"运费到付（Freight Collect）"或"运费预付/已付（Freight Prepaid/Paid）"。CIF、CFR 术语填"Freight Prepaid/Paid"，FOB 术语填"Freight Collect"。

若填了"Freight Prepaid/Paid"，则在"Prepaid at"一栏内填写装运港名称；若填了"Freight Collect"，则在"Collect at"一栏内填写目的港名称。

（22）委托人签字（Entrusting Party Signature）

出口企业盖章，并注明出口企业地址和电话号码，由出口企业经办人签字。

2. 订舱委托书的操作注意事项

①订舱委托书的填制必须符合合同和信用证规定的发货人、收货人、通知人，特别是收货人抬头必须符合合同、信用证规定。

②装运港、目的港的填制须符合信用证和合同规定，且与实际装运港、目的港相符。

③船名、航次号按实际装船的情况填写。

④唛头、包装件数及种类、货物描述、毛重、尺码等须按实际情况填写，且与合同、信用证保持一致。

⑤装运期、有效期、分批装运和转运等内容须按实际情况填写，且与合同、信用证规定相符。

⑥提单份数按要求填写。

⑦运费及支付地点须与使用的贸易术语相符。

任务二 海运提单

一、海运提单的概念

海运提单(Bill of Lading)简称提单,是承运人收到货物后出具的货物收据,也是承运人所签署的运输契约的证明。海运提单还代表所载货物的所有权,是一种具有物权特性的凭证。

二、海运提单的作用

1.货物收据

海运提单证明承运人已按提单所载内容收到货物。

2.物权凭证

海运提单代表着货物的所有权,提单持有人可以凭提单提货,也可以将提单背书转让,还可以将提单做抵押。

3.运输契约证明

海运提单背面载有承运人和托运人双方权利与义务、责任与豁免的规定,所以,提单起到了运输契约证明的作用。

海运提单样例见表6.2。

三、海运提单缮制方法与操作注意事项

1.海运提单缮制方法

(1)托运人(Shipper)

与海运托运委托书相应栏目填法相同。一般填写卖方的名称,有时也可以是第三方。《UCP600》规定:"除非 L/C 另有规定,银行将接受表明以 L/C 受益人以外的第三人作为发货人的运输单据。"目前实际业务中,有些货运代理公司将自己的公司名称写在这一栏。

(2)收货人(Consignee or Order)

与海运托运委托书相应栏目填法相同,必须严格与信用证规定的一致。如果 L/C 规定"…Bill of Lading made out ABC CO. ",则"提单收货人"一栏应填写"ABC CO. ";如果 L/C 规定"…Bill of Lading made out to order",则"提单收货人"一栏应填写"To order"。

如果收货人是做成"To order""To order of shipper"或"To order of negotiating bank",则托运人或议付行应在提单背面作空白背书。

(3)通知人(Notify Party)

通知人与海运委托书相应栏目填法相同,要与信用证的规定一致。例如,信用证提单条款

中规定："…Bill of Lading…notify applicant"，则提单通知人栏中要打上开证申请人的详细名称和地址。

表 6.2　海运提单样例

1. Shipper (1)		B/L No.
2. Consignee or Order (2)		**SINOTRANS** **中国外运广东公司** SINOTRANS GUANGDONG COMPANY **OCEAN BILL OF LADING**
3. Notify Party (3)		SHIPPED on board in apparent good order and condition (unless otherwise indicated) the goods or packages specified herein and to be discharged at the mentioned port of discharge or as near there to as the vessel may safely get and be always afloat. 　The weight, measure, marks and numbers, quality, contents and value, being particulars furnished by the Shipper, are not checked by the Carrier on loading.
4. Place of Receipt (4)	5. Port of Loading (5)	**The Shipper, Consignee and the Holder of this Bill of Lading hereby expressly accept and agree to all printed, written or stamped provisions, exceptions and conditions of this Bill of Lading, including those on the back hereof.** 　IN WITNESS whereof the number of original Bills of Lading stated below have been signed, one of which being accomplished the other(s) to be void.
6. Vessel Voyage No. (6)	7. Port of Transshipment (7)	
8. Port of Discharge (8)	9. Place of Delivery (9)	

10. Container Seal No. or Marks and Nos. (10)	11. Number and Kind of Package (11)	12. Description of Goods (12)	13. Gross Weight (KGS) (13)	14. Measurement (CBM) (14)

15. Freight and Charges (15)			REGARDING TRANSSHIPMENT INFORMATION PLEASE CONTACT
Ex. Rate	Prepaid at	Freight Payable at	16. Place and Date of Issue (16)
	Total Prepaid	17. Number of Original B/L (17)	18. Signed for or on Behalf of the Master (18)
			As Agent

如果收货人是做成"To order of issuing bank"或"To order of applicant"，则托运人不必进行背书。

（3）通知人（Notify Party）

几乎所有的提单上都有通知人名称这一项，但在记名提单上就没有必要填写通知人了，因此这时可以填写"Same as Consignee"。通知人有时是作为预定收货人或代理人，必须与信用证规定的完全一致，如果信用证没有规定，此栏可以不填，即使已经填写了内容，银行也可以接受但不必进行审核。

（4）收货地（Place of Receipt）

此栏填报实际收货地点，如工厂、仓库等。在一般海运提单中，没有此栏目，但在多式联运提单中就有此栏目。如果提单注明的收货地与装货港不同，例如，收货地为"Nanjing"，装货港为"Shanghai"，则不管是已装船提单还是收妥备运提单都必须加注已装船批注、装船日期、实际装船的船名和装货港名称。

（5）装运港（Port of Loading）

与海运托运单相应栏目填法相同，必须与信用证规定的装货港一致。例如，信用证规定装货港为"Shanghai"，应把"Shanghai"显示在"装货港（Port of Loading）"处，不能将其显示在"收货地（Place of Receipt）"处，而把装货港写成另一个港口名，同时应填写实际港口的名称。例如，信用证规定"From Chinese Port"，则提单上的装货港应显示具体港口的名称，如"Shanghai Port"。如果信用证规定"From Tianjin Port/ Shanghai Port"，则装货港处只需填写一个港口即可。如果提单上显示了"Intended port of loading/intended port of discharge"，则不管是已装船提单还是收妥备运提单都必须加注已装船批注、装船日期和实际装货港或卸货港名称。

（6）船名和航次（Vessel and Voyage No. ）

若是已装船提单，须注明船名和航次；若是收妥待运提单，待货物实际装船完毕后记载船名。该项记载的意义有多个方面，如便于购买保险，便于跟踪查询，便于发生合同纠纷法院有确定的客体、可采取诉讼保全等。只要符合信用证条款，可以接受任何船名的海运提单。

如果在提单上显示了"Intended vessel：A vessel"，则不管是已装船提单还是收妥备运提单，都必须加注已装船批注、装船日期和实际装船的船名。此栏必须填写船名和航次（Vessel and Voyage No. ），如没有航次，可以不显示。

（7）转运港（Port of Transshipment）

只有货物在海运途中进行转运时才填写此栏。例如，信用证规定"Shipment from Shanghai to Hamburg with transshipment at Hong Kong"，则提单可以这样填写："装货港：Shanghai，卸货港：Hamburg with transshipment at Hong Kong"，转运港可不填；或者"卸货港：Hamburg，转运港：Hong Kong。"

如果信用证允许转运，在同一提单全程海运前提下，银行可以接受货物将被转运的提单。即使信用证禁止转运，银行也可接受以下提单。

①表明转运将发生，前提是提单上已证实有关的货物是由集装箱（Container）、拖车（Trailer）或"子母船"（"LASH" barge）装运，而且同一提单包括全程海运运输。

②含有承运人有权转运的条款，但不包括诸如"Transshipment has taken place"等明确表示已转运的提单。

（8）卸货港（Port of Discharge）

此项与海运托运单相应栏目填法相同，必须与信用证规定的卸货港一致。例如，信用证规定卸货港为"Hamburg"，应把"Hamburg"显示在"卸货港（Port of Discharge）"处，不能将其显示在"目的地（Place of Delivery）"处，而把卸货港写成另一个港口名。又如，当信用证规定"From Shanghai to Hamburg via Singapore"时，则应将"Hamburg"显示在"卸货港"处，不能将"Singapore"写在"卸货港"处，而把"Hamburg"标注在"目的地"处；同时，应填写实际港口的名称。例如，信用证规定"To European Main Port"，则提单上的卸货港应显示具体港口的名称，如"Hamburg Port"。

（9）交付地（Place of Delivery）

可根据实际情况填写具体的交货地名称。在此，如果收货地与交货地都空白，就是普通的海运提单，而不是多式联运提单了。

（10）唛头与封志号（Container Seal No. or Marks and Nos.）

与海运托运单相应栏目填法相同，应与信用证、商业发票和其他单据一致。当没有唛头时，用"N/M"表示。

（11）包装件数及种类（Number and Kind of Package）

与海运托运单相应栏目填法相同。提请注意，此栏也是一旦发生赔偿时计算赔偿费的一个计量数，即"件数×赔偿费率"。

（12）货物描述（Description of Goods）

与海运订舱委托书相应栏目填法相同。应是信用证规定的货物，但在与信用证规定的货物描述不矛盾的前提下可以用商品的统称。例如，信用证的品名为"Lady's shirts"，而提单显示"Garment"是可以接受的。

（13）毛重（Gross Weight）

与海运托运单相应栏目填法相同。此处显示货物的毛重，当货物无毛重时，可以在标有毛重的栏目加注净重"N. W：×××　KGS"。

（14）体积（Measurement）

与海运订舱委托书相应栏目填法相同，一般以 CBM 为计量单位，小数点后保留 3 位小数。

（15）运费的支付（Freight and Charges）

与海运订舱委托书相应栏目填法相同。一般有运费预付（Freight Prepaid）和运费到付（Freight Collect）两种情况。当使用 CIF 或 CFR 时，应填写"运费预付（Freight Prepaid）"；使用 FOB 时，应填写"运费到付（Freight Collect）"。

（16）签发的提单日期和地点（Place and Date of Issue）

与海运托运单相应栏目填法相同。签发地点一般是装货港的所在地，如与该地不一致，也可以接受。每张提单必须有签发日期。

（17）正本的提单份数（Number of Original B/L）

与海运托运相应栏目填法相同，但必须显示签发了几份正本。如果提单上标注有"Duplicate"和"Triplicate"，其效力等同于"Second original""Third original"，可以被接受。

（18）承运人或承运人代理人签字、盖章（Signed for or on Behalf of the Master）

根据《UCP600》的规定：海运提单应由承运人或代表承运人的具名代理人签署证实，或由船长或代表船长的具名代理人签署证实。

另外，海运提单必须是已装船提单，即使信用证仅要求"B/L"而未标明"Shipped on board B/L"，提单也一定要有"已装船（On Board）"的表示。

提单要显示装船日期，而且此日期不能迟于信用证规定的最迟装运日。

实务中可分成两种情况。

①提单上预先印就"已装船"文字或相同意思，如"Shipped on board the vessel named here in apparent good order and condition…"或"Shipped in apparent good order and condition…"。这种提单通常被称为"已装船提单"，不必另行加注"已装船"批注，提单的签发日期就是装船日期和装运日期。

②提单上只有"Received by the carrier from the shipper in apparent good order and condition…"。这种通常被称为"收妥备运提单"，这时需在提单上加注"已装船（On board）"的批注，并在旁边显示装船日期，该装船日期即为装运日期；而提单的签发日期不能视作装船日期和装运日期。

2. 海运提单的操作注意事项

①填制操作同订舱委托书。

②如海运提单的收货人抬头为"To order"或"To order of ×××"，交单时背书人不要忘记在提单背面背书，否则，海运提单的所有权并未得到转移。

此外，运输相关的单据还有装船通知、装船指示等，这些单据详情见项目十。

单证员殷实根据项目二中的信用证样例和信用证修改书缮制的海运提单见表6.3。

G. W：9 KGS/CTN

N. W：8 KGS/CTN

MEAS：0.5 CBM/CTN

PACKED IN 50 CARTONS, 100 PCS/CTN

PACKED IN ONE 20' CONTAINER（集装箱号：TEXU2263888）

表6.3 缮制好的海运提单

1. Shipper WILL SHANGHAI TRADING CO.,LTD NO.2009 CHENGNAN ROAD, PUDONG, SHANGHAI,P.R.CHINA	B/L No. **ENSIGN FREIGHT (CHINA)LTD.** **OCEAN BILL OF LADING**

2. Consignee or Order TO ORDER	SHIPPED on board in apparent good order and condition (unless otherwise indicated) the goods or packages specified herein and to be discharged at the mentioned port of discharge or as near there to as the vessel may safely get and be always afloat. 　　The weight, measure, marks and numbers, quality, contents and value, being particulars furnished by the Shipper, are not checked by the Carrier on loading.
3. Notify Party NU BONNETERIE DE GROOTE AUTOSTRADEWEG 69090 MELLE BELGIUM	**The Shipper, Consignee and the Holder of this Bill of Lading here by expressly accept and agree to all printed, written or stamped provisions, exceptions and conditions of this Bill of Lading, including those on the back here of.** 　　IN WITNESS where of the number of original Bills of Lading stated below have been signed, one of which being accomplished the other(s) to be void.

4. Place of Receipt	5. Port of Loading 　SHANGHAI PORT	
6. Vessel Voyage No.	7. Port of Transshipment	
8. Port of Discharge 　ANTWERP PORT	9. Place of Delivery	

10. Container. seal No. or Marks and Nos.	11. Number and Kind of Package	12. Description of Goods	13. Gross Weight (KGS)	14. Measurement (CBM)
N/M 1×20FCL CONTAINER NO: TEXU2263888	5000 PCS 50 CARTONS	SHORT TROUSERS	450 KGS	25 CBM

15. Freight and Charges FREIGHT PREPAID	REGARDING TRANSSHIPMENT INFORMATION PLEASE CONTACT

Ex. Rate	Prepaid at SHANGHAI	Freight Payable at	16. Place and Date of Issue 　SHANGHAI JULY 20, 2021
	Total Prepaid	17. Number of Original B/L 　THREE(3)	18. Signed for or on Behalf of the Master **ENSIGN FREIGHT (CHINA)LTD.** DELIA LAN As Agent

任务三 进口换单

一、进口换单和提货单的概念

　　进口换单是指进口货物到达目的港后,买方凭海运提单到目的港处换提货单,然后持提货单、商业发票、装箱单等办理进口清关和提货。

提货单(Delivery Order,缩写为 D/O),又称小提单。它是收货人凭正本提单或副本提单随同有效的担保向承运人或其代理人换取的,可向港口装卸部门提取货物的凭证。

提货单样例见表6.4。

表 6.4 提货单样例

上海中远集装箱运输船务代理有限公司

COSCO SHANGHAI CONTAINER SHIPPING AGENCY CO., LTD

进口集装箱货物提货单

NO. 0135790

港区场站:				船档号:
收货人名称:上海联兴对外贸易有限公司			收货人开户银行与账号	
船名: HUANYU	航次: V48S	起运港: FRANKFURT	目的港: SHANGHAI	船舶预计到达时间 OCT. 30, 2021
提单号:DLC56712567	交付条款 CFS-CFS	卸货地点 SHANGHAI	进库日期 OCT. 30, 2021	第一程运输
标记与集装箱号	货名	集装箱数或件数	重量(KGS)	体积(CBM)
LX08056G SHANGHAI, CHINA MADE IN GERMANY TRBU90876523	CNC LATHES	1 CASE	6120	25.02
船代公司重要提示: (1)本提货单中有关船、货内容按照提单的相关显示填制。 (2)请当场核查本提货单内容错误之处,否则本公司不承担由此产生的责任和损失。 (3)本提货单仅为向承运人或承运人委托的雇用人或替承运人保管货物订立合同的人提货的凭证,不得买卖转让。 (4)在本提货单下,承运人代理人及雇用人的任何行为,均应视为代表承运人的行为,均应享受承运人享有的免责、责任限制或其他任何抗辩理由。 (5)本提单所列船舶预计到达时间,不作为申报进境和计算滞报金、滞箱费、疏港费等起算的依据,货主不及时换单和提货造成的损失,责任自负。 (6)本提货单中的中文译文仅供参考。 　　　　上海中远集装箱运输船务代理有限公司 　　　　　　　　(盖章有效) 　　　　2021 年 11 月 2 日		收货人章 检验检疫章	海关章	

续表

注意事项： （1）本提货单需盖有船代放货章和海关放行章后有效。凡属法定检验、检疫的进口商品，必须向检验检疫机构申报。 （2）提货人到码头公司办理提货手续时，应出示单位证明或经办人身份证。提货人若非本提货单记名收货人时，还应出示提货单记名收货人开具的证明，以表明其为有权提货的人。 （3）货物超过港存期，码头公司可以按《上海港口货物疏运管理条例》的有关规定处理。在规定期间无人提取的货物，按《中华人民共和国海关法》和国家有关规定处理。		

二、进口换单操作和进口换单操作注意事项

1. 进口换单操作

①进口商到船公司缴清相关费用，并提供缴费凭证。

②备齐换单所需单据（正本提单或无正本提单提货保函和提单副本或电放保函）到船代处换取提货单。

2. 进口换单应注意的问题

①确认船舶是否已经到港和是否可以换单。

②确认应缴纳费用。

③确认是凭正本提单换单，还是凭电传副本换单。

④海运提单如需背书，是否已经背书。

⑤确认该票换单是整箱或是拼箱，如是整箱，船公司是否要求压箱。

⑥进口换单后，核对品名、件数、毛重、体积等是否正确。

【实操训练】

1. 请根据以下所给信用证及补充资料的内容缮制出口货物订舱委托书。

（1）信用证。

SEQUENCE OF TOTAL	*27:	1/1
FORM OF DOC CREDIT	*40A:	IRREVOCABLE
DOC CREDIT NUMBER	*20:	210911
DATE OF ISSUE	31C:	210925
DATE AND PLACE OF EXPIRY	*31D:	DATE 211220 PLACE IN THE COUNTRY OF BENEFICIARY
APPLICANT	*50:	YAMADA TRADE CO., LTD
		310-224 SKURAMAJI OSAKA, JAPAN
ISSUING BANK	52A:	FUJI BANK LTD
		1013 SAKULA OTOLIKINGZA MACHI TOKYO, JAPAN
BENEFICIARY	*59:	SHANGHAI TOY IMPORT & EXPORT CORPORATION
		530 ZHONGSHAN ROAD SHANGHAI, CHINA
AMOUNT	*32B:	CURRENCY USD AMOUNT 19800.00
AVAILABLE WITH/BY	*41D:	ANY BANK IN CHINA BY NEGOTIATION
DRAFTS AT	42C:	30 DAYS AFTER SIGHT FOR FULL INVOICE COST
DRAWEE	42A:	FUJI BANK LTD
PARTIAL SHIPMENT	43P:	PROHIBITED
TRANSSHIPMENT	43T:	PROHIBITED
LOADING ON BOARD	44A:	SHANGHAI
FOR TRANSPORATION TO	44B:	OSAKA PORT
LATEST DATE OF SHIPMENT	44C:	211031
DESCRIPTION OF GOODS	45A:	PLUSH TOY
		ART NO. 818 (PANDA) 300000 PCS USD0.33/PC
		ART NO. 518 (BEAR) 300000 PCS USD0.33/PC
		CIF OSAKA
DOCUMENTS REQUIRED	46A:	+SIGNED COMMERCIAL INVOICE IN TRIPLICATE
		+PACKING LIST IN TRIPLICATE
		+CERTIFICATE OF ORIGIN, ISSUED BY THE CHAMBER OF COMMERCE OR OTHER AUTHORITY DULY ENTITLED FOR THIS PURPOSE.
		+3/3 SET OF CLEAN ON BOARD OCEAN BILL OF LADING MADE OUT TO ORDER OF SHIPPER AND BLANK ENDORSED AND MARKED "FREIGHT PREPAID" AND NOTIFY APPLICANT.
		+FULL SET OF NEGOTIABLE INSURANCE POLICY OR CERTIFICATE BLANK ENDORSED FOR 110 PCT OF INVOICE VALUE COVERING ALL RISKS AND WAR RISK AS PER CIC.
		+ NO SOLID WOOD PACKING CERTIFICATE ISSUED BY MANUFACTURER
CHARGES	71B:	ALL BANKING CHARGES OUTSIDE JAPAN ARE FOR ACCOUNT OF BENEFICIARY.
PERIOD FOR PRESENTATION	48:	DOCUMENTS MUST BE PRESENTED WITHIN 15 DAYS AFTER THE DATE OF SHIPMENT BUT WITHIN THE VALIDITY OF THE CREDIT.

（2）补充资料。

①INVOICE NO.：WJ061088

②PACKING：　　　　G. W.　　　　　N. W.　　　　　MEAS.

ART NO. 818　　　　10. 2 KGS/CTN　　10 KGS /CTN　　0. 2 CBM/CTN

ART NO. 518　　　　11. 2 KGS/CTN　　11 KGS /CTN　　0. 2 CBM/CTN

PACKED IN ONE CARTON OF 100PCS EACH

PACKED IN TWO 40' CONTAINER（集装箱号：TEXU2263456；TEXU2263458）

③H. S. CODE：95039000. 00

④货运委托书编号：JF0387145

⑤VESSEL：XIANG DONG V. 009

⑥B/L NO.：COCSO 611866

⑦B/L DATE：OCT. 28，2021

⑧委托日期：OCT. 18，2021

⑨FREIGHT FEE：USD810

⑩唛头：N/M

海运订舱委托书

委托编号 (Entrusting Serial)	提单号 (B/L No.)	合同号 (Contract No.)	委托日期 (Entrusting Date)	
发货人名称地址(Shipper's Full Name and Address)				
收货人名称地址(Consignee's Full Name and Address)				
通知方名称地址(Notify Party's Full Name and Address)				
装货港(Port of Loading)		目的港(Port of Destination)	船名(Vessel)航次(Voy.)	
唛头标记 (Marks & No.)	包装件数及种类 (No. & Kind of Packages)	货物说明 (Description of Goods)	毛重(Gross Weight in KGS)	体积(Measurement in CBM)
装船日期(Loading Date)		可否转船(Transshipment)	可否分批(Partial Shipment)	
信用证有效期（L/C Expiry Date）	提单份数 (Copies of B/L)		正本 (Original)	副本 (Copy)
运费及支付地点(Freight Payable at)：				
备注(Remarks)：				
委托人签字(Entrusting Party Signature)： 地址(Address)： 电话(Telephone)：				

2. 根据所给资料和信用证缮制海运提单。

（1）信用证。

MT 700		ISSUE A DOCUMENTARY CREDIT
SENDER		EMIRATES BANK INTERNATIONAL LIMITED
RECEIVER		BANK OF CHINA, ZHENGZHOU, CHINA
SEQUENCE OF TOTAL	*27:	1/1
FORM OF DOC CREDIT	*40A:	IRREVOCABLE
DOC CREDIT NUMBER	*20:	CD082519
DATE OF ISSUE	31C:	210403
DATE AND PLACE OF EXPIRY	*31D:	DATE 210525 PLACE IN THE COUNTRY OF BENEFICIARY
APPLICANT	*50:	ALOSMNY INTERNATIONAL TRADE CO., LTD. P. O. BOX 2002, DUBAI, U. A. E
BENEFICIARY	*59:	HENAN LIANXIN FOREIGN TRADE CO., LTD NO. 59 JIANKANG ROAD, ZHENGZHOU, CHINA
AMOUNT	*32B:	CURRENCY USD AMOUNT 17280.00
AVAILABLE WITH/BY	*41D:	ANY BANK IN CHINA BY NEGOTIATION
DRAFTS AT	42C:	SIGHT FOR 100 PCT INVOICE VALUE
DRAWEE	42A:	EMIRATES BANK INTERNATIONAL LIMITED
PARTIAL SHIPMENT	43P:	ALLOWED
TRANSSHIPMENT	43T:	ALLOWED
LOADING ON BOARD	44A:	SHANGHAI
FOR TRANSPORATION TO	44B:	DUBAI
LATEST DATE OF SHIPMENT	44C:	210505
DESCRIPTION OF GOODS	45A:	7500 DOZEN PAIRS OF MEN'S COTTON SOCKS SIZE: 26 CM× 27 CM STANDARD, COLOURS: 6 COLOURS EQUALLY ASSORTED, BRAND: GOLDEN PINE MADE IN SHANGHAI, CHINA.　　　　　　　　　DESIGN NO. N3004-D33 AND N3004-D92 EACH 3750 DOZEN PAIRS AT USD2.304/DOZEN PAIR CIF DUBAI. SHIPPING MARK: A. I. T. C. L/DUBAI/NOS. 1-150
DOCUMENTS REQUIRED	46A:	+SIGNED COMMERCIAL INVOICE IN 6 COPIES +PACKING LIST IN 6 COPIES +CERTIFICATE OF ORIGIN, ISSUED BY THE CHAMBER OF COMMERCE OR OTHER AUTHORITY DULY ENTITLED FOR THIS PURPOSE. +FULL SET OF CLEAN ON BOARD OCEAN BILL OF LADING MADE OUT TO ORDER OF SHIPPER AND BLANK ENDORSED AND MARKED "FREIGHT PREPAID" AND NOTIFY APPLICANT. +FULL SET OF NEGOTIABLE INSURANCE POLICY OR CERTIFICATE BLANK ENDORSED FOR 110 PCT OF INVOICE VALUE COVERING ALL RISKS AND WAR RISK AS PER CIC.

续表

		+BENEFICIARY'S CERTIFICATE CERTIFYING THAT THEY HAVE SENT COPIES OF COMMERCIAL INVOICE, PACKING LIST AND MARINE BILLS OF LADING TO THE APPLICANT BY COURIER SERVICE WITHIN 5 DAYS FROM DATE OF SHIPMENT. +SHIPPING ADVICE SHOWING THE NAME OF CARRYING VESSEL, DATE OF SHIPMENT, MARKS, QUANTITY, NET WEIGHT AND GROSS WEIGHT OF THE SHIPMENT TO APPLICANT WITHIN 3 DAYS AFTER THE DATE OF BILL OF LADING.
ADDITIONAL CONDITION	47A:	+ALL REQUIRED DOCUMENTS ARE NOT TO BE DATED PRIOR TO THE ISSUANCE DATE OF THIS CREDIT. + TRANSPORT DOCUMENTS ISSUED BY FREIGHT FORWARDERS ARE NOT ACCEPTABLE. +COMMERCIAL INVOICES ISSUED FOR AMOUNTS IN EXCEEDS OF D/C VALUE ARE NOT ACCEPTABLE. ALL BANKING CHARGES OUTSIDE JAPAN ARE FOR ACCOUNT OF BENEFICIARY.
CHARGES	71B:	DOCUMENTS MUST BE PRESENTED WITHIN 15 DAYS AFTER THE DATE OF SHIPMENT BUT WITHIN THE VALIDITY OF THE CREDIT.
PERIOD FOR PRESENTATION	48:	
CONFIRMATION	49:	WITHOUT
INSTR TO PAY/ACCEP/NEG	78:	THE AMOUNT OF EACH DRAWING MUST BE ENDORSED ON THE REVERSE OF PAGE 1 OF THIS CREDIT.
DOCUMENTS MUST BE FORWARDED DERECTLY TO US IN ONE LOT BY COURIER. IN REIMBURSEMENT, THE NEGOTIATING BANK IS AUTHORIZED TO DRAW ON OUR ACCOUNT WITH CHEMICAL BANK,15th FLOOR, 55 WATER STREET, NEW YORK, N. Y. 10014-0199, UAS		

------------------------ End of Messa ------------------------

（2）制单参考资料。

①INVOICE NO.：LX-005

②发票日期:2021 年 5 月 5 日

③CONTRACT NO.：LX-12120

④B/L NO.：C021806

⑤装船日期:2021 年 5 月 5 日

⑥VESSEL:"RED STAR"，VOY. NO. V506

⑦CONTAINER NO/SEAL NO.：GEGU3163669/1051088

⑧INSURANCE POLICY NO.：HMP11076531

⑨TOTAL GROSS WEIGHT： 9000 KGS

⑩TOTAL NET WEIGHT：8700 KGS

⑪MEASUREMENT：48 CBM

⑫PACKING：IN CARTONS OF 50 PCS EACH

⑬H. S. CODE NO. ：61159500. 19

⑭授权签字人:李丽

1. Shipper	B/L No.

SINOTRANS

中 国 外 运 广 东 公 司
SINOTRANS GUANGDONG COMPANY

2. Consignee	

OCEAN BILL OF LADING

3. Notify Party	SHIPPED on board in apparent good order and condition (unless otherwise indicated) the goods or packages specified herein and to be discharged at the mentioned port of discharge or as near there to as the vessel may safely get and be always afloat. The weight, measure, marks and numbers, quality, contents and value, being particulars furnished by the Shipper, are not checked by the Carrier on loading. **The Shipper, Consignee and the Holder of this Bill of Lading hereby expressly accept and agree to all printed, written or stamped provisions, exceptions and conditions of this Bill of Lading, including those on the back here of.**
4. Place of Receipt / **5. Port of Loading**	IN WITNESS where of the number of original Bills of Lading stated below have been signed, one of which being accomplished the other(s) to be void.
6. Vessel Voyage No. / **7. Port of Transshipment**	
8. Port of Discharge / **9. Place of Delivery**	

10. Container Seal No. or Marks and Nos.	11. Number and Kind of Package	12. Description of Goods	13. Gross Weight (KGS)	14. Measurement (CBM)

15. Freight and Charges	REGARDING TRANSSHIPMENT INFORMATION PLEASE CONTACT

Ex. Rate	Prepaid at	Freight Payable at	16. Place and Date of Issue
	Total Prepaid	17. Number of Original B/L	18. Signed for or on Behalf of the Master
			As Agent

项目七　保险单据缮制与操作

【项目目标】

知识目标
- 掌握投保单的概念、主要内容与缮制方法
- 掌握保险单的概念、类别、主要内容与缮制方法
- 掌握预约保险单的概念、主要内容与缮制方法

能力目标
- 能够熟练缮制投保单
- 能够熟练缮制保险单

思政目标
- 通过对保险单的概念等内容的学习,引导学生了解保险"分散风险、补偿损失"的基本功能,承载社会稳定器和经济助推器的独特功能,从而激发学生的社会责任感和学习热情,坚定学生的报国之志

【工作情景】

上海威尔进出口公司与 NU BONNETERIE DE GROOTE 公司签订的合同中采用了 CIF 术语成交,因此需要在装船前办理出口货物运输保险事宜。于是,单证员殷实着手填制国际货运保险投保单,备齐商业发票等单据,向中国人民保险公司上海分公司办理海运保险手续。

【工作任务】

任务一　投保单缮制与操作

一、投保单的概念

投保单是发货人或被保险人在货物发运前,确定装运工具并缮制发票以后,向保险公司(保险人)办理投保手续所填制和提交的单据。

投保单由出口公司在投保时填写,其内容应按合同或信用证要求仔细、认真填写,不能有错,保险公司根据投保单的内容来缮制和签发保险单。

投保单样例见表 7.1。

表7.1　投保单样例

中保财产保险有限公司

The People's Insurance（Property）Company of China，Ltd

出口货物运输保险投保单

APPLICATION FORM FOR MARINE CARGO TRANSPORTATION INSURANCE

1. 发票号 （Invoice No.）	（1）	2. 合同号 （Contract No.）	（2）	3. 信用证号 （L/C No.）	（3）
4. 被保险人 （Insured）	（4）				
5. 唛头 （Marks & Numbers）	6. 包装及数量 （Quantity）		7. 保险货物项目 （Description of Goods）		8. 保险金额 （Insured Amount）
（5）	（6）		（7）		（8）
9. 总保险金额 （Total Amount Insured）			（9）		
10. 装载运输工具 （Conveyance）	（10）	11. 起运日期 （Date of Commencement）	（11）	13. 赔款偿付 地点 （Loss if Any Payable）	（13）
12. 运输路线 （Voyage） （12）	自　　　　到 （From）　　（To）．	转载地点 （Port of Transshipment）			
14. 投保险别（14） （Insurance Coverage Required）			15. 投保人（签名盖章）（15） （Applicant's Signature & Stamp）		
申请保险单正本份数为:3 ［Issued in 3 Original（s）On- ly．］	□保险单（Insurance Policy） □保险凭证（Insurance Certificate）		16. 投保日期 （Date）	（16）	

二、投保单缮制方法与操作注意事项

1. 投保单缮制方法

各保险公司的投保单格式不尽相同,但内容基本一致,内容如下。

（1）发票号（Invoice No.）

填写投保标的的商业发票号码。

（2）合同号（Contract No.）

填写投保标的的买卖合同号码。

（3）信用证号（L/C No.）

填写本次交易中买方开来的信用证号码。若采用托收方式支付，则此栏空白不填。

（4）被保险人（Insured）

托收项下，填写出口商的名称。信用证若无特别规定，一般应为信用证的受益人或合同的卖方（即发货人）。

（5）唛头（Marks & Numbers）

此栏填写装运唛头，与发票、提单上的相同栏目内容一致。此栏也可以填写"AS PER IN-VOICE NO. ×××"。

（6）包装及数量（Quantity）

数量即出口货物的总数量，如总重或总包装数。

（7）保险货物项目（Description of Goods）

保险物资项目即货物的品名或规格，一般按提单的填法，填大类名称或货物的统称，不必详细列明各种规格等细节。

（8）保险金额（Insured Amount）

填写计算投保加成后的总保险金额，或成交金额，但需标明成交价格条件。

（9）总保险金额（大写）（Total Amount Insured）

将保险金额以大写的形式填入。计价货币也应以全称形式填入。注意保险金额使用的货币应与信用证使用的货币一致，保险总金额大写应与保险金额的阿拉伯数字一致。

（10）装载运输工具（Conveyance）

此栏填写运输的名称，如果是海运，填写船名；如果中途转运，各程运输的船名都应填写在该栏。

（11）起运日期（Date of Commencement）

此栏填写本保险单项下货物运输单据的签发日期，或填写"AS PER B/L NO."。

（12）起讫地点（Voyage，From… To…）

在"FROM"后面填写装运港名称，"TO"后面填写目的港名称，如有转运，在"VIA"后面填写转运港名称。

（13）赔款偿付地点（Loss if Any Payable）

此栏填写保险赔款的支付地点和赔付的货币名称，根据合同或信用证规定的保险条款填写。如果信用证未作规定，或是托收方式支付，则填写目的港，赔付货币为投保金额相同的货币。

（14）投保险别（Insurance Coverage Required）

按合同规定或信用证条款填写。

（15）投保人签章（Applicant's Signature & Stamp）

上述内容填写完毕后，投保人需签字盖章才能生效。

（16）投保日期（Date）

此栏填写投保的日期。

2.投保单操作注意事项

①投保单的填写和提交要及时，否则会影响按时投保。

②投保单的内容填制需与合同和信用证的保险条款相符，特别是唛头、包装及数量、货物描述、投保加成和投保险别、起运日期、装载的运输工具等。

任务二　保险单缮制与操作

一、保险单的概念

保险单（Insurance Policy）俗称"大保单"，是使用最广泛的正式保险单据，是证实保险人与被保险人建立保险契约的正式文件。

保险凭证（Insurance Certificate）又称"小保单"，是一种简化的保险单据，与保险单具有相同的法律效力。保险凭证正面所列内容与海上保险单是一样的，背面空白没有条款，但保险条款仍应以保险单的保险条款为准。如果信用证要求提供保险单，不能提供保险凭证；如果信用证要求提供保险凭证，可以提供保险单。

保险单样例见表7.2。

表7.2　保险单样例

中保财产保险有限公司

The People's Insurance（Property）Company of China, Ltd

发票号码　　（2）　　　　　　　　　　　　　　　　保险单号次

Invoice No.　　　　　　　　　　　　　　　　　　　Policy No.

海 洋 货 物 运 输 保 险 单

MARINE CARGO TRANSPORTATION INSURANCE POLICY

被保险人：

Insured：　　（1）

中保财产保险有限公司（以下简称本公司）根据被保险人的要求，及其所缴付约定的保险费，按照本保险单承担险别和背面所载条款与下列特别条款承保下列货物运输保险，特签发本保险单。

This Policy of Insurance witnesses that the People's Insurance（Property）Company of China, Ltd.（hereinafter called "The Company"）, at the request of the Insured and in consideration of the agreed premium paid by the Insured, undertakes to insure the undermentioned goods in transportation subject to conditions of the Policy as per the Clauses printed overleaf and other special clauses attached here on.

唛 头 Marks & Nos	包装及数量 Quantity	保险货物项目 Descriptions of Goods	保险金额 Amount Insured
（3）	（4）	（5）	（6）

承保险别

Conditions _____ （7） _____

总保险金额：

Total Amount Insured：_____ （8） _____

保费 费率 装载运输工具 开航日期

Premium （9） Rate Per conveyance S. S （10） Slg. on or abt （11）

起运港 目的港

From_____ To_____

所保货物,如发生本保险单项下可能引起索赔的损失或损坏,应立即通知本公司下述代理人查勘。如有索赔,应向本公司提交保险单正本(本保险单共有____份正本)及有关文件。如一份正本已用于索赔,其余正本则自动失效。

In the event of loss or damage which may result in a claim under this Policy, immediate notice must be given to the Company's Agent as mentioned here under. Claims, if any, one of the Original Policy which has been issued in original（s）together with the relevant documents shall be surrendered to the Company. If one of the Original Policy has been accomplished, the others to be void.

赔款偿付地点

Claim payable at_____ （12）

日期 在

Date _____ （13） _____ at_____

地址： 中国人民保险公司

Address： The People's Insurance Company of China

（14）

（Authorized Signature）

二、保险单缮制方法与操作注意事项

1.保险单缮制方法

（1）被保险人（Insured）

在国际贸易业务中,买卖双方对货物的权利因单据的转移而转移,保险单的可保利益也会由卖方转移给买方,保险索赔通常是由买方办理。按照习惯,被保险人一栏,一般填写出口商的名称,若信用证另有规定,则按规定填写。

（2）发票号码（Invoice No.）

按实际号码填写。

（3）唛头（Marks & Nos）

按信用证规定,唛头应与发票、提单相一致,可单独填写,也可填"AS PER INV. NO."。

（4）包装及数量（Quantity）

填写商品外包装的种类和数量。如以单位包装件数计价者,可只填总件数;若为散装货,则应注明"IN BULK",再填重量。

（5）保险货物项目（Description of Goods）

本栏填写商品的名称,根据投保单填写,要与提单一致。

（6）保险金额（Amount Insured）

保险金额应为发票金额加上投保加成后的金额投保。信用证支付方式下,严格按信用证规定。大小写要一致,币种要用英文全称,币制应与信用证规定相符。保险金额按加成计算,如有小数,应采取"进一法",如保险金额为 USD785.22,应填写"USD786"。

（7）承保险别（Conditions）

按信用证规定或双方约定填写。

（8）保险总金额（Total Amount Insured）

此栏需将保险金额以大写的形式填入。计价货币也写全称,并与信用证使用的金额一致。

（9）保费和保率（Premium & Rate）

一般由保险公司在保险单印刷时填入"AS ARRANGED",出口公司无须填写。

（10）装载运输工具（Per Conveyance S.S）

此栏内容要与运输单据一致。海运填船名航次,转运时,填"一程船/二程船",可填"AS PER B/L";陆运填"BY RAILWAY"或"BY TRAIN:WAGON NO.××";空运填"BY AIR";邮包运输填"BY PARCEL POST"。

（11）开行日期及起讫地点（Slg. on or abt & From…To…）

一般填提单签发日,也可填写提单签发日前 5 天内的任一日期,或填"AS PER B/L"。

（12）赔款偿付地点（Claim payable at）

应填地点和币种两项内容。地点按信用证或投保单填写,一般为目的地;币种应与保险金额一致。

（13）签发地点和日期（Address & Date）

签发日期需早于运输单据的签发日期,才能证明是在装运前办理的投保。

（14）保险公司签章（Authorized Signature）

经签章后保险单才能生效。

2. 保险单操作

①保险单操作同投保单。

②如按 CIF、CIP 术语成交,卖方交单时,不要忘记在保险单背面背书,否则,保险单并没有转让。

单证员殷实根据项目二中的信用证样例和信用证修改书样例缮制的保险单见表7.3。

表7.3 缮制的保险单

中保财产保险有限公司

The People's Insurance（Property）Company of China，Ltd

发票号码

（2） WT980

Invoice No.

保险单号次

Policy No.

海 洋 货 物 运 输 保 险 单
MARINE CARGO TRANSPORTATION INSURANCE POLICY

被保险人：WILL SHANGHAI TRADING CO. LTD

Insured：WILL SHANGHAI TRADING CO. LTD

中保财产保险有限公司（以下简称本公司）根据被保险人的要求,及其所缴付约定的保险费,按照本保险单承担险别和背面所载条款与下列特别条款承保下列货物运输保险,特签发本保险单。

This Policy of Insurance witnesses that the People's Insurance（Property）Company of China，Ltd.（hereinafter called "The Company"）, at the request of the Insured and in consideration of the agreed premium paid by the Insured, undertakes to insure the undermentioned goods in transportation subject to conditions of the Policy as per the Clauses printed overleaf and other special clauses attached hereon.

标 记 Marks & Nos	包装及数量 Quantity	保险货物项目 Descriptions of Goods	保险金额 Amount Insured
N/M	5000 PCS 50 CTNS ONE 20 FCL	SHORT TROUSERS	USD69575.00

承保险别

Conditions

COVERING ALL RISKS AND WAR RISKS

总保险金额：

Total Amount Insured： SAY U. S. DOLLARS SIXTY NINE THOUSAND FIVE HUNDRED AND SEVENTY FIVE ONLY

保费 费率 装载运输工具 开航日期

Premium AS ARRANGED Rate Per conveyance S. S "DONGFENG" V128 Slg. on or abt JULY 20, 2021

起运港 目的港

From SHANGHAI To ANTWERP

所保货物,如发生本保险单项下可能引起索赔的损失或损坏,应立即通知本公司下述代理人查勘。如有索赔,应向本公司提交保险单正本(本保险单共有____份正本)及有关文件。如一份正本已用于索赔,其余正本则自动失效。

In the event of loss or damage which may result in a claim under this Policy, immediate notice must be given to the Company's Agent as mentioned here under. Claims, if any, one of the Original Policy which has been issued in 2 original(s) together with the relevant documents shall be surrendered to the Company. If one of the Original Policy has been accomplished, the others to be void.

赔款偿付地点

Claim payable at　　ANTWERP　IN U.S.D

日期　　　　　　　　　　在

Date　JULY 17, 2021　　　　　at　　SHANGHAI

地址：　　　　　　　　　　　　　中国人民保险公司

Address：　　　　　　　　　　　The People's Insurance Company of China

　　　　　　　　　　　　　　　　　　　　　　（14）

任务三　预约保险单缮制与操作

一、预约保险单的概念

预约保险单(Open Policy/Open Cover)，又称"开口保险单"或"预约保险单"，是一种长期的货物运输保险合同，一般适用于经常有相同类型货物需要陆续装运的保险。办理预约保险，在货物出运前，双方先签订预约保险合同，规定保险范围、货物种类、保险费率等条件，保险人一接到被保险人的装船通知，保险立即生效。

预约保险的优点在于减少了逐笔订立保险合同的烦琐手续，并可以防止因漏保或迟保而造成的无法弥补的损失。保险公司一般对使用预约保险的投保人提供更优惠的保险费率，因而也吸引了不少投保人。

预约保险单样例见表7.4。

表7.4　预约保险单样例
进口货物运输预约保险合同

合同号：（1）　　　　　　　　　　　　　　　　日期：（2）
甲方：　（3）
乙方：　（4）
双方就进口货物的运输预约保险拟定以下条款以资共同遵守：

一、保险范围(5)

甲方从国外进口全部货物，不论运输方式，凡贸易条件规定由进口商办理保险的，都属于本合同范围之内，甲方应根据本合同规定，向乙方办理投保手续并支付保险费。

乙方对上述保险范围内的货物，负有自动承保责任，在发生本合同规定范围内的损失时，均按本合同的规定，负责赔偿。

二、保险金额(6)

保险金额以货物的 CIF 价为准。

续表

三、保险险别和费率(7)

各种货物需要投保的险别由甲方选定并在投保单中填明。乙方根据不同的险别规定不同的费率。现暂定如下：

货物种类	运输方式	保险险别	保险费率

四、保险责任(8)

各种险别的责任范围,按照所属乙方制定的"海洋货物运输保险条款""海洋货物运输战争险条款""海洋进口货物国内转运期间保险责任扩展条款""航空运输一切险条款"和其他有关条款的规定为准。

五、投保手续(9)

甲方一经掌握货物发运情况,即应向乙方寄送启运通知书,办理投保。通知书一式五份,由保险公司签认后,退回一份。如不办理投保,货物发生损失,乙方不予理赔。

六、保险费的支付(10)

乙方按照甲方寄送的启运通知书照前列相应的费率逐笔计收保险费,甲方应及时付费。

七、索赔手续和期限(11)

本合同所保货物发生保险责任范围内的损失时,乙方应按制定的"关于海运进口保险货物残损检验的赔款给付办法"和"进口货物施救整理费用支付方法"迅速处理。甲方应尽力采取防止货物扩大受损的措施,对已遭受损失的货物必须积极抢救,尽量减少货物的损失。向乙方办理索赔的有效期限,以保险货物卸离海轮之日起满一年终止。如有特殊需要,可向乙方提出延长索赔期限。

八、合同期限(12)

本合同自 2021 年 6 月 26 日起生效。

甲方： 乙方：

(13)

二、预约保险单缮制方法与操作注意事项

1.预约保险单缮制方法

(1)合同号

保险公司填写。

（2）日期

填写预约保险单的日期。

（3）甲方

填写被保险人的名称。

（4）乙方

填写保险公司的名称。

（5）保险范围

双方约定。

（6）保险金额

双方约定，一般为货物的 CIF 价。

（7）保险险别和费率

对应相应的货物种类和运输方式，双方约定保险险别和费率。

（8）保险责任

双方约定。

（9）投保手续

双方约定。

（10）保险费的支付

双方约定，一般为货物起运前支付。

（11）索赔手续和期限

双方约定。

（12）合同期限

双方约定。

（13）签字盖章

保险人和被保险人双方签字盖章。

2.预约保险单操作

①双方需就保险范围、保险金额、保险险别、保险费率、保险费支付等内容作出明确规定。

②被保险人在每次货物出运后，需及时将装船通知的内容告知保险公司，以便保险公司承保。

【实操训练】

1.请根据以下所给信用证及补充资料的内容缮制投保单。

（1）信用证。

SEQUENCE OF TOTAL	*27:	1/1
FORM OF DOC CREDIT	*40A:	IRREVOCABLE
DOC CREDIT NUMBER	*20:	210911
DATE OF ISSUE	31C:	210925
DATE AND PLACE OF EXPIRY	*31D:	DATE 211220 PLACE IN THE COUNTRY OF BENEFICIARY
APPLICANT	*50:	YAMADA TRADE CO. , LTD
		310-224 SKURAMAJI OSAKA, JAPAN
ISSUING BANK	52A:	FUJI BANK LTD
		1013 SAKULA OTOLIKINGZA MACHI TOKYO, JAPAN
BENEFICIARY	*59:	SHANGHAI TOY IMPORT & EXPORT CORPORATION
		530 ZHONGSHAN ROAD SHANGHAI, CHINA
AMOUNT	*32B:	CURRENCY USD AMOUNT 19800. 00
AVAILABLE WITH/BY	*41D:	ANY BANK IN CHINA BY NEGOTIATION
DRAFTS AT	42C:	30 DAYS AFTER SIGHT FOR FULL INVOICE COST
DRAWEE	42A:	FUJI BANK LTD
PARTIAL SHIPMENT	43P:	PROHIBITED
TRANSSHIPMENT	43T:	PROHIBITED
LOADING ON BOARD	44A:	SHANGHAI
FOR TRANSPORATION TO	44B:	OSAKA PORT
LATEST DATE OF SHIPMENT	44C:	211031
DESCRIPTION OF GOODS	45A:	PULASH TOY
		ART NO. 818（PANDA）300000 PCS USD0. 33/PC
		ART NO. 518（BEAR） 300000 PCS USD0. 33/PC
		CIF OSAKA
DOCUMENTS REQUIRED	46A:	+SIGNED COMMERCIAL INVOICE IN TRIPLICATE
		+PACKING LIST IN TRIPLICATE
		+CERTIFICATE OF ORIGIN, ISSUED BY THE CHAMBER OF COMMERCE OR OTHER AUTHORITY DULY ENTITLED FOR THIS PURPOSE.
		+3/3 SET OF CLEAN ON BOARD OCEAN BILL OF LADING MADE OUT TO ORDER OF SHIPPER AND BLANK ENDORSED AND MARKED "FREIGHT PREPAID" AND NOTIFY APPLICANT.
		+FULL SET OF NEGOTIABLE INSURANCE POLICY OR CERTIFICATE BLANK ENDORSED FOR 110 PCT OF INVOICE VALUE COVERING ALL RISKS AND WAR RISK AS PER CIC.
		+ NO SOLID WOOD PACKING CERTIFICATE ISSUED BY MANUFACTURER
CHARGES	71B:	ALL BANKING CHARGES OUTSIDE JAPAN ARE FOR ACCOUNT OF BENEFICIARY.
PERIOD FOR PRESENTATION	48:	DOCUMENTS MUST BE PRESENTED WITHIN 15 DAYS AFTER THE DATE OF SHIPMENT BUT WITHIN THE VALIDITY OF THE CREDIT.

（2）补充资料。

①INVOICE NO.：WJ211088

②PACKING：　　　　G. W.　　　　　　N. W.　　　　　　　MEAS

ART NO. 818　　10. 2 KGS/CTN　　10 KGS /CTN　　　0. 2 CBM/CTN

ART NO. 518　　11. 2 KGS/CTN　　11 KGS /CTN　　　0. 2 CBM/CTN

PACKED IN ONE CARTON OF 100 PCS EACH ,PACKED IN TWO 40' CONTAINER（集装箱号：TEXU2263456；TEXU2263458）

③投保单编号：TB2336112

④VESSEL：XIANG DONG V. 009

⑤B/L NO. ：COCSO 611866

⑥B/L DATE：OCT. 28，2021

出口货物运输保险投保单

发票号码			投保条款和险别			
被保险人	客户抬头		（　）PICC CLAUSE			
			（　）ICC CLAUSE			
			（　）ALL RISKS			
			（　）W. P. A. /W. A.			
			（　）F. P. A.			
	过户		（　）WAR RISKS			
			（　）S. R. C. C.			
			（　）STRIKE			
			（　）ICC CLAUSE A			
			（　）ICC CLAUSE B			
			（　）ICC CLAUSE C			
保险金额	USD　（　　　　　　）		（　）AIR TPT ALL RISKS			
	HKD　（　　　　　　）		（　）AIR TPT RISKS			
	（　）（　　　　　　）		（　）O/L TPT ALL RISKS			
起运港			（　）O/L TPT RISKS			
目的港			（　）TRANSSHIPMENT RISKS			
转内陆			（　）W TO W			
开航日期			（　）T. P. N. D.			
船名航次			（　）F. R. E. C.			
赔款地点			（　）R. F. W. D.			
赔付币别			（　）RISKS OF BREAKAGE			
正本份数			（　）I. O. P.			
其他特别条款						
以　下　由　保　险　公　司　填　写						
	保单号码			费　率		
	签单日期			保　费		

投保日期：　　　　　　　　　　　　　　　　　　　　　投保人签章：

2. 根据所给资料和信用证缮制保险单。

（1）信用证。

MT 700	ISSUE A DOCUMENTARY CREDIT	
SENDER	EMIRATES BANK INTERNATIONAL LIMITED	
RECEIVER	BANK OF CHINA, ZHENGZHOU, CHINA	
SEQUENCE OF TOTAL	*27：	1/1
FORM OF DOC CREDIT	*40A：	IRREVOCABLE
DOC CREDIT NUMBER	*20：	CD082519
DATE OF ISSUE	31C：	210403
DATE AND PLACE OF EXPIRY	*31D：	DATE 210525 PLACE IN THE COUNTRY OF BENEFICIARY
APPLICANT	*50：	ALOSMNY INTERNATIONAL TRADE CO. , LTD. P. O. BOX 2002, DUBAI, U. A. E
BENEFICIARY	*59：	HENAN LIANXIN FOREIGN TRADE CO. , LTD NO. 59 JIANKANG ROAD, ZHENGZHOU, CHINA
AMOUNT	*32B：	CURRENCY USD AMOUNT 17280. 00
AVAILABLE WITH/BY	*41D：	ANY BANK IN CHINA BY NEGOTIATION
DRAFTS AT	42C：	SIGHT FOR 100 PCT INVOICE VALUE
DRAWEE	42A：	EMIRATES BANK INTERNATIONAL LIMITED
PARTIAL SHIPMENT	43P：	ALLOWED
TRANSSHIPMENT	43T：	ALLOWED
LOADING ON BOARD	44A：	SHANGHAI
FOR TRANSPORATION TO	44B：	DUBAI
LATEST DATE OF SHIPMENT	44C：	210505
DESCRIPTION OF GOODS	45A：	7500 DOZEN PAIRS OF MEN'S COTTON SOCKS SIZE：26 CM× 27 CM STANDARD, COLOURS：6 COLOURS EQUALLY ASSORTED, BRAND：GOLDEN PINE MADE IN SHANGHAI, CHINA. DESIGN NO. N3004-D33 AND N3004-D92 EACH 3750 DOZEN PAIRS AT USD2. 304/DOZEN PAIR CIF DUBAI. SHIPPING MARK：A. I. T. C. L/DUBAI/NOS. 1-150
DOCUMENTS REQUIRED	46A：	+SIGNED COMMERCIAL INVOICE IN 6 COPIES +PACKING LIST IN 6 COPIES +CERTIFICATE OF ORIGIN, ISSUED BY THE CHAMBER OF COMMERCE OR OTHER AUTHORITY DULY ENTITLED FOR THIS PURPOSE.

续表

		+FULL SET OF CLEAN ON BOARD OCEAN BILL OF LADING MADE OUT TO ORDER OF SHIPPER AND BLANK ENDORSED AND MARKED "FREIGHT PREPAID" AND NO-TIFY APPLICANT. +FULL SET OF NEGOTIABLE INSURANCE POLICY OR CER-TIFICATE BLANK ENDORSED FOR 110 PCT OF INVOICE VALUE COVERING ALL RISKS AND WAR RISK AS PER CIC OF PICC. +BENEFICIARY'S CERTIFICATE CERTIFYING THAT THEY HAVE SENT COPIES OF COMMERCIAL INVOICE, PACKING LIST AND MARINE BILLS OF LADING TO THE APPLICANT BY COURIER SERVICE WITHIN 5 DAYS FROM DATE OF SHIPMENT. +SHIPPING ADVICE SHOWING THE NAME OF CARRYING VESSEL, DATE OF SHIPMENT, MARKS, QUANTITY, NET WEIGHT AND GROSS WEIGHT OF THE SHIPMENT TO AP-PLICANT WITHIN 3 DAYS AFTER THE DATE OF BILL OF LADING.
ADDITIONAL CONDITION	47A:	+ALL REQUIRED DOCUMENTS ARE NOT TO BE DATED PRIOR TO THE ISSUANCE DATE OF THIS CREDIT. +TRANSPORT DOCUMENTS ISSUED BY FREIGHT FOR-WARDERS ARE NOT ACCEPTABLE. +COMMERCIAL INVOICES ISSUED FOR AMOUNTS IN EX-CEEDS OF D/C VALUE ARE NOT ACCEPTABLE.
CHARGES	71B:	ALL BANKING CHARGES OUTSIDE JAPAN ARE FOR AC-COUNT OF BENEFICIARY.
PERIOD FOR PRESENTATION	48:	DOCUMENTS MUST BE PRESENTED WITHIN 15 DAYS AFTER THE DATE OF SHIPMENT BUT WITHIN THE VALIDI-TY OF THE CREDIT.
CONFIRMATION	49:	WITHOUT
INSTR TO PAY/ACCEP/NEG	78:	THE AMOUNT OF EACH DRAWING MUST BE ENDORSED ON THE REVERSE OF PAGE 1 OF THIS CREDIT.

DOCUMENTS MUST BE FORWARDED DERECTLY TO US IN ONE LOT BY COURIER.

IN REIMBURSEMENT, THE NEGOTIATING BANK IS AUTHORIZED TO DRAW ON OUR ACCOUNT WITH CHEMICAL BANK,15th FLOOR, 55 WATER STREET, NEW YORK, N. Y. 10014- 0199, UAS

（2）制单参考资料。

INVOICE NO.：LX- 005

发票日期：2021 年 4 月 20 日

CONTRACT NO.：LX-12120

B/L NO.：C021806

装船日期：2021 年 5 月 5 日

VESSEL："RED STAR"，VOY. NO. V506

CONTAINER NO/SEAL NO.：GEGU3163669/1051088

INSURANCE POLICY NO.：HMP11076531

TOTAL GROSS WEIGHT：9 KGS

TOTAL NET WEIGHT：8.7 KGS

MEASUREMENT：48 CBM

PACKING：IN CARTONS OF 50 PCS. EACH

H. S. CODE NO.6115950019

授权签字人：李丽

中保财产保险有限公司

The People's Insurance（Property）Company of China，Ltd

发票号码	保险单号次
Invoice No.	Policy No.

海 洋 货 物 运 输 保 险 单
MARINE CARGO TRANSPORTATION INSURANCE POLICY

被保险人：

Insured：

　　中保财产保险有限公司（以下简称本公司）根据被保险人的要求，及其所缴付约定的保险费，按照本保险单承担险别和背面所载条款与下列特别条款承保下列货物运输保险，特签发本保险单。

　　This Policy of Insurance witnesses that the People's Insurance（Property）Company of China, Ltd.（hereinafter called "The Company"），at the request of the Insured and in consideration of the agreed premium paid by the Insured，undertakes to insure the undermentioned goods in transportation subject to conditions of the Policy as per the Clauses printed overleaf and other special clauses attached here on.

标 记 （Marks & Nos）	包装及数量 （Quantity）	保险货物项目 （Descriptions of Goods）	保险金额 （Amount Insured）

承保险别

Conditions：

总保险金额

Total Amount Insured: _____

保费	费率	装载运输工具	开航日期

Premium: _____ Rate: _____ Per conveyance S. S: _____ Slg. on or abt: _____

起运港   目的港

From: _____ To: _____

所保货物,如发生本保险单项下可能引起索赔的损失或损坏,应立即通知本公司下述代理人查勘。如有索赔,应向本公司提交保险单正本(本保险单共有____份正本)及有关文件。如一份正本已用于索赔,其余正本则自动失效。

In the event of loss or damage which may result in a claim under this Policy, immediate notice must be given to the Company's Agent as mentioned here under. Claims, if any, one of the Original Policy which has been issued in original (s) together with the relevant documents shall be surrendered to the Company. If one of the Original Policy has been accomplished, the others to be void.

赔款偿付地点

Claim payable at

日期   在

Date: _____ at: _____

地址

Address: _____

项目八 报检报关单证缮制与操作

【项目目标】

知识目标

- 熟悉出境商品检验检疫单证
- 熟悉出口货物报检报关的程序
- 掌握出口报关单的概念
- 掌握出口报关单的缮制方法

能力目标

- 能够熟练填写出境货物报关单

思政目标

- 通过对查验技术的学习,告诫学生需要具备不断学习和进取的精神,快速掌握新技术、更新知识结构,以便更好地适应将来工作的需要
- 通过对报检报关基本知识的学习,培养学生知法、守法、爱国、敬业和诚信的思想意识

【工作情景】

关检融合统一申报系统于 2018 年 8 月 1 日正式上线,原报检单和原报关单合并为一张新报关单,将原报关和报检共 229 个申报项目精简融合为 105 个,企业可以通过"中国国际贸易单一窗口"标准版系统或者"互联网+海关"渠道进行申报。在上海威尔进出口公司与 NU BONNETERIE DE GROOTE 公司的出口交易中,因出口的商品 SHORT TROUSERS 根据《中华人民共和国进出口商品检验法》的规定属于法定检验的商品,税号为 62046200.99,海关监管条件为"B",所以,上海威尔进出口公司应在规定的时限和地点就该批出口货物向海关申报。请以单证员殷实的身份填写出口货物报关单。

【工作任务】

任务一 出口货物检验检疫单证

一、报检基础知识

1.商品检验(商检)的含义

商品检验是指对商品的品质、重量、包装、残损及货物装运技术条件进行检验和鉴定,以

确定交货的品质、数量和包装等是否与合同规定相一致,并出具证明文件作为买卖双方交接货物、支付货款和处理索赔的依据。

2. 货物的报检范围

①国家法律法规规定必须检验检疫的。

②有关国际条约规定必须要检验检疫的。

③申请签发普惠制产地证或一般原产地证的。

④对外贸易关系人申请的鉴定业务和委托检验。

⑤对外贸易合同、信用证规定需要出具检验检疫证书的。

⑥报检单位对海关出具的检验检疫结果有异议的,可申请复验。

3. 出口货物检验检疫申请的一般程序

出口货物检验检疫申请是指有关当事人根据法律、行政法规的规定,对外贸易合同的约定或证明履约的需要,向海关申请检验检疫、鉴定、准出入境或取得销售使用的合法凭证及某种公证证明所必须履行的法定程序。

二、出口货物检验检疫申请所需主要单证

当货物的监管条件为"A"或者"B"时,需要对进、出境货物进行商检。以监管条件为"B"、需要进行出口商检为例。当出口商备妥货物和办理租船订舱后,需要在网上向海关提交报检申请,然后准备收集报检单证和相关信息:装箱单、发票、购销合同、报检委托书、厂检单、生产企业备案证明、发货人及生产厂家海关备案回执、货物中英文品名、H. S. 编码、离境口岸、离境海关、报关海关、施检海关和货物合格证明等。

1. 报检委托书

报检委托书是委托人与受托人进行代理报检业务的协议。报检单位是经海关注册登记,依法接受有关关系人委托,代理有关关系人办理报检业务,在工商行政管理部门注册登记的境内企业法人。报检单位主要有专业代理报检单位、国际货运代理报检单位、国际船务运输代理报检单位等。

2. 出境货物检验检疫申请单

出境货物检验检疫申请时,报检单位应按照出口贸易合同、商业发票等内容准确填写出境货物检验检疫申请单,不得涂改。

出境货物检验检疫申请单样例见表8. 1。

表 8.1 出境货物检验检疫申请单

中华人民共和国海关
出境货物检验检疫申请

申请单位（加盖公章）： (1)　　　　电子底账数据号：　　　　　　*编　号＿＿＿＿＿＿

申请单位登记号： (2)　联系人：　　　电话：　　　　　　申请日　年　月　日

发货人	（中文）(3)				
	（外文）				
收货人	（中文）(4)				
	（外文）				
货物名称（中/外文）(5)	H.S.编码(6)	产地(7)	数/重量(8)	货物总值(9)	包装种类及数量(10)

运输工具名称号码	(11)		贸易方式	(12)	货物存放地点	(13)
合同号	(14)		信用证号	(15)	用途	(16)
发货日期	(17)	输往国家(地区)	(18)	许可证/审批号		(19)
起运地	(20)	到达口岸	(21)	生产单位注册号		(22)
集装箱规格、数量及号码			(23)			

合同、信用证订立的检验检疫 条款或特殊要求	标记及号码	随附单据（画"✓"或补填）(26)	
(24)	(25)	□合同 □信用证 □发票 □装箱单 □厂检单	□包装性能结果单 □许可/审批文件 □报检委托书 □其他单据 □

需要证单名称（画"✓"或补填）(27)		*检验检疫费	
□品质证书　＿正＿副	□植物检疫证书　＿正＿副	总金额	
□重量证书　＿正＿副	□熏蒸/消毒证书　＿正＿副	（人民币元）	
□数量证书　＿正＿副	□		
□兽医卫生证书　＿正＿副	□	计费人	
□健康证书　＿正＿副	□		
□卫生证书　＿正＿副	□	收费人	
□动物卫生证书　＿正＿副	□		

续表

申请人郑重声明:(28) 　　1. 本人被授权申请检验检疫。 　　2. 上列填写内容正确属实,货物无伪造或冒用他人的厂名、标志、认证标志,并承担货物质量责任。 　　　　　　　　　　签名:_____	领 取 证 单	
	日期	
	签名	(29)

注:有"＊"号栏由海关填写

3. 出境货物检验检疫申请单缮制方法

①申请单位:指向海关申报检验检疫、鉴定业务的单位;申请单应加盖公章。

②申请单位登记号:指在海关的报检注册登记号。

③发货人:指本批货物贸易合同中的卖方名称或信用证中的受益人名称,如需要出具英文证书的,填写中英文。

④收货人:指本批出境货物贸易合同中或信用证中的买方名称,如需要出具英文证书的,填写中英文。

⑤货物名称:按外贸合同、信用证上所列名称及规格填写。

⑥H. S. 编码:指货物对应的当年海关《商品名称及编码协调制度》中的代码,填写10位数。

⑦产地:指货物的生产/加工地,填写省、市、县名。

⑧数/重量:填写报检货物的数/重量,重量一般以净重填写,如填写毛重,或以毛重作净重则需注明。

⑨货物总值:按本批货物合同或发票上所列的总值填写(以美元计),如同一检验检疫申请单报检多批货物,需列明每批货物的总值。

⑩包装数量及种类:指本批货物运输包装的数量及种类。

⑪运输工具名称号码:填写货物实际装载的运输工具类别名称(如船、飞机、货柜车、火车等)及运输工具编号(船名、飞机航班号、车牌号码、火车车次)。报检时,未能确定运输工具编号的,可只填写运输工具类别。

⑫贸易方式:A. 一般贸易;B. 三来一补;C. 边境贸易;D. 进料加工;E. 其他贸易。

⑬货物存放的地点:指本批申请检验检疫货物存放的地点。

⑭合同号:指贸易双方就本批货物出境而签订的贸易合同、订单或形式发票的编号。

⑮信用证号:指本批货物所对应的信用证编号。

⑯用途:指本批货物出境用途,如种用、食用、观赏或演艺、实验、药用、饲用、加工等。

⑰发货日期:按本批货物信用证或合同所列的出境日期填写。

⑱输往国家(地区):指贸易合同中买方(进口方)所在国家或地区。

⑲许可证/审批单号:对国家已实施出口商品质量许可证制度目录下的出口货物和其他已实行许可制度、审批制度管理的货物,申请检验检疫时填写出口商品许可证编号或审批单

编号。

　　⑳启运地:指装运本批货物离境的交通工具的启运口岸/地区城市名称。

　　㉑到达口岸:指装运本批货物的交通工具最终抵达目的地停靠的口岸名称。

　　㉒生产单位注册号:指生产/加工本批货物的单位在海关的注册登记编号。

　　㉓集装箱规格、数量及号码:填写装载本批货物的集装箱规格(如40英尺、20英尺等)及分别对应的数量和集装箱号码全称。

　　㉔合同、信用证订立的检验检疫条款或特殊要求:指贸易合同或信用证中贸易双方对本批货物特别约定而订立的质量、卫生等条款,以及报检单位对本批出境货物的其他检验检疫特别要求。

　　㉕标记及号码:按出境货物运输包装的实际标记填写,如没有标记,填 N/M,标记填写不下时可用附页填报。

　　㉖随附单据:按实际提供的单据,在对应的窗口打"√"。

　　㉗需要证单名称:按需要由海关出具的证单,在对应的窗口打"√",并应注明所需证单的正副本数量。

　　㉘报检人郑重声明:必须有报检人的亲笔签名。

　　㉙领取证单:由领证人在领证时填写实际领证日期并签名。

三、检验检疫证书的种类和作用

1. 种类

①品质检验证书(Inspection Certificate of Quality)。

②重量或数量检验证书(Inspection Certificate of Weight or Quantity)。

③兽医检验证书(Veterinary Inspection Certificate)。

④卫生检验证书(Sanitary Inspection Certificate)。

⑤消毒检验证书(Inspection Certificate of Disinfection or Sterilization)。

⑥温度检验证书(Inspection Certificate of Temperature)。

⑦熏蒸检验证书(Inspection Certificate of Fumigation)。

⑧包装检验证书(Inspection Certificate of Packing)。

⑨衡量证书(Certificate of Measurement & /or Weight)。

⑩船舶检验证书(Inspection Certificate of Hold/Tank)。

⑪集装箱检验证书(Inspection Certificate on Container)。

⑫价值证明书(Certificate of Value)。

⑬生丝品级及公量检验证书(Inspection Certificate for Raw Silk Classificaton & Condition Weight)。

2. 作用

①检验检疫证书是出口人凭以交单结汇和银行凭以议付或付款的结汇单据之一。

②检验检疫证书是证明卖方交货的品质、数(重)量、包装的安全及卫生条件等是否符合合同规定的依据。

③检验检疫证书是明确责任的有效证件。

任务二　报关单证缮制与操作

一、报关的基础知识

1.报关的概念

报关是进出口货物的收发货人、进出境运输公司的负责人、进出境物品的所有人或其代理人向海关办理货物、物品或运输工具进出境手续及相关海关事务的全过程。

2.进出口货物报关的一般程序

进出口货物报关的程序大致分为前期阶段、进出境阶段和后续阶段3个不同阶段。根据海关对进出口货物的监管要求不同,货物报关的程序有所不同。对监管类货物,海关有特定的监管要求,此类货物在实际进出境前需要向海关办理备案、登记等手续,并在此类货物完成进出境储存、加工、装配、使用和维修后,还要在规定的时限按规定的要求,向海关办理核销、销案、申请解除监管手续。

进出口申报是指进出口货物收发货人或其代理人在海关规定的期限内,按照海关规定的形式,向海关报告进出口货物的情况,提请海关按其申报的内容放行货物的工作环节。申报前需要做好3项准备工作,即单证准备、货物准备和运输准备。其中,单证准备是指报关单位应按照海关规定准备好货物报关所需要的进出口货物报关单及随附单证。常见出口报关单证有合同或通关手册/账册、商业发票、装箱单、出口报关单、电子委托(海关"单一窗口"或电子口岸操作即可,无须提供纸质资料)、货代运单、随货资料(随货发给客户清关的资料,如发票、装箱单、产地证等)。

二、出口货物报关单的概念与缮制方法

1.出口货物报关单的概念

出口货物报关单由海关总署规定统一格式和填制规范,是进出口企业或代理人申报货物状况的法律文书,是海关依法监管货物出口、征收关税及其他税费、编制海关统计以及处理其他海关业务的重要凭证。

出口货物报关单样例见表8.2。

表8.2 出口货物报关单样例

中华人民共和国海关出口货物报关单

预录入编号(1)   海关编号(2)

境内发货人(3)	出境关别(4)	出口日期(5)		申报日期(6)	备案号(7)
境外收货人(8)	运输方式(9)	运输工具名称及航次号(10)		提运单号(11)	
生产销售单位(12)	监管方式(13)	征免性质(14)		许可证号(15)	
合同协议号(16)	贸易国(地区)(17)	运抵国(地区)(18)		指运港(19)	离境口岸(20)
包装种类(21)	件数(22)	毛重(千克)(23)	净重(千克)(24)	成交方式(25)	运费(26)	保费(27)	杂费(28)
随附单证及编号(29)							
标记唛码及备注(30)							

项号(31)	商品编号(32)	商品名称及规格型号(33)	数量及单位(34)	单价/总价/币制(35)	原产国/地区(36)	最终目的国(地区)(37)	境内货源地(38)	征免(39)
1								
2								
3								

报关人员申报单位	报关人员证号	电话	兹申明以上内容承担如实申报、依法纳税之法律责任(签章)	海关批注及签章

预录入编号: 海关编号:

2.出口货物报关单的缮制方法

出口货物报关单有各种形式,但主要的内容大致相同,下面就介绍一下报关单的填制方法。

(1)预录入编号

填写申报单位或预录入单位对该单位填制录入的报关单的编号,用于该单位与海关之间引用其申报后尚未批准放行的报关单。报关单录入凭单的编号规则由申报单位自行决定,预录入报关单或 EDI 报关单的预录入编号由接受申报的海关决定。

（2）海关编号

海关接受申报后所做的报关单标志号，一般为9位数码。此栏由海关填写。

（3）境内发货人

填报在海关备案的对外签订并执行进出口贸易合同的中国境内法人、其他组织名称及编码。编码填报18位法人和其他组织统一社会信用代码，没有统一社会信用代码的，填报其在海关的备案编码。

（4）出境关别

根据货物实际进出境的口岸海关，填报海关规定的"关区代码表"中相应口岸海关的名称及代码。

（5）出口日期

填写运载出口货物的运输工具申报进境/出境的日期，顺序为年、月、日，如2021年1月20日填为"2021.01.20"。

（6）申报日期

填写海关接受发货人或其代理人申报货物出口的日期，填写方法与第5栏出口日期的填写方法相同。

（7）备案号

填报进出口货物收发货人、消费使用单位、生产销售单位在海关办理加工贸易合同备案或征、减、免税审核确认等手续时，海关核发的"加工贸易手册"、海关特殊监管区域和保税监管场所保税账册、"征免税证明"或其他备案审批文件的编号。一份报关单只允许填报一个备案号。

（8）境外收发货人

填报境外收发货人的名称及编码。非互认国家（地区）AEO企业等其他情形，编码免于填报。境外收发货人通常指签订并执行出口贸易合同中的买方或合同指定的收货人，境外发货人通常指签订并执行进口贸易合同中的卖方。名称一般填报英文名称，检验检疫要求填报其他外文名称的，在英文名称后填报，以半角括号分隔；对于AEO互认国家（地区）企业的，编码填报AEO编码，填报样式按照海关总署发布的相关公告要求填报（如新加坡AEO企业填报样式为：SG123456789012，韩国AEO企业填报样式为KR1234567，具体见相关公告要求）。

（9）运输方式

本栏目应根据实际运输方式，按海关规定的"运输方式代码表"选择填报相应的运输方式。例如："江海运输""航空运输""铁路运输"等。

（10）运输工具名称

填写运输该货物进出境的运输工具的名称或编号。一份报关单只允许填报一个运输工具名称。

（11）提运单号

填写出口货物提单或运单的编号。一份报关单只允许填报一个提运单号，一票货物对应多个提运单时，应分单填报。

（12）生产销售单位

填报出口货物在境内的生产或销售单位的名称,包括自行出口货物的单位、委托进出口企业出口货物的单位。

（13）监管方式

根据海关"贸易方式代码表"中确定的贸易方式简称或代码填写。一份贸易报关单只允许填报一种贸易方式。例如,一般贸易,代码为"0110";来料加工,代码为"0214";进料加工,代码为"0615"等。

（14）征免性质

按照海关核发的征免税证明中批注的征免性质填报,或根据进出口货物的实际情况,参照"征免性质代码表"选择填报相应的征免性质简称或代码。加工贸易货物应按海关核发的登记手册中批注的征免性质填报相应的征免性质简称或代码。征免性质一般由海关填写,一份报关单只允许填报一种征免性质。

（15）许可证号

填报进（出）口许可证、两用物项和技术进（出）口许可证、两用物项和技术出口许可证（定向）、纺织品临时出口许可证、出口许可证（加工贸易）、出口许可证（边境小额贸易）的编号。一份报关单只允许填报一个许可证号。

（16）合同协议号

填报进出口货物合同（包括协议或订单）编号。未发生商业性交易的免予填报。

（17）贸易国（地区）

发生商业性交易的进口填报购自国（地区）,出口填报售予国（地区）。未发生商业性交易的填报货物所有权拥有者所属的国家（地区）。

（18）运抵国（地区）

运抵国（地区）填报出口货物离开我国关境直接运抵或者在运输中转国（地区）未发生任何商业性交易的情况下最后运抵的国家（地区）。经过第三国（地区）转运的进出口货物,如在中转国（地区）发生商业性交易,则以中转国（地区）作为起运/运抵国（地区）。

（19）指运港

指运港填报出口货物运往境外的最终目的港;最终目的港不可预知的,按尽可能预知的目的港填报。

（20）离境口岸

离境口岸填报出口货物始发港。

（21）填报进出口货物的所有包装材料

填报资料包括运输包装和其他包装,按海关规定的"包装种类代码表"选择填报相应的包装种类名称及代码。运输包装指提运单所列货物件数单位对应的包装,其他包装包括货物的各类包装,以及植物性铺垫材料等。

（22）件数

填报进出口货物运输包装的件数（按运输包装计）。特殊情况填报要求如下:舱单件数为集装箱的,填报集装箱个数;舱单件数为托盘的,填报托盘数;不得填报为零,裸装货物填报为"1"。

（23）毛重

填报进出口货物及其包装材料的重量之和，计量单位为千克，不足1千克的填报为"1"。

（24）净重

填报进出口货物的毛重减去外包装材料后的重量，即货物本身的实际重量，计量单位为千克，不足1千克的填报为"1"。

（25）成交方式

根据进出口货物实际成交价格条款，按海关规定的"成交方式代码表"选择填报相应的成交方式代码。无实际进出境的货物，进口填报 CIF，出口填报 FOB。

（26）运费

填报进口货物运抵我国境内输入地点起卸前的运输费用，出口货物运至我国境内输出地点装载后的运输费用。运费可按运费单价、总价或运费率三种方式之一填报，注明运费标记（运费标记"1"表示运费率，"2"表示每吨货物的运费单价，"3"表示运费总价），并按海关规定的"货币代码表"选择填报相应的币种代码。

（27）保费

填报进口货物运抵我国境内输入地点起卸前的保险费用，出口货物运至我国境内输出地点装载后的保险费用。保费可按保险费总价或保险费率两种方式之一填报，注明保险费标记（保险费标记"1"表示保险费率，"3"表示保险费总价），并按海关规定的"货币代码表"选择填报相应的币种代码。

（28）杂费

填报成交价格以外的、按照《中华人民共和国进出口关税条例》相关规定应计入完税价格或应从完税价格中扣除的费用。可按杂费总价或杂费率两种方式之一填报，注明杂费标记（杂费标记"1"表示杂费率，"3"表示杂费总价），并按海关规定的"货币代码表"选择填报相应的币种代码。应计入完税价格的杂费填报为正值或正率，应从完税价格中扣除的杂费填报为负值或负率。

（29）随附单证

根据海关规定的"监管证件代码表"和"随附单据代码表"选择填报除本规范第十六条规定的许可证件以外的其他进出口许可证件或监管证件、随附单据代码及编号。本栏目分为随附单证代码和随附单证编号两栏，其中代码栏按海关规定的"监管证件代码表"和"随附单据代码表"选择填报相应证件代码；随附单证编号栏填报证件编号。

（30）标记唛码及备注

标记唛码按照发票中的唛头，用除图形以外的文字和数字填制。

与本报关单有关联关系的，同时在业务管理规范方面又要求填报的备案号，填报在电子数据报关单中"关联备案"栏。集装箱体信息填报集装箱号（在集装箱箱体上标示的全球唯一编号）、集装箱规格、集装箱商品项号关系（单个集装箱对应的商品项号，半角逗号分隔）、集装箱货重（集装箱箱体自重+装载货物重量，单位为千克）。

（31）项号

分两行填报。第一行填报报关单中的商品顺序编号；第二行填报备案序号，专用于加工贸易及保税、减免税等已备案、审批的货物，填报该项货物在"加工贸易手册"或"征免税证明"等备案、审批单证中的顺序编号。有关优惠贸易协定项下报关单填制要求按照海关总署相关规定执行。

（32）商品编号

填报由13位数字组成的商品编号。前8位为《中华人民共和国进出口税则》和《中华人民共和国海关统计商品目录》确定的编码，9，10位为监管附加编号，11—13位为检验检疫附加编号。

（33）商品名称及规格型号

分两行填报。第一行填报进出口货物规范的中文商品名称，第二行填报规格型号。品牌类型为必填项目。可选择"无品牌""境内自主品牌""境内收购品牌""境外品牌（贴牌生产）""境外品牌（其他）"如实填报。其中"境内自主品牌"是指由境内企业自主开发、拥有自主知识产权的品牌；"境内收购品牌"是指境内企业收购的原境外品牌；"境外品牌（贴牌生产）"是指境内企业代工贴牌生产中使用的境外品牌；"境外品牌（其他）"是指除代工贴牌生产以外使用的境外品牌。出口享惠情况为出口报关单必填项目。可选择"出口货物在最终目的国（地区）不享受优惠关税""出口货物在最终目的国（地区）享受优惠关税""出口货物不能确定在最终目的国（地区）享受优惠关税"如实填报。进口货物报关单不填报该申报项。

（34）数量及单位

分三行填报。第一行按进出口货物的法定第一计量单位填报数量及单位，法定计量单位以《中华人民共和国海关统计商品目录》中的计量单位为准。凡列明有法定第二计量单位的，在第二行按照法定第二计量单位填报数量及单位。无法定第二计量单位的，第二行为空。成交计量单位及数量填报在第三行。

（35）单价/总价/币制

填报同一项号下进出口货物实际成交的商品单位价格。无实际成交价格的，填报单位货值。按海关规定的"货币代码表"选择相应的货币名称及代码填报，如"货币代码表"中无实际成交币种，需将实际成交货币按申报日外汇折算率折算成"货币代码表"列明的货币填报。

（36）原产国（地区）

原产国（地区）依据《中华人民共和国进出口货物原产地条例》《中华人民共和国海关总署关于非优惠原产地规则中实质性改变标准的规定》以及海关总署关于各项优惠贸易协定原产地管理规章规定的原产地确定标准填报。同一批进出口货物的原产地不同的，分别填报原产国（地区）。进出口货物原产国（地区）无法确定的，填报"国别不详"。

（37）最终目的国（地区）

最终目的国（地区）填报已知的进出口货物的最终实际消费、使用或进一步加工制造国家（地区）。不经过第三国（地区）转运的直接运输货物，以运抵国（地区）为最终目的国（地区）；经过第三国（地区）转运的货物，以最后运往国（地区）为最终目的国（地区）。同一批进出口货物的最终目的国(地区)不同的,分别填报最终目的国(地区)。进出口货物不能确定最终目的国(地区)时,以尽可能预知的最后运往国(地区)为最终目的国(地区)。

(38)境内货源地

境内货源地填报出口货物在国内的产地或原始发货地。出口货物产地难以确定的,填报最早发运该出口货物的单位所在地。

(39)征免

按照海关核发的"征免税证明"或有关政策规定,对报关单所列每项商品选择海关规定的"征减免税方式代码表"中相应的征减免税方式填报。加工贸易货物报关单根据"加工贸易手册"中备案的征免规定填报;"加工贸易手册"中备案的征免规定为"保金"或"保函"的,填报"全免"。

【实操训练】

1.请根据以下所给信用证及补充资料的内容,缮制出口货物报关单。

(1)信用证

SEQUENCE OF TOTAL	*27:	1/1
FORM OF DOC CREDIT	*40A:	IRREVOCABLE
DOC CREDIT NUMBER	*20:	2109111
DATE OF ISSUE	31C:	210925
DATE AND PLACE OF EXPIRY	*31D:	DATE 211220 PLACE IN THE COUNTRY OF BENEFICIARY
APPLICANT	*50:	YAMADA TRADE CO., LTD
		310-224 SKURAMAJI OSAKA, JAPAN
ISSUING BANK	52A:	FUJI BANK LTD
		1013 SAKULA OTOLIKINGZA MACHI TOKYO, JAPAN
BENEFICIARY	*59:	SHANGHAI TOY IMPORT & EXPORT CORPORATION
		530 ZHONGSHAN ROAD SHANGHAI, CHINA
AMOUNT	*32B:	CURRENCY USD AMOUNT 19800.00
AVAILABLE WITH/BY	*41D:	ANY BANK IN CHINA BY NEGOTIATION
DRAFTS AT	42C:	30 DAYS AFTER SIGHT FOR FULL
		INVOICE COST
DRAWEE	42A:	FUJI BANK LTD
PARTIAL SHIPMENT	43P:	PROHOBITED
TRANSSHIPMENT	43T:	PROHIBITED
LOADING ON BOARD	44A:	SHANGHAI
FOR TRANSPORATION TO	44B:	OSAKA PORT
LATEST DATE OF SHIPMENT	44C:	211031
DESCRIPTION OF GOODS	45A:	PLUSH TOY
		ART NO. 818(PANDA) 300000 PCS USD0.33/PC
		ART NO. 518(BEAR) 300000 PCS USD0.33/PC
		CIF OSAKA

续表

DOCUMENTS REQUIRED	46A：	+SIGNED COMMERCIAL INVOICE IN TRIPLICATE +PACKING LIST IN TRIPLICATE +CERTIFICATE OF ORIGIN, ISSUED BY THE CHAMBER OF COMMERCE OR OTHER AUTHORITY DULY ENTITLED FOR THIS PURPOSE. +3/3 SET OF CLEAN ON BOARD OCEAN BILL OF LADING MADE OUT TO ORDER OF SHIPPER AND BLANK ENDORSED AND MARKED "FREIGHT PREPAID" AND NOTIFY APPLICANT. +FULL SET OF NEGOTIABLE INSURANCE POLICY OR CERTIFICATE BLANK ENDORSED FOR 110 PCT OF INVOICE VALUE COVERING ALL RISKS AND WAR RISK AS PER CIC. + NO SOLID WOOD PACKING CERTIFICATE ISSUED BY MANUFACTURER
CHARGES	71B：	ALL BANKING CHARGES OUTSIDE JAPAN ARE FOR ACCOUNT OF BENEFICIARY.
PERIOD FOR PRESENTATION	48：	DOCUMENTS MUST BE PRESENTED WITHIN 15 DAYS AFTER THE DATE OF SHIPMENT BUT WITHIN THE VALIDITY OF THE CREDIT.

（2）补充资料

①S/C NO. WJ060125

②PACKING：　　　　G. W.　　　　　　N. W.　　　　　MEAS

ART NO. 818　　10. 2 KGS/CTN　　10 KGS/CTN　　0. 2 CBM/CTN

ART NO. 518　　11. 2 KGS/CTN　　11 KGS/CTN　　0. 2 CBM/CTN

PACKED IN ONE CARTON OF 100PCS EACH

PACKED IN TWO 40' CONTAINER（集装箱号：TEXU 2263456；TEXU 2263458）

③H. S. CODE：95039000. 00

④B/L DATE：OCT. 28，2021

⑤VESSEL：XIANG DONG V. 009

⑥许可证号：785455661

⑦报关单编号：568881222

⑧报关单位登记号：1234567855

⑨生产单位注册号：56422P

⑩预录人编号：611250886

⑪海关编号：4561233770

⑫出口口岸：上海海关，代码（2200）

⑬境内货源地：上海

⑭生产厂家：上海玩具进出口公司

⑮海关注册号：8546221147

⑯报关申报日期：2021 年 10 月 26 日

⑰批准文号：2999456

⑱境内货源地：上海其他，代码（31909）

⑲运输方式：江海运输

⑳贸易方式：一般贸易，代码（0110）

㉑征免性质：一般征税，代码（101）

㉒目的国：日本，代码（116）

㉓指运港：大阪，代码（1303）

中华人民共和国海关出口货物报关单

预录入编号：（1）   海关编号：（2）

境内发货人(3)	出境关别(4)		进口日期(5)		申报日期(6)	备案号(7)
境外收货人(8)	运输方式(9)		运输工具名称及航次号(10)		提运单号(11)	
生产销售单位(12)	监管方式(13)		征免性质(14)		许可证号(15)	
合同协议号(16)	贸易国(地区)(17)		运抵国(地区)(18)		指运港(19)	离境口岸(20)
包装种类(21)	件数(22)	毛重（千克）(23)	净重（千克）(24)	成交方式(25)	运费(26)	保费(27)	杂费(28)
随附单证及编号(29)						
标记唛码及备注(30)						

项号(31)	商品编号(32)	商品名称及规格型号(33)	数量及单位(34)	单价/总价/币制(35)	原产国/地区(36)	最终目的国(地区)(37)	境内货源地(38)	征免(39)
1								
2								
3								

报关人员申报单位	报关人员证号	电话	兹申明以上内容承担如实申报、依法纳税之法律责任（签章）	海关批注及签章

项目九　原产地证书缮制与操作

【工作情景】

在上海威尔进出口公司与 NU BONNETERIE DE GROOTE 公司达成的短裤出口交易中,NU BONNETERIE DE GROOTE 公司申请开立的信用证条款中要求"由权威机构出具一般原产地证书/普惠制产地证书"。请以单证员殷实的身份填制普惠制产地证书。

【工作任务】

任务一　原产地证书概述

一、原产地证书的定义与作用

1. 原产地证书的定义

原产地证书(Certificate of Origin),是出口商应进口商要求而提供的、由出口国特定机构出具的证明其出口货物为该国家(或地区)原产或制造的一种证明文件。中华人民共和国出口货物原产地证明书是证明有关出口货物原产地为中华人民共和国的证明文件。

2. 原产地证书的作用

①证明货物的原产地或制造地。

②作为进口国允许货物进口通关的文件之一。

③作为进口国海关征收关税的依据。

④作为进口国对不同出口国实行不同贸易政策的工具。

⑤作为贸易关系人交接货物、结算货款、索赔理赔的凭证之一。

⑥作为出口国享受配额待遇的凭证。

⑦作为一国贸易统计和制定贸易政策的依据之一。

二、原产地证书的出具人

在我国,原产地证书的出具人有以下几种情况。

①海关出具的原产地证书。例如,中华人民共和国海关出具的中华人民共和国原产地证书。

②民间商会出具的原产地证书。例如,中国国际贸易促进委员会出具的一般原产地证书。

③中华人民共和国商务部出具的原产地证书。

④出口商或制造商出具的原产地证书。

在国际贸易实务中,需要由谁出具原产地证书,主要依据合同或信用证的要求。如果合同或信用证并未明确规定原产地证书的出具者,那么银行应该接受上述任何一方出具的原产地证书。

三、原产地证书的种类

根据原产地证书的不同用途和范围,国际上通常将原产地证书分为 4 类。

1. 非优惠原产地证书

(1)一般原产地证书

一般原产地证书(Certificate of Origin)是最常用的非优惠原产地证书,是证明货物原产于某一特定国家或地区,享受进口国正常关税(最惠国)待遇的证明文件。通常用于不使用海关发票或领事发票的国家(地区),以确定对货物征税的税率。

(2)加工装配证书

加工装配证书(Certificate of Processing)是指对全部或部分使用了进口原料或零部件而在中国进行了加工、装配的出口货物,当其不符合中国出口货物原产地标准、未能取得原产地证书时,由签证机构根据申请单位的申请所签发的证明中国为出口货物加工、装配地的一种证明文件。

(3)转口证书

转口证书(Certificate of Re-Export)是指经中国转口的外国货物,由于不能取得中国的原产地证,而由中国签证机构出具的证明货物系他国原产、经中国转口的一种证明文件。

2. 普惠制原产地证书

普惠制原产地证书(Generalized System of Preferences Certificate of Origin)即 GSP 原产地证书,简称 FORM A。普遍优惠制度是发达国家给予发展中国家出口制成品和半制成品(包括某些初级产品)普遍的、非歧视性的、非互惠的一种关税优惠制度。普惠制产地证是一种受惠国有关机构就本国出口商向给惠国出口受惠商品而签发的用以证明货物原产地的证明文件。在我国,普惠制原产地证书由各口岸的检验检疫机构负责办理签证、发证和管理工作。

普惠制产地证主要有 3 种格式:普惠制产地证格式 A、普惠制产地证格式 59A 和普惠制产地证格式 APR。其中,"格式 A"(FORM A)使用范围最广。

3. 区域性优惠贸易协定项下原产地证书

区域性优惠贸易协定项下原产地证书是指订有区域性优惠贸易协定的国家官方机构签发的,证明货物符合相关协定规定的享受相互减免关税待遇的原产地证书。目前主要有以下10 种。

(1)《亚太贸易协定》原产地证书(FORM B)

目前适用于对印度、韩国、孟加拉国和斯里兰卡出口并符合相关规定的产品。

(2)《中国—东盟自由贸易协定》原产地证书(FORM E)

目前适用于对印度尼西亚、泰国、马来西亚、越南、菲律宾、新加坡、文莱、柬埔寨、缅甸、老挝等国出口并符合相关规定的产品。

(3)《中国—巴基斯坦自由贸易协定》原产地证书(FORM P)

目前适用于对巴基斯坦出口并符合相关规定的产品。

(4)《中国—智利自由贸易协定》原产地证书(FORM F)

目前适用于对智利出口并符合相关规定的产品。

(5)《中国—新西兰自由贸易协定》原产地证书(FORM N)

目前适用于对新西兰出口并符合相关规定的产品。

(6)《中国—新加坡自由贸易协定》原产地证书(FORM X)

目前适用于对新加坡出口并符合相关规定的产品。

(7)《中国—秘鲁自由贸易协定》原产地证书(FORM R)

目前适用于对秘鲁出口并符合相关规定的产品。

(8) CEPA 原产地证书

CEPA(Closer Economic Partnership Arrangement)即《关于建立更紧密经贸关系的安排》。目前适用于从我国香港特别行政区及我国澳门特别行政区输入并符合相关规定的产品。

(9) ECFA 原产地证书

ECFA(Economic Cooperation Framework Agreement),即《海峡两岸经济合作框架协议》。

目前适用于对我国台湾地区输出并符合相关规定的产品。

(10)《中国—哥斯达黎加自由贸易协定》原产地证明书(FORM L)

目前适用于对哥斯达黎加出口并符合相关规定的产品。

4.专用原产地证书

专用原产地证书是国际组织和国家根据政策和贸易措施的特殊需要,针对某一特殊行业的特定产品签发的原产地证书。专用原产地证书上所列的商品均属某一特殊行业的某项特定产品,这些产品符合特定的原产地证规则,签证依据为我国政府与外国政府签订的协议规定,如金伯利进程国际证书、输欧农产品原产地证明书、烟草真实性证书等。

任务二　原产地证书缮制与操作

一、原产地证书申领手续

根据我国有关规定,出口企业最迟于货物出运 3 天前,打开"中国国际贸易单一窗口"网站(图 9.1),单击门户网站"标准版应用"页签,单击"原产地证",普惠制产地证选择"海关原产地证申请"进入,一般原产地证选择"贸促会原产地证申请"进入(图 9.2)。原产地证书申请成功后,可以单击"原产地证书自助打印"打印原产地证书(图 9.2)。

图 9.1　原产地选择

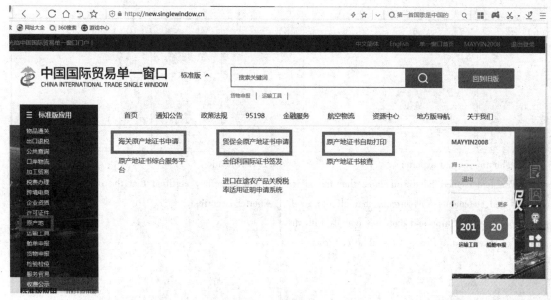

图9.2 打印原产地证书

二、一般原产地证书缮制规范

一般原产地证书样例见表9.1。

表9.1 一般原产地证书样例

ORIGINAL

1. Exporter （1）			Certificate No. **CERTIFICATE OF ORIGIN** **OF** **THE PEOPLE'S REPUBLIC OF CHINA**		
2. Consignee （2）					
3. Means of transport and route （3）			5. For certifying authority use only （5）		
4. Country / region of destination （4）					
6. Marks and numbers	7. Number and kind of packages; description of goods		8. H. S. Code	9. Quantity	10. Number and date of invoices

续表

(6)	(7)	(8)	(9)	(10)

11. Declaration by the exporter The undersigned hereby declares that the above details and statements are correct, that all the goods were produced in China and that they comply with the Rules of Origin of the People's Republic of China. (11) Place and date, signature and stamp of authorized signatory.	12. Certification It is hereby certified that the declaration by the exporter is correct. (12) Place and date, signature and stamp of certifying authority.

一般原产地证书共有12项内容,除证书号(Certificate No.)由发证机构指定、第5栏签证机构使用、第12栏签证机构证明以外,其余各栏均由出口企业用英文规范打印。

(1)出口方(Exporter)

此栏填写出口方名称、详细地址及国家(地区),此栏不得留空。出口方名称是指出口申报方名称,必须是中国境内已办理产地证书注册的企业,且公司英文名称应与检验检疫机构注册备案的名称一致,详细地址包括街道名、门牌号码等。一般填有效合同的卖方或发票的出票人。例如:

"NINGBO SKYLAND GROUP CO.,LTD.

"ROOM 1209, FT MANSION, 93 EAST ZHONGSHAN ROAD NINGBO CHINA"。

若中间商要求显示其名称,可按如下方式填写:"出口商名称、地址 VIA 中间商名称、地址",不能直接填写中间商名称、地址。例如:

"SINOCHEM INTERNATIONAL CHEMICALS CO.,LTD.

"NO.40,FUCHENG ROAD,BEIJING,CHINA VIA HONG KONG DAMING CO. LTD.

"NO.656,GUANGDONG ROAD, HONG KONG"。

此栏不得填写国外出口商名称。

(2)收货方(Consignee)

此栏应填写最终收货人的名称、详细地址及国家(地区),通常是外贸合同中的买方或信

用证上规定的提单通知人或特别声明的收货人,如果最终收货人不明确,可填写发票抬头人。例如:

"JENSON & JESSON TRADING

"LANGE MUHREN 9, F-2000, FIAMBURG, GERMANY"。

有时由于贸易的需要,信用证规定所有单证收货人一栏留空,在这种情况下,此栏应加注"TO WHOM IT MAY CONCERN(致有关人)"或"TO ORDER(凭指示)",也可声明"空白",填写"BLANK"或一行"＊"(星号)。本栏不得空白。

(3)运输方式及路线(Means of transport and route)

此栏填写装货港、到货港及运输路线(海运、陆运、空运等)。如经转运,还应注明转运地。此栏装货港应为中国内地境内最后离境的港口,不得填写国(境)外的港口。例如,通过海运,由上海港经香港转运至鹿特丹港,英文为:"FROM SHANGHAI TO HONG KONG, THEN TRANSSHIPPED TO ROTTERDAM BY VESSEL"或"FROM SHANGHAI TO ROTTERDAM BY SEA VIA HONG KONG"。

(4)目的国/地区(Country/region of destination)

此栏填写货物最终运抵的国家(地区),如"GERMANY"。也可依据有关方面要求填写国内的保税区,不能填写中间商所在国家(地区)名称。

(5)签证机构专用(For certifying authority use only)

此栏不需要证书申领单位填写,是签证机构在签发后发证书、重发证书或加注商会印章及其他声明时使用的专用栏目,是原产地证书中唯一可以并且经常性留空的一个栏目。如属"后发"证书,签证机构会在此栏加打"ISSUED RETROSPECTIVELY";如属签发"复本"(重发证书),签证机构会在此栏注明原发证书的编号和签证日期,并声明原发证书作废,其文字是:"THIS CERTIFICATE IS IN REPLACEMENT OF CERTIFICATE OF ORIGIN NO…DATED…WHICH IS CANCELLED",并加打"DUPLICATE"字样。

(6)唛头和号码(Marks and numbers)

此栏应按照出口发票上所列唛头填写完整,内容及格式必须与实际货物的外包装箱上所刷的内容一致。唛头中处于同一行的内容不要换行打印。例如:

"JENSON & JESSON

"ORDER NO.123456

"HAMBURG

"C/N 1-270"。

唛头不得出现"R. O. C."等中国以外其他产地制造字样,不能简单填写"AS PER INVOICE NO. …"(按照发票)或"AS PER B/L NO. …"(按照提单)。无唛头应填写"NO MARK"(或"N/M"),此栏不得留空。如唛头多,本栏填写不开,可填写在第7、8、9栏的空白处;如还不够,可在该栏填写"SEE ATTACHMENT",并另加附页。附页上方填写"ATTACH-MENT TO THE CERTIFICATE OF ORIGIN NO. …(证书号码)",附页下方两边分别打上申报地点、申报日期和签证地点、签证日期,左下方盖上申报单位签章并由申报单位申报员签名。附页应与原产地证书大小一致,由签证机构签章并加盖骑缝章。

（7）商品名称、包装数量及种类（Number and kind of packages；description of goods）

商品名称要填写具体名称，如"睡袋（SLEEPING BAGS）""杯子（CUPS）""网球拍（TENNIS RACKET）"；不得用概括性表述，如"服装（GARMENT）""运动用品（SPORTING GOODS）"。包装数量及种类要填写具体，并在包装数量的英文数字描述后用括号加上阿拉伯数字。例如，100 箱彩电，填写为"ONE HUNDRED （100） CARTONS OF COLOUR TV SET"。散装货物应加注"IN BULK"。本栏内容结束后，要在下一行填打表示结束的截止线"＊＊＊＊＊＊"，以防再添加内容。例如，"SIX HUNDRED （600） CTNS OF SHRIMPS ＊＊＊＊＊＊＊＊＊＊＊＊＊＊＊"。有时信用证要求在所有单证上加注合同号、信用证号码等，可加在此栏截止线下方，并以"REMARKS："作为开头。例如"FIVE HUNDRED （500） CTNS OF SHRIMPS

"＊＊＊＊＊＊

"REMARKS：L/C：12345678"。

（8）H. S. 编码（H. S. Code）

此栏要求准确填写 H. S. 编码，应与出口报关单一致。如同一发票项下同时出运的货物包含多种商品，应将每一种商品相应的税目号全部填打。此栏不得留空。

（9）数量（Quantity）

填写出口货物的数量或重量，如"1200 KGS G. W."或"500 PCS"。应在商品的具体数量后面填写明确的计量单位（个数、重量、长度、面积、体积、容积单位等）。以重量计算的要注明毛重或净重，如为毛重须加注"G. W.（GROSS WEIGHT）"，净重则加注"N. W.（NET WEIGHT）"，若同一证书包含有多种商品，则此栏的填制必须与第 7、8 栏中商品名称、商品编码相对应，必要时还需要填写总数。

（10）发票号码及日期（Number and date of invoices）

必须按照所申请出口货物的商业发票填写。该栏日期应早于或同于实际出口日期。为避免对日期的误解，日期一律用英文表述。例如，2021 年 8 月 10 日，用英文表述为"AUG. 10,2021"。此栏不得留空。在同一发票号项下的货物只能出具一份原产地证书。同一合同项下分批出运的货物若发票号不同，应分别申办原产地证书；若发票号相同，则只能出具一份原产地证书。

（11）出口商声明、签字、盖章（Declaration by the exporter）

出口商声明已经印就，内容如下："The undersigned hereby declares that the above details and statement are correct, that all the goods were produced in China and that they comply with the Rules of Origin of the People's Republic of China."在出口商声明下方由申请单位在签证机构注册备案的手签人签字，并填写申请地点和申请日期，同时加盖申请单位在签证机构备案的中英文合璧签证章，印章和签字不要重合、申请日期不要填法定休息日，且不得早于第 10 栏的发票日期。一般也不要迟于提单日期，如迟于提单日期，则要申请后发证书。

（12）签证机构证明、签字、盖章（Certification）

签证机构证明已经印就，内容如下："It is thereby certified that the declaration by the exporter is correct."在签证机构证明下方由签证机构授权的签证人员签字，并加盖签证机构印章,注明签署地点和日期,签字和盖章不能重合。此栏日期不得早于第10栏的发票日期和第11栏的申请日期。如信用证对签证机构有明确要求,需仔细核对,要求准确无误。

殷实根据项目二中信用证样例和信用证修改书样例缮制的原产地证见表9.2。

表9.2　缮制的原产地证

ORIGINAL

1. Exporter WILL SHANGHAI TRADINGG CO. ,LTD NO. 2021CHENGNAN ROAD,PUDONG SHANGHAI, CHINA			Certificate No. CERTIFICATE OF ORIGIN OF THE PEOPLE'S REPUBLIC OF CHINA		
2. Consignee NU BONNETERIE DE GROOTE. AUTOSTRADEWEG 69090 MELLE BELGIUM					
3. Means of transport and route SHIPMENT FROM SHANGHAI PORT, CHINA TO ANTWERP PORT, BELGIUM BY SEA			5. For certifying authority use only		
4. Country / region of destination BELGIUM					
6. Marks and numbers	7. Number and kind of packages; description of goods	8. H. S. Code	9. Quantity		10. Number and date of invoices
N/M	FIFTY （ 50 ） CARTONS OF SHORT TROUSERS	62046200. 99	5000 PCS		WT980 July1 , 2021
SAY TOTAL：FIFTY CARTONS ONLY. WE HEREBY CERTIFY THAT GOODS EXPORTED ARE WHOLLY OF CHINESE ORIGIN.					
11. Declaration by the exporter 　　The undersigned hereby declares that the above details and statements are correct, that all the goods were produced in China and that they comply with the Rules of Origin of the People's Republic of China.			12. Certification 　　It is hereby certified that the declaration by the exporter is correct.		
SHANGHAI, CHINA　JULY 17, 2021 Place and date, signature and stamp of authorized signatory			SHANGHAI, CHINA　JULY 17, 2021 Place and date, signature and stamp of certifying authority		

三、普惠制原产地证书缮制规范

普惠制原产地证书样例见表9.3。

表9.3 普惠制原产地证书样例

ORIGINAL

1. Exporter's name、address and country (1)	Certificate No.　　GZ07/2345/12345 CERTIFICATE OF ORIGIN					
2. Producer's name and address (2)	FORM A Issued in 　THE　PEOPLE'S REPUBLIC OF CHINA 　　　　　　　　　　(country)					
3. Importer's name、address and country (3)						
4. Means of transport and route (4)	For official use only 　　　　　　　　(15) 5. Remarks 　　　　　＊ ＊ ＊ ＊ ＊ ＊ ＊ ＊(5) Verification：origin. customs. gov. cn					
6. Item number (max. 20) (6)	7. Marks and numbers on packages (7)	8. Number and kind of packages; description of goods (8)	9. H. S. code (9)	10. Origin criterion (10)	11. Gross or net weight or other quantity (e. g. Quantity Unit, litres, m3.) (11)	12. Invoice number and date (12)
13. Declaration by the exporter or producer The undersigned hereby declares that the above-stated information is correct and that the goods exported to _____. 　　　　　Importing Party 　　　　　(13) Place, date and signature of authorized person	14. Certification On the basis of the control carried out, it is hereby certified that the information herein is correct and that the described goods comply with the origin requirements of the China-Australia Free Trade Agreement. Place, date, and signature and stamp of the Authorised Body. 　　　　　　　　(14)					

普惠制原产地证书共有 14 项内容,其中,证书右上角标题栏内证书号(Certificate No.)由发证机构指定,在标题横线上方必须填上"中华人民共和国"的英文字样,即"Issued in The People's Republic of China"。其他除第 15 栏签证机构使用,第 13 栏签证机构证明以外,其余各栏均由出口企业用英文规范打印,证书一律不得涂改,不得加盖校对章。

(1)出口商名称、地址、国家(Exporter's name, address, country)

此栏不得留空,应填明出口商详细地址,包括街道名、门牌号码等。例如,"CHINA ARTEX(HOLDINGS)CORP. GUANGDONG CO.""119(2ND BUILDING), LIUHUA ROAD, GUANGZHOU, CHINA"。

在信用证项下,一般填写信用证规定的受益人全称、地址、国别。中国地名的英文译音应采用汉语拼音,如"SHANGHAI(上海)""GUANGZHOU(广州)""TIANJIN(天津)""NANJING(南京)""QINGDAO(青岛)""DALIAN(大连)"等。

(2)制造商名称、地址(Producer's name and address)

此栏填写制造商名称、地址。

(3)进口商名称、地址和国家(地区)(Importer's name、address and country)

在信用证项下,一般填写开证申请人。如果预先不确定最终收货人,则可显示提单上通知人、发票抬头人或特别声明的收货人,一般银行也接受下列表述"TO WHOM IT MAY CONCERN",但不可填写中间转口商的名称。欧盟国家及挪威对此栏无强制性要求,如果商品直接运往上述给惠国,而且进口商要求将此栏留空时,可以不填。

(4)运输方式及路线(就所知而言)[Means of transport and route(as far as known)]

此栏一般应填写本批货物最终装运港、目的港或到货地点的名称及运输方式(海运、陆运、空运等)。例如,"FROM SHANGHAI TO HAMBURG BY SEA."。

货物涉及转运时应加上转运港名称,如"VIA HONG KONG"。不明确转运地时用"W/T"表示。若目的地为内陆地,则允许产地证上目的地名称与海运提单上卸货港名称不一致。对输往内陆给惠国(如瑞士、奥地利)的商品,由于这些国家没有海岸,因此如确系海运,填写时需注明:"从××港口经转××港口抵达××给惠国"。

此栏一般还需要加注预计离开中国的日期,此日期必须真实,不得捏造。例如,2021 年 8 月 6 日,从上海港经汉堡港转运至瑞士:"ON/AFTER 6 AUG., 2021 BY SEA FROM SHANGHAI TO HAMBURG TRANSIT TO SWITZERLAND."。

(5)注意事项(Remarks)

注意事项可以不填写内容,也可以填写"Verification:origin. customs. gov. cn."。

(6)商品顺序号(Item number)

如同批出口货物有不同种类商品品种,则按每一项商品归类品种后,用阿拉伯数字"1""2""3"顺序编号填入此栏。单项商品用"1"表示,或省略不填。

(7)唛头及包装号(Marks and numbers of packages)

此栏与一般原产地证书相应栏目填法相同。

(8)包件数量及种类(Number and kind of packages;description of goods)

商品名称与一般原产地证书相应栏目填法相同。

（9）H. S. 码（H. S. CODE）

填写商品的六位数 H. S. 编码。

（10）原产地标准（Origin criterion）

此栏用字最少，但却是国外海关审证的核心项目。对含有进口成分的商品，因情况复杂，国外要求严格，极易弄错而造成退证，故应认真审核。现将一般规定说明如下：

①完全原产品，不含任何进口成分，出口到所有给惠国，填"P"。

②含有进口成分的产品，出口到欧盟、挪威、瑞士和日本，填"W"，其后加上出口产品的 H. S. 税目号，如"W"42. 02。

条件一：产品列入了上述给惠国的"加工清单"并符合其加工条件。

条件二：产品未列入"加工清单"，但产品生产过程中使用的进口原材料和零部件经过充分加工，产品的 H. S. 税目号不同于原材料或零部件的 H. S. 税目号。

③含有进口成分的产品，出口到加拿大，填"F"。条件：进口成分的价值未超过产品出厂价的 40%。

④含有进口成分的产品，出口到加拿大，适用全球性原产地累计标准，填"G"。

⑤含有进口成分的产品，出口到波兰、俄罗斯、乌克兰、白俄罗斯、哈萨克斯坦、捷克、斯洛伐克 7 国，填"Y"，其后加上进口成分价值占该产品离岸价格的百分比，如"Y"38%。条件：进口成分的价值未超过产品离岸价格的 50%。

⑥含有进口成分的产品，出口到美国，适用区域性原产地累计标准，填"Z"，其后加上本国成分占产品出厂价的百分比。例如，"Z"35%。

⑦出口到澳大利亚、新西兰的商品，此栏可以留空。

（11）毛重或其他数量（Gross weight or other quantity）

此栏填写商品的毛重或其他数量及计量单位。例如，"3200 DOZ"或"6270 KG"。如商品只有净重，此栏填净重也可，但要标注"N. W. （NET WEIGHT）"。

（12）发票号码及日期（Invoice umber and date）

与一般原产地证书相应栏目填法相同。

（13）出口商声明（Declaration by the exporter）

出口商声明已事先印制，内容为"The undersigned hereby declares that the above detail and statements are correct that the goods were produced in _____（exporting country）and that they comply with the original requirements specified for those goods in the Generalized System of Preferences for goods exported to _____（importing country）."。

在生产国横线上填写"CHINA"。进口国横线上填最终进口国，如"GERMANY"。进口国必须与第 3 栏目的港的国别一致，货物运往欧盟成员国，进口国不明确时，进口国可填"E. U."。由申请单位在签证机构注册备案的手签人签字，并填写申请地点和申请日期，如"TIANJIN AUG. 18, 2021"，同时加盖申请单位在签证机构备案的中英文合璧签证章。印章和签字不要重合，申请日期不要填法定休息日且不得早于第 10 栏的发票日期。

（14）签证机构证明（Certification）

签证机构证明已事先印制，内容为"It is hereby certified, on the basis of control carried out, the declaration by the exporter is correct"，此栏填写检验检疫机构的签证地点和签证日期。例如，"TIANJIN AUG.18,2021"。同时，检验检疫机构签证人经审核后在此栏(正本)签名,盖签证印章。此栏日期不得早于第10栏的发票日期和第12栏的申报日期,而且应早于第3栏的货物的出运日期。

（15）供官方使用（For official use only）

此栏由签证当局填写,申请签证的单位应将此栏留空。正常情况下此栏空白,特殊情况下,签证当局在此栏加注。如属货物已出口,签证日期迟于出货日期的"后发"证书时,此栏加盖"ISSUED RETROSPECTIVELY"红色印章。如属证书遗失、被盗或损毁,签发"复本"证书时,加盖"DUPLICATE"红色印章,在此栏注明原证书的编号和签证日期,并声明原发证书作废,其文字是"THIS CERTIFICATE IS IN REPLACEMENT OF CERTIFICATE OF ORIGIN NO. … DATED … WHICH IS CANCELLED."日本一般不接受"后发"证书,除非有不可避免的原因。

单证员殷实根据项目二中的信用证样例和信用证修改书样例缮制的普惠制产地证书见表9.4。

表9.4 **ORIGINAL**

1. Goods consigned from (Exporter's business name, address, country) WILL SHANGHAI TRADINGG CO., LTD NO.2021CHENGNAN ROAD, PUDONG SHANGHAI, CHINA	Crertificate No. GZ07/2345/12345				
2. Goods consigned to (Consignee's name, address, country) SHITAYA KINZOKU CO., LTD NU BONNETERIE DE GROOTE. AUTOSTRADEWEG 69090 MELLE BELGIUM	GENERALIZED SYSTEM OF PREFERENCES CERTIFICATE OF ORIGIN (Combined declaration and certificate) FORM A Issued in THE PEOPLE'S REPUBLIC OF CHINA (country)				
3. Means of transport and route (as far as known) SHIPMENT FROM SHANGHAI PORT, CHINA TO ANTWERP PORT, BELGIUM BY SEA	4. For official use only				
5. Item number	6. Marks and numbers of packages	7. Number and kind of packages; description of goods	8. Origin criterion	9. Gross weight or other quantity	10. Number and date of invoices

续表

1	N/M	FIFTY（50）CAR-TONS OF SHORT TROUSERS ＊＊＊＊ ＊＊＊＊＊＊＊＊＊＊＊＊ ＊＊＊＊＊＊＊＊＊＊＊＊ ＊＊＊＊＊＊＊＊＊＊	"P"	5000 PCS	WT980 JULY 1，2021

11. Certification	12. Declaration by the exporter
It is hereby certified, on the basis of control carried out, that the declaration by the exporter is correct.	The undersigned hereby declares that the above details and statements are correct, that all the goods were produced in _____CHINA_____（country）and that they comply with the origin requirements specified for those goods in the Generalized System of Preferences for goods exported to ____BELGIUM____
_____SHANGHAI JULY 17,2021_____	_____SHANGHAI JULY 17,2021_____
Place and date, signature and stamp of certifying authority	Place and date, signature and stamp of authorized signatory

【实操训练】

商业发票。根据所给的商业发票和信用证缮制普惠制产地证书。

ISSUER NANJING TANG TEXTILE GARMENT CO.，LTD. HUARONG MANSION RM2901 NO. 85 GUAN-JIAQIAO， NANJING 210005，CHINA	**商业发票** COMMERCIAL INVOICE	
TO FASHION FORCE CO.，LTD P. O. BOX 8935 NEW TERMINAL, ALTA， VISTA OTTAWA，CANADA	NO. NT01FF004	DATE MAR. 9，2021
TRANSPORT DETAILS SHIPMENT FROM SHANGHAI PORT, P. R. CHINA TO MONTREAL PORT, CANADA BY VESSEL	S/C NO. F01LCB05127	L/C NO. 63211020049
	TERMS OF PAYMENT L/C AT SIGHT	

续表

MARKS AND NUMBERS	NUMBER AND KIND OF PACKAGE DESCRIPTION OF GOODS	QUANTITY	UNIT PRICE USD	AMOUNT
FASHION FORCE F01LCB05127 CTN NO. MONTREAL MADE IN CHINA	CIF MONTREAL, CANADA LADIES COTTON BLAZER （100% COTTON, 40SX20/140X60）	2550 PCS	USD12.80	USD32640.00

TOTAL：
               2550 PCS   USD32640.00

SAY TOTAL：USD THIRTY TWO THOUSAND SIX HUNDRED AND FORTY ONLY

SALES CONDITIONS：CIF MONTREAL/CANADA
SALES CONTRACT NO. F01LCB05127
LADIES COTTON BLAZER (100% COTTON, 40SX20/140X60)

STYLE NO.	PO NO.	QTY/PCS	USD/PC
46-301A	10337	2550	12.80

PAKAGE.	N. W.	G. W.
85CARTONS	17 KGS.	19 KGS.

TOTAL PACKAGE：85 CARTONS
TOTAL MEAS：21.583 CBM

（出口商签字和盖单据章）

信用证。

2021 AN31 15:23:46		LOGICAL TERMINAL E102

MT S700   ISSUE OF A DOCUMENTARY CREDIT   PAGE   00001

FUNC   MSG700

UMR   06607642

MSGACK   DWS765I AUTH OK,KEY B110106173BAOC53B, BKCHCNBJ BNPA ∗∗∗∗ RECORO

BASIC HEADER   F 01 BKCHCNBJA940 0542 725524

APPLICATION HEADER   0 700   1122 010129 BNPACAMMA※※ 4968 839712 010130 0028 N

* BNP PARIBAS（CANADA）

* MONTREAL

USER HEADER   SERVICE CODE   103:

BANK PRIORITY   113:

MSG USER REF. 108:   （银行盖信用证通知专用章）

INFO. FROM CI   115:

SEQUENCE OF TOTAL	*27:	1／1
FORM OF DOC. CREDIT	*40 A:	IRREVOCABLE
DOC. CREDIT NUMBER	*20:	63211020049
DATE OF ISSUE	31 C:	210129
EXPIRY	*31 D:	DATE 210410 PLACE IN BENEFICIARY'S COUNTRY
APPLICANT	*50:	FASHION FORCE CO., LTD
		P. O. BOX 8935 NEW TERMINAL, ALTA, VISTA OTTAWA, CANADA
BENEFICIARY	*59:	NANJING TANG TEXTILE GARMENT CO., LTD.
		HUARONG MANSION RM2901 NO. 85 GUANJIAQIAO, NANJING 210005, CHINA
AMOUNT	*32 B:	CURRENCY USD AMOUNT 32640
AVAILABLE WITH/BY	*41 D:	ANY BANK
		BY NEGOTIATION
DRAFTS AT...	42 C:	SIGHT
DRAWEE	42 A:	BNPACAMM×××
		* BNP PARIBAS（CANADA）
		* MONTREAL
PARTIAL SHIPMTS	43 P:	NOT ALLOWED
TRANSSHIPMENT	43 T:	ALLOWED
LOADING ON CHARGE	44 A:	
CHINA		

FOR TRANSPORT TO…　　　44 B：

MONTREAL

LATEST DATE OF SHIP.　　　44 C：　　　　210325

DESCRIPTION OF GOODS　　　45 A：

　　　SALES CONDITIONS：CIF MONTREAL/CANADA

　　　SALES CONTRACT NO. F01LCB05127

　　　LADIES COTTON BLAZER（100% COTTON, 40SX20/140X60）

STYLE NO.	PO NO.	QTY/PCS	USD/PC
46-301A	10337	2550	12.80

DOCUMENTS REQUIRED　　46 A：

+COMMERCIAL INVOICES IN 3 COPIES SIGNED BY BENEFICIARY'S REPRESENTATIVE.

+CANADA CUSTOMS INVOICES IN 4 COPIES.

+FULL SET OF ORIGINAL MARINE BILLS OF LADING CLEAN ON BOARD PLUS 2 NON NEGOTIABLE COPIES MADE OUT OR ENDORSED TO ORDER OF BNP PARIBAS（CANADA）MARKED FREIGHT PREPAID AND NOTIFY APPLICANT'S FULL NAME AND ADDRESS.

+DETAILED PACKING LISTS IN 3 COPIES.

+COPY OF CERTIFICATE OF ORIGIN FORM A.

+COPY OF EXPORT LICENCE.

+BENEFICIARY'S LETTER STATING THAT ORIGINAL CERTIFICATE OF ORIGIN FORM A, ORIGINAL EXPORT LICENCE, COPY OF COMMERCIAL INVOICE, DETAILED PACKING LISTS AND A COPY OF BILL OF LADING WERE SENT DIRECTLY TO APPLICANT BY COURIER WITHIN 5 DAYS AFTER SHIPMENT.
THE RELEATIVE COURIER RECEIPT IS ALSO REQUIRED FOR PRESENTATION.

+COPY OF APPLICANT'S FAX APPROVING PRODUCTION SAMPLES BEFORE SHIPMENT.

+LETTER FROM SHIPPER ON THEIR LETTERHEAD INDICATING THEIR NAME OF COMPANY AND ADDRESS, BILL OF LADING NUMBER, CONTAINER NUMBER AND THAT THIS SHIPMENT, INCLUDING ITS CONTAINER, DOES NOT CONTAIN ANY NON-MANUFACTURED WOODEN MATERIAL, DUNNAGE, BRACING MATERIAL, PALLETS, CRATING OR OTHER NON-MANUFACTURED WOODEN PACKING MATERIAL.

+INSPECTION CERTIFICATE ORIGINAL SINGED AND ISSUED BY FASHION FORCE CO., LTD STATING THE SAMPLES OF FOUR STYLE GARMENTS HAVE BEEN APPROVED, WHICH WILL BE SENT THROUGH DHL BEFORE 15 DAYS OF SHIPMENT.

续表

	+INSURANCE POLICY OR CERTIFICATE IN 1 ORIGINAL AND 1 COPY ISSUED OR ENDORSED TO THE ORDER OF BNP PARIBAS (CANADA) FOR THE CIF INVOICE PLUS 10 PERCENT COVERING ALL RISKS, INSTITUTE STRIKES, INSTITUTE WAR CLAUSES AND CIVIL COMMOTIONS CLAUSES.
ADDITIONAL COND. 47 A:	
	+IF DOCUMENTS PRESENTED ARE FOUND BY US NOT TO BE UN FULL COMPLIANCE WITH CREDIT TERMS. WE WILL ASSESS A CHARGE OF USD 55.00 PER SET OF DOCUMENTS.
	+ALL CHARGES IF ANY RELATED TO SETTLEMENTS ARE FOR ACCOUNT OF BENEFICIARY.
	+3 PCT MORE OR LESS IN AMOUNT AND QUANTITY IS ALLOWED.
	+ALL CERTIFICATES/LETTERS/STATEMENTS MUST BE SIGNED AND DATED
	+FOR INFORMATION ONLY, PLEASE NOTE AS OF JANUARY 4, 2021 THAT ALL SHIPMENTS FROM CHINA THAT ARE PACKED WITH UNTREATED WOOD WILL BE BANNED FROM CANADA DUE TO THE THREAT POSED BY THE ASIAN LONGHORNED BEETLE.
	+THE CANADIAN GOVERNMENT NOW INSIST THAT EVERY SHIPMENT ENTERING CANADA MUST HAVE THE ABOVE DOCUMENTATION WITH THE SHIPMENT.
	+BILL OF LADING AND COMMERCIAL INVOICE MUST CERTIFY THE FOLLOWING: THIS SHIPMENT, INCLUDING ITS CONTAINER DOES NOT CONTAIN ANY NON-MANUFACTURED WOODEN MATERIAL, DUNNAGE, BRACING MATERIAL PALLETS, CRATING OR OTHER NON MANUFACTURED WOODEN PACKING MATERIAL.
	+BENEFICIARY'S BANK ACCOUNT NO. 07773108201140121
CHARGES	71 B: OUTSIDE COUNTRY BANK CHARGES TO BE BORNE BY THE BENEFICIARY OPENING BANK CHARGES TO BE BORNE BY THE APPLICANT
CONFIRMATION	* 49 : WITHOUT
INSTRUCTIONS	78 :
	+WE SHALL COVER THE NEGOTIATING BANK AS PER THEIR INSTRUCTIONS
	+FORWARD DOCUMENTS IN ONE LOT BY SPECIAL COURIER PREPAID TO BNP PARIBAS (CANADA) 1981 MCGILL COLLECE AVE. MONTREAL QC H3A 2W8 CANADA.

续表

SEND. TO REC. INFO.	72: THIS CREDIT IS SUBJECT TO UCP FOR DOCUMENTARY CREDIT 1993 REVISION ICC PUBLICATION 600 AND IS THE OPERATIVE INSTRUMENT
TRAILER	ORDER IS <MAC:> <PAC:> <ENC:> <CHK:><TNG:> <PDE:> MAC: F344CA36 CHK: AA6204FFDFC2

项目十　装运通知与船公司证明缮制与操作

【项目目标】

知识目标
- 掌握装运通知的含义及作用
- 掌握船公司证明相关内容

能力目标
- 能够熟练制作装运通知
- 能够审核船公司证明

思政目标
- 通过对装运通知的学习,培养学生良好的时间观念
- 通过对船公司证明相关内容的学习,培养学生踏实细致的工作作风和谨慎的工作态度

【工作情景】

在上海威尔进出口公司与 NU BONNETERIE DE GROOTE 公司达成的短裤出口交易中,上海威尔进出口公司在完成货物出口通关各项工作后,货物得以顺利装船。威尔进出口公司立刻给 NU BONNETERIE DE GROOTE 公司发送装船通知,以便其办理进口手续并按时接货,同时上海威尔进出口公司还应按照信用证中的要求提示船公司给买方出具船公司证明。请以单证员殷实的身份,完成装运通知与船公司证明缮制操作。

【工作任务】

任务一　装运通知缮制与操作

一、装运通知的含义与作用

1.装运通知的含义

装运通知(Shipping Advice)也称为装船通知,是出口商在货物装运/装船后发给进口方的包括货物详细装运情况的通知。

2.装运通知的作用

①通知买方办理保险手续。在使用 FOB/FCA 或 CFR/CPT 等术语出口时,如卖方未按合同或信用证约定及时发送或漏发装运通知,导致买方未能及时办理保险手续,卖方应负责赔偿买方由此而引起的一切损害及/或损失。有时,买方会要求卖方将装运通知直接或同时发给其指定的进口国保险公司,买方应提供保险公司详细准确的联系方式,如传真号、电子邮件地址等。在使用 CIF 术语出口时,虽然由卖方办理投保手续,但有时买方需要额外投保,也需要以装运通知的形式提供相关信息。

②便于买方作好接货的准备。买方可以根据装运通知提供的信息适时申请进口许可证、租订仓库、作好清关准备、安排提货运输或转售等。

③在信用证项下,装运通知副本通常作为向银行交单议付的单据之一。

④便于买方适时筹措资金,作好付款准备。

二、装运通知发送的时间及方式

1.装运通知发送的时间

装运通知发送的时间应以合同或信用证的约定为准,常见的有以小时为准和以天为准两种情形。例如,"within 24/48 hours after loading(装船后 24/48 小时内)";"within 2 days after shipment date(装运日后两天内)";合同或信用证没有明确规定发送时间时,应在装船后当天或转天及时发出;如合同或信用证规定"immediately after shipment"(装船后立即通知),按照国际贸易的习惯做法应掌握在提单日期后 3 天之内进行。

2.装运通知发送的方式

目前实际业务中,多采用传真(Fax)、电子邮件方式(E-mail),也可以采用快递(Express)、邮件(Mail)、电报(Cable)、电传(Telex)等方式。

三、装运通知的名称和签署

1.装运通知的名称

装运通知并无固定名称,在实际业务中常用"Shipping Advice",也有用"Shipping Statement/Declaration/Note"或"Shipment Advice""Notice of Shipment"等,如果合同或信用证有具体要求,应从其规定。

2.装运通知的签署

装运通知一般可以不签署,如果信用证要求"certified copy of shipping advice",通常要加盖受益人条形章。

装运通知样例见表 10.1。

表 10.1　装运通知样例

SHIPPING ADVICE

From：(1)
To：(2)

Issue Date： (3)
Contract No. ： (4)

Dear Sir or Madam,

　　We are pleased to advise you that the following mentioned goods has been shipped out. Full details were shown as follows：

Invoice No. ：(5)

Bill of Lading No. ： (6)

Ocean Vessel：(7)

Port of Loading：(8)

Date of Shipment：(9)

Port of Destination：(10)

Estimated Date of Arrival：(11)

Containers/Seals No. ：(12)

Commodity：(13)

Shipping Marks：(14)

Quantity：(15)

Packing：(16)

Gross Weight：(17)

Total Value：(18)

四、出口商装运通知缮制规范

　　装运通知通常以英文制作,可以采用上述格式,也可以缮制在印有公司函头的信笺或白纸上,一般只提供一份。其内容一定要符合合同或信用证的规定。

1. 装运通知条款操作分析

　　(1)Original fax from beneficiary to our applicant evidencing B/L No. , name of shipment, date of shipment, quantity and value of goods.

　　该条款要求信用证受益人向开证申请人提交正本装运通知一份,列明提单号、船名、装运日期、货物的数量和金额。该条款并未明确规定装运通知的名称,制作单据时上述内容必不可少,但通常并不仅限于显示上述内容,而是同时显示其他必要的内容,如货物名称等。装运通知的名称可以采用"Shipment/Shipping Advice"或其他常用名称。

（2）Shipment advice to be made to the said insurance Co. indicating policy No. ,email No. and details of shipment, a copy of which is to be accompanied by the original documents.

该条款要求装运通知应注明保险公司名称、保险单号码、电子邮箱号码及货物详情，一份副本随正本单据向银行提交。制作单据时上述内容必不可少，但货物详情还应包括装运通知通常的内容，如与货物本身及货物运输相关的内容。装运通知的名称为"Shipment Advice"。

（3）Shipping advice with full details including shipping marks, carton numbers, vessel's name, B/L number, value and quantity of goods must be sent on the date of shipment to applicant.

该条款要求装运通知应列明包括运输标志、箱号、船名、提单号、货物金额和数量在内的详细情况，并在货物发运当天寄给开证申请人。制作单据时装运通知的名称为"Shipping Advice"。除上述必不可少的内容外，货物详情还应包括装运通知通常的内容。

（4）Beneficiary must fax advice to the applicant for the particulars before shipment effected and a copy of the advice should be presented for negotiation.

该条款项下受益人发出装运通知的方式是传真，发出时间是在货物装运前，通知对象是开证申请人，通知内容为装运详情，一份传真副本作为议付单据提交。制作单据时装运通知的名称可以为"Shipping Advice"或"Shipment Advice"，装运详情应包括装运通知通常的内容。

（5）Insurance covered by the applicant. All shipments under this credit must be advised by beneficiany immediately after shipment direct to ABC insurance Co. And to the applicant referring to cover note No. CA364 giving full details of shipment. A copy of this advice should be accompanied each set of documents.

该条款规定货物保险由开证申请人负责，货物装运后立即由受益人直接发装运通知给ABC保险公司和申请人，装运通知上应注明暂保单号码为"CA364"，并说明货物的详细情况。每次交单都应随附该装运通知副本一份。该条款并未明确规定该通知的名称，制作单据时装运通知的名称可以采用"Shipment Advice""Shipping Advice"或其他常用名称。除暂保单号码必不可少外，货物详情还应包括装运通知通常的内容，如与货物本身及货物运输相关的内容。

（6）Beneficiary's certified copy of fax sent to applicant within 48 hours after shipment indicating contract No. ,L/C No. ,the name of goods, quantity, invoice value, vessel's name, package/container No. , loading port, shipping date and ETA.

该信用证条款要求受益人出具的装运通知必须签署，装运通知应在发货后48小时内以传真方式发给开证申请人，注明合同号、信用证号、货物名称、数量、发票金额、船名、包装件号/集装箱号、装货港、装运日期和船舶预计抵港时间。

（7）Shipment advice quoting the name of the carrying vessel, date of shipment, number of packages, shipping marks, amount, letter of credit number, policy number must be sent to applicant by fax, copies of transmitted shipment advice accompanied by fax transmission report must accompany the documents.

该条款要求装运通知要注明船名、装船日期、包装件号、唛头、金额、信用证号、保险单号，并以传真的方式发给开证申请人，装船通知副本和传真发送报告必须随附议付单据提交。制作单据时上述内容必不可少，装运通知的名称应为"Shipment Advice"。

（8）Beneficiary's certificate certifying that they have despatched the shipment advice to applicant by fax(fax No. 2838-0983) within 1 day after B/L date advising shipment details including contract No. , invoice value, name of the vessel, loading port, quantity of goods loaded, B/L date, the vessel movement including time of arrival, time of berthed, time of start loading, time of finish loading and departure time from Dalian and this credit No. .

该信用证条款对装船通知的要求：受益人在提单日期后一天内以传真方式按给定的传真号发给开证申请人，内容包括合同号、发票金额、船名、装货港、货物数量、提单日期，船舶动态包括抵达时间、靠泊时间、开始装货时间、装货完毕时间和驶离大连港的时间及信用证号码。制作单据时装运通知的名称应采用"Shipment Advice"并严格按信用证所要求的内容缮制，同时受益人还必须缮制一份受益人证明，以证明自己按信用证要求完成了装运通知的相关操作。

2. 装运通知缮制规范

虽然装运通知的内容因合同或信用证的具体要求而不尽相同，但通常包含以下内容。

（1）From

填写装运通知的出具人，应为合同中出口商名称及地址或信用证受益人名称及地址。

（2）To

填写装运通知的抬头人，即接收该通知的人。应为合同中进口商名称及地址或信用证开证申请人名称及地址或指定的保险公司或代理人的名称及地址。

（3）Issue Date

填写装运通知的出单日期。应符合合同或信用证要求。

（4）Contract No.

填写相关合同号。应与其他单据显示的一致。

（5）Invoice No.

填写出口发票号。应与发票及其他单据显示的一致。

（6）Bill of loading No.

填写相关提/运单号。应与提/运单及其他单据显示的一致。

（7）Ocean Vessel

填写船名及航次号。应与提/运单显示的一致。

（8）Port of Loading

填写装货港名称。应与提/运单显示的一致。

（9）Date of Shipment

填写装运日期。应与提/运单显示的一致。

（10）Port of Destination

填写卸货港名称。应与提/运单显示的一致。

（11）Estimated Date of Arrival

填写船舶预计抵港时间（ETA）。

（12）Containers/Seals No.

填写集装箱/封签号。应与提/运单显示的一致。

（13）Commodity

填写品名及必要的货物描述。应与提/运单显示的一致。

（14）Shipping Marks

填写详细唛头或"N/M"，集装箱货物填写集装箱号。应与其他单据显示的一致。

（15）Quantity

填写货物数量、毛重、净重等。应与其他单据显示的一致。

（16）Packing

填写货物包装类型及件数。应与其他单据显示的一致。

（17）Gross Weight

填写毛重。应与其他单据显示的一致。

（18）Total Value

填写货物总值。应与发票显示的一致。

五、进口商装船指示缮制规范

在进口业务中，为便于买卖双方做好船货衔接工作，在进口方派船接货的交易条件下，如使用 FOB 术语进口，特别是使用程租船方式进口大宗散货时，进口方为了使船、货衔接得当，也会向出口方发出有关通知，报告货物租船订舱详情，以便卖方做好装船准备。通常称为"装船指示（Shipping Instruction）"。

装船指示通常以英文制作，无统一格式，可以缮制在印有公司函头的信笺或白纸上，一般只提供一份，多以传真或电子邮件方式发出。在 FOB 术语下装船指示由买方在完成租船订舱之后向卖方发出，用于提供租船订舱的相关信息，核心内容通常包括买方指定的承运人名称、船名、航次、装货港口、卸货港口、预计到达装货港的时间以及其他需要说明的情况等。买方及时发出装船指示有利于卖方有充分的时间作好备货及装船准备。

装船指示样例见表 10.2。

表 10.2 装船指示样例

SHIPPING INSTRUCTION

Date:_____(1)_____ From:_____(2)_____

To:_____(3)_____

Contract No.:_____(4)_____

L/C No.:_____(5)_____

Dear Sirs,

    We wish to advise that the following stipulated vessel will arrive at_____(6)_____port, on/a-bout the vessel_____(7)_____

Vessel's name:_____(8)_____

Voy. No.:_____(9)_____

Carrier:_____(10)_____

Port of discharge:_____(11)_____

    We will appreciate to see that the covering goods would be shipped on the above vessel on the date of L/C (Contract) called.

                   Importer stamp and signature:_____(12)_____

装船指示缮制规范流程如下。

(1)Date

填写装船指示的出单日期。买方应在完成租船订舱后尽早发出装船指示。

(2)From

填写装船指示的出具人,应为合同中进口商名称及地址或信用证开证申请人名称及地址。

(3)To

填写装船指示的抬头人,即接收该指示的人。应为合同中出口商名称及地址或信用证受益人名称及地址。

(4)Contract No.

填写相关合同号。

(5)L/C No.

填写相关信用证号。

(6)at… port

填写装货港名称。应与合同或信用证规定的一致。

(7)on/about the vessel

填写船舶预计到达装货港的时间。

(8)Vessel's name

填写船名。

（9）Voy. No.

填写航次号。

（10）Carrier

填写船公司相关资料，如承运人名称、联系方式等。

（11）Port of discharge

填写卸货港口名称。应与合同或信用证规定的一致。

（12）Importer stamp and signature

填写进口商或信用证开证申请人名称及法人代表或由经办人签字。进口商或信用证开证申请人名称应与"From"栏或信笺函头一致。

任务二　船公司证明缮制与操作

一、船公司证明的定义和种类

1. 船公司证明的定义

船公司证明（Shipping Company's Certificate）是船公司应出口商（托运人）要求出具给进口商（收货人或通知人）有关载货船舶或货物运输情况的证明，用以满足进口商的要求，通常也是信用证项下交单议付的单据之一。在实际业务中，根据合同或信用证的内容及相关证明的性质，某些有关载货船舶或货物运输情况的证明也可以由出口商/受益人出具。

2. 船公司证明的种类

（1）船舶本身的证明

①船龄证明（Certificate of Age of Vessel）。

船龄是自船舶建造完毕时起计算的船舶使用年限。船龄在某种程度上表明船舶的现有状况，因此在有关船舶和海上运输的交易中，是一个重要因素。因为海洋运输环境恶劣，所以航行15年以上的船舶就属于"高龄危险"船舶。国际上有些保险公司拒绝理赔产生在这种"高危"船舶上的意外，或者必须事先通知、收取较高保险费后才理赔。

有些进口商担心自己的货物被装入此种"高危"船舶，就会在合同或信用证中提出要求承运人出具船龄证明，证明载货船舶的船龄不超过15年。出口商或受益人应要求船代或船公司出具载货船舶的船龄证明。

②船籍证明（Certificate of Registry）。

船籍指船舶的国籍。商船的所有人向本国或外国有关管理船舶的行政部门办理所有权登记，取得本国或登记国国籍后才能取得船舶的国籍。有些国家/地区来证规定载货船舶必须是哪个国家的船或者不能是哪个国家的船。这种要求出具说明载货船舶之国籍的证明文件一般由承运人出具。进口商要求出口商提供船籍证明往往是因为一些特殊原因,如巴基斯坦银行开来的信用证会要求出口商提供载货船舶的船籍不属于印度的证明,阿拉伯国家银行开来的信用证会要求出口商提供载货船舶的船籍不属于以色列的证明等。

③船级证明(Confirmation of classification)。

船级是表示船舶技术状态的一种指标。在国际航运界,凡注册总吨在 100 吨以上的海运船舶,必须在某船级社或船舶检验机构监督之下进行监造。在船舶开始建造之前,船舶各部分的规格须经船级社或船舶检验机构批准。每艘船建造完毕,由船级社或船舶检验局对船体、船上机器设备、吃水标志等项目和性能进行鉴定,发给船级证书。证书有效期一般为 4 年,期满后需重新予以鉴定。船舶入级可保证船舶航行安全,有利于国家对船舶进行技术监督,便于租船人和托运人选择适当的船只,以满足进出口货物运输的需要,也便于保险公司决定船、货的保险费用。

船级证明是一种证明载货船舶符合一定船级标准的文书。按照惯例船级证明由船级社(Classification Society)出具。国际上著名的船级社有英国劳合社(Lloyd's Register of Shipping,LR)、德国船级社(Germanischer Lloyd,GL)、挪威船级社(Det Norske Veritas,DNV)、法国船级社(Bureau Veritas,BV)、日本海事协会(Nippon Kaiji Kyokai,NK)、美国船级社(American Bureau of Shipping,ABS)等。有的信用证规定提供英国劳合社船级证明,如"Class certificate certifying that the shipment is made by a seaworthy vessel which are classified 100 A1 issued by Lloyd's or equivalent classification society",对这样的要求通常应予以满足。

④集装箱船证明(Certificate of Container Vessel)。

证明货物采用集装箱船运输。如进口商或银行在合同/信用证中规定货物须装集装箱船并要求出具相应证明,可由出口商或受益人自行制作并加盖有关签发人的图章,也可在运输单据上加以注明。

(2)运输和航行证明

①航程证明(Certificate of Itinerary)。

航程证明用于说明航程中载货船舶航行的路线和停靠的港口,多见于一些阿拉伯或中东国家和地区开来的信用证中。这些国家和地区的买方通常出于特殊原因或为了避免航行途中货船被扣的风险,对装货船舶的航行路线、停靠港口予以限制,要求船只不经过某些地区或不在某些港口停靠,并要求卖方提供相应证明。

②转船证明(Certificate of Transshipment)。

出口方出具转船证明书,说明出口货物将在中途转船且已联系妥当,并由托运人负责将有关转船事项通知收货人。

③指定船公司证明。

采用 FOB 术语出口时,有时进口方要求货物经由其指定的船公司装运,并由出口方提供相关证明。例如,信用证要求"A certificate from the shipping company or its agent stating that goods are shipped by APL",意思是指定由 APL 承运货物,并要求出口方提供由船公司或其代理出具的货装美国总统轮船公司的证明。劳合社的船级符号为"LR",标志"IOOAI""IOOA"

表示该船的船体和机器设备是根据劳氏规范和规定建造的,"I"表示船舶的装备如船锚、锚链和绳索等处于良好和有效的状态。

④船长收据(Captain's Receipt)。

船长收据是指船长收到随船带交给收货人单据时的收单证明。内容一般是收到单据的种类、份数,并声明在船舶到达目的港后交给指定人。在实际业务中,有时为便于进口方及时提货,需要将全套或一份正本提单随船,或需要将样品、单据副本交载货船只的船长带交进口商,合同或信用证通常规定提供船长收据,如委托船长带去而未取得船长收据将影响出口商收汇,常见于近洋运输。

(3)航运组织和公约证明

①班轮公会证明(Conference Line Certificate)。

班轮公会(FREIGHT CONFERENCE)又称航运工会,是由两家以上在同一航线上经营班轮运输的轮船公司,为维护共同利益,避免相互间的竞争,建立统一的运价和统一的办法制度所组成的国际航运垄断组织。

有的信用证规定货物必须使用班轮公会船只装运,受益人向银行所交单据中应包括船公司或船代出具的证明。

②SMC 和 DOC 证书。

SMC (Safety Management Certificate)船舶安全管理证书、DOC (Document of Compliance)船/港安全符合证书,是按照国际安全管理规则(ISM Code)的规定载货船舶应在船上拥有的必要证书。

这两种证书近年来常常出现在信用证要求提供的单证中。"9·11 事件"后国际海事组织修订了《国际海上人命安全公约》(*Convention on the Safety of Life at Sea*)(简称"SOLAS 公约"),并于 2004 年 7 月 1 日起开始实施。SOLAS 公约规定船舶应持有"安全管理证书"正本,其船名与国籍证书一致,所载公司名称与"符合证书"中的公司名称相一致。

信用证中的一般要求是:"The carrying vessel should comply with the provisions of the ISM Code which necessitates that such vessel must have on board, copies of the two (SMC and DOC) valid Certificates and copies of such certificate must be presented with the original documents."也可表述为:"Certificate issued, signed and stamped by the owner/carrier/master of the carrving vessel holds valid ISM certificate and ISPS [*International Ship and Port Facility Security Code*《国际船舶和港口设施保安规则》]。"

此外,船公司还包括进港证明、运费已交收据、港口费用单(Port Charges Documents)、装卸准备就绪通知书(Notice of Readiness,N/R NOR)和装卸时间事实记录等。

二、船公司证明条款操作分析

如果合同或信用证中要求由船公司或其代理人出具证明,托运人必须在向船公司订舱时就将相关条款提交给他们。如果他们承诺可以按照该条款出具船公司证明,就可以在此船公司租船订舱,否则必须另寻能够出具相应证明的船公司。托运人必须仔细审核船公司证明,确保其与合同或信用证要求相符,与海运提单一致。

合同或信用证中要求由船公司或其代理人出具的证明样例展示如下。

样例 1　Vessel should not be more than 15 years of age and is subject to institute classfications clauses. A certificate to this effect from the shipping company/agent must accompay documents presented for negotiation.

根据伦敦协会船级条款,载货船舶不应该超过 15 年船龄,船公司/代理出具的船龄证明在议付时应随同单据一起提交。

样例 2　A certificate issued by the carrier, shipping Co. or their agents certifying that shipment has been effected by conference line and/or regular line vessels only covered by institute classification clause to accompany the documents.

由承运人、船公司或他们的代理签发证明,证实货物业已装运在符合伦敦协会船级条款的班轮公会船只或定期船上,该船证随单据提交。

样例 3　Shipping company's certificate stating that the carrying vessel has entered P&I Club and should be attached with the original documents.

要求船公司签发证明,明确载货船舶系船东保赔协会成员且该证明应随附正本单据一起。

样例 4　某信用证中要求:Certificate from the shipping agents issued at the port of shipment stating that cargo and/or interests are carried by a mechanically self propelled seaworthy vessel classified under Lloyd's register of shipping as IOOAI or equivalent provided such vessels are not over fifteen years of age or over fifteen years but not over twenty five years of age and have established and maintained a regular pattern of trading on an advertised schedule to load and unload at specific ports or equivalent.

船证由船代在装运港制作,明确货物系由英国劳合社或其他相应机构确认的 IOOAI 级、机械驱动、适航的船舶运输,船龄应在 15 年以下,或能按预先公布的船期表在特定港口持续定期投入装卸货物的商业运营的,船龄也可在 15 年以上、25 年以下。证明内容以证内文字及船舶的实际情况加以叙述即可。

样例 5　Shipping company's or their agent's certificate(in duplicate) stating that the carrying vessel mentioned in the Bill of Lading is a seaworthy vessel not more than twenty years old, has been approved under institute classification clause (class maintained equivalent to Llyod 's IOOAI) and has been registered with an approved classification society (certificate to specify the name of classification society).

船公司或者船代理的证明书(一式两份),应声明:提单上的承运船是适航船舶,船龄不超过 20 年,符合协会船级条款(维护船级相当于劳埃德 IOOAI),并且已经在经核准的船级协会注册(证明书应列明船级协会的名称)。

三、船公司证明的基本内容

船公司证明通常用英文制作,具体内容应以合同或信用证中要求为准,所有船证必须签署。各类船公司证明的主要栏目内容通常包括以下内容。

1. 出证日期和地址

一般为签发提单的日期和地址。

2. 合同或信用证号

不论信用证是否明确要求，都应表明与本证明关联的合同号或信用证号，以及信用证要求的其他必须显示的内容。

3. 船名和提单号

表明本次运输的运载船只及其提单号。

4. 证明函标题

按照合同或信用证要求提供不同种类的证明，标题常为"Certificate of …（……证明）"或"Statement of…（……声明）"。如果信用证未限定标题，此项可以省略。若信用证内规定了是何种证明函，则一定要加注标题。

5. 抬头人

一般都笼统打印为"TO WHOM IT MAY CONCERN（致有关人士）"。

6. 证明内容

按照合同或信用证要求，根据实际情况作出相应证明。

7. 出证人签章

应与提单签单人一致，通常为承运货物的船公司或其代理人、外轮代理公司或承担联运业务的外运公司等。船证上，通常要盖船公司的提单章或公章。

【实操训练】

1. 根据相关说明和下列提单内容填制货物装运通知书。

（1）相关说明。

①传真：56489542

②电话：56489545

③发票号码：JS03256

④信用证号码：H2108

⑤销售合同号码：ST355

（2）提单。

Shipper NANJING FOREIGN TRADE IMP. AND EXP. CORP.	B/L NO. HJSHB142323  **PACIFIC INTERNATION LINES（PTE）LTD** （Incorporated in Singapore） **COMBINED TRANSPORT BILL OF LADING**
Consignee TO ORDER	Received in apparent good order and condition except as otherwise noted the total number of container or other packages or units enumerated below for transportation from the place of receipt to the place of delivery subject to the terms hereof. One of the signed Bills of Lading must be surrendered duly endorsed in exchange for the Goods or delivery order. On presentation of this document（duly）Endorsed to the Carrier by or on behalf
Notify Party EAST AGENT COMPANY 126ROOM STREET, ANTERWEIP, BELGIUM	of the Holder, the rights and liabilities arising in accordance with the terms hereof shall（without prejudice to any rule of common law or statute rendering them binding on the Merchant）become binding in all respects between the Carrier and the Holder as though the contract evidenced hereby had been made between them. SEE TERMS ON ORIGINAL B/L

Vessel and Voyage Number	Port of Loading	Port of Discharge
DAFENG E002	NANJING	LONDON

Place of Receipt	Place of Delivery	Number of Original B/L THREE

PARTICULARS AS DECLARED BY SHIPPER-CARRIER NOT RESPONSIBLE

Container Nos/Seal Nos. Marks and/ Numbers	No. of Container / Packages / Description of Goods	Gross Weight （Kilos）	Measurement （cu-metres）
CBD LONDON NOS1-200	LADIES LYCRA LONG PANT	2000 KGS	6 CBM
	SHIPPED IN ONE 20' CY TO CY CONTAINER FREIGHT：USD2635.00		

FREIGHT & CHARGES FREIGHT PREPAID	Number of Containers/Packages （in words）
	Shipped on Board Date： OCT. 20, 2021
	Place and Date of Issue： NANJING OCT. 20, 2021
	In witness where of this number of Original Bills of Lading stated above all of the tenor and date one of which being accomplished the others to stand void. for PACIFIC INTERNATIONAL LINES （PTE）LTD as Carrier

2. 根据下列信用证，制作装船通知。

SEQUENCE OF TOTAL	*27：	1/1
FORM OF DOC. CREDIT	*40A：	IRREVOCABLE
DOC. CREDIT NUMBER	*20：	DC LDI700954
DATE OF ISSUE	31C：	210624
EXPIRY	*31D：	DATE 210824 PLACE IN COUNTRY OF BENEFICIARY
APPLICANT	*50：	VIRSONS LIMITED
		23 COSGROVE WAY
		LUTON, BEDFORDSHIRE
		LU1 1XL
BENEFICIARY	*59：	HANGZHOU WANSHILI IMP. AND EXP. CO. LTD. ,
		309 JICHANG ROAD,
		HANGZHOU,
		CHINA
AMOUNT	*32B：	CURRENCY USD AMOUNT 74150.00
POS. / NEG. TOL. (%)	39A：	05/05
AVAILABLE WITH/BY	*41D：	ANY BANK
		BY NEGOTIATION
DRAFT AT ...	42C：	AT SIGHT
DRAWEE	*42D：	HSBC BANK PLC (FORMERLY MIDLAND)
PARTIAL SHIPMENT	43P：	ALLOWED
TRANSSHIPMENT	43T：	NOT ALLOWED
LOADING IN CHARGE	44A：	CHINA
FOR TRANSPORT TO...	44B：	FELIXSTOWE PORT
LATEST DATE OF SHIP.	44C：	210809
DESCRIPT. OF GOODS	45A：	

CUSHION COVERS AND RUGS AS PER VIRSONS ORDER NO. RAP-599/2021.

CIF FELIXSTOWE PORT

DOCUMENTS REQUIRED	46A：

+ORIGINAL SIGNED INVOICE PLUS THREE COPIES.

+FULL SET OF ORIGINAL CLEAN ON BOARD MARINE BILL OF LADING MADE OUT TO SHIPPERS ORDER AND BLANK ENDORSED, MARKED "FREIGHT PREPAID" AND NOTIFY APPLICANT QUOTING FULL NAME AND ADDRESS.

+ORIGINAL PACKING LIST PLUS THREE COPIES INDICATING DETAILED PACKING OF EACH CARTON.

+MARINE INSURANCE POLICY FOR 110PCT OF INVOICE VALUE, BLANK ENDORSED, COVERING ALL RISKS AND WAR RISK, CLAIMS PAYABLE AT DESTINATION.

+ORIGINAL CERTIFICATE OF ORIGIN PLUS ONE COPY ISSUED BY CHAMBER OF COMMERCE.

		+ORIGINAL GSP FORM A CERTIFICATE OF ORIGIN IN OFFICIAL FORM ISSUED BY A TRADE AUTHORITY OR GOVERNMENT BODY PLUS ONE COPY.
		+SHIPPING ADVICES MUST BE SENT TO APPLICANT ON THE DATE OF SHIPMENT ADVISING SHIPPING MARKS, COMMODITY NAME, CARTON NUMBERS, TOTAL GROSS WEIGHT, VESSEL NAME, BILL OF LADING NO., PORT OF LOADING, DESTINATION, CONTRACT NO., INVOICE NO., LETTER OF CREDIT NO.
		+COPY OF FAX SENT BY BENEFICIARY TO APPLICANT, EVIDENCING THAT COPIES OF INVOICE, BILL OF LADING AND PACKING LIST HAVE BEEN FAXED TO APPLICANT ON FAX NO. 01582. 434708 WITHIN 3 DAYS OF BILL OF LADING DATE.
ADDITIONAL COND.	47A:	+VIRSONS ORDER NUMBER MUST BE QUOTED ON ALL DOCUMENTS.
		+UNLESS OTHERWISE EXPRESSLY STATE, ALL DOCUMENTS MUST BE IN ENGLISH.
		+EXCEPT SO FAR AS OTHERWISE EXPRESSLY STATE, THIS DOCUMENTARY CREDIT IS SUBJECT TO UNIFORM CUSTOMS AND PRACTICE FOR DOCUMENTARY CREDIT ICC PUBLICATION NO. 500.
		+ALL BANK CHARGES IN CONNECTION WITH THIS DOCUMENTARY CREDIT EXCEPT ISSUING BANK'S OPENING COMMISSION AND TRANSMISSION COSTS ARE FOR THE BENEFICIARY.
		PRESENTATION PERIOD 48: WITHIN 15 DAYS AFTER THE DATE OF SHIPMENT BUT WITHIN THE VALIDITY OF THE CREDIT.
CONFIRMATION	*49:	WITHOUT
INSTRUCTION	78:	ON RECEIPT OF DOCUMENTS CONFIRMING TO THE TERMS OF THIS DOCUMENTARY CREDIT, WE UNDERTAKE TO REIMBURSE YOU IN THE CURRENCY OF THE CREDIT IN ACCORDANCE WITH YOUR INSTRUCTIONS, WHICH SHOULD INCLUDE YOUR UID NUMBER AND THE ABA CODE OF THE RECEIVING BANK.
SEND. TO REC. INFO.	72:	DOCUMENTS TO BE DESPATCHED BY COURIER SERVICE IN ONE LOT TO HSBC BANK PLC, TRADE SERVICES, LD1 TEAM. LEVEL 26, 8 CANADA SQUARE, LONDON E14 5HQ.

项目十一 出口商证明缮制与操作

【项目目标】

知识目标

- 掌握出口商证明的基本内容
- 掌握出口商证明的缮制方法与操作注意事项

能力目标

- 能够熟练缮制各种出口商证明

思政目标

- 通过对出口商证明基本知识的学习,培养学生诚信、友善和爱国的思想品质,以及高度的社会责任感

【工作情景】

上海威尔进出口公司业务员在安排货物装船出运后,即着手开立相关的证明文件。要求单证员殷实根据信用证的规定备好各项证明文件。

【工作任务】

任务一 出口商证明概述

一、出口商证明的定义

出口商证明(EXPORTER'S CERTIFICATE)是一种由出口商自己出具的书面证明,在信用证项下也称为"受益人证明(BENEFICIARY'S CERTIFICATE)"。它的作用是证明自己履行了合同/信用证规定的任务或证明自己按照合同/信用证的要求处理了相关事项或证实了某件事,如证明所交货物的品质、证明运输包装的处理、证明按要求寄单等。

出口商证明一般无固定格式,内容多种多样,可以出具在有出口公司信头的信笺上,也可以出具在一张白纸上,多以英文制作,通常签发一份。

二、出口商证明的基本内容与缮制注意事项

1. 出口商证明的基本内容

出口商证明的内容一般包括单据名称、出证日期、抬头人、事由、证明文句、出口商(受益

人)名称及签章等。

（1）单据名称

单据名称通常位于单据正上方,可根据合同/信用证的要求确定具体名称。较为常见的有：“Beneficiary's Certificate（受益人证明）”“Beneficiary's Statement（受益人声明）”“Beneficiary's Declaration（受益人申明）”或“Exporter's Certificate（出口商证明）”“Manufacturer's Certificate（制造商证明）”。

（2）出证日期

按照实际签发日期填写，一般而言,需与所证明的内容相匹配,根据需证实的内容而定,但必须符合合同/信用证的规定。例如,信用证要求受益人证明一套副本单据已经在装船后3天内寄给开证申请人,如果装运日期为3月15日,那么受益人证明的签发日期应为3月16、17或18日。

（3）抬头人

类似这样的公开证明或申明,一般都填写笼统的抬头人。即“TO WHOM IT MAY CONCERN（致有关人士）”,也可以写具体的开证申请人或进口商名称、地址。

（4）事由

事由是指该证明出具的依据或表明与其他单据的关系,一般填写发票号、合同或信用证号。

（5）证明文句

这部分是该单据的核心内容,必须对应于合同/信用证的要求填写。

（6）出口商（受益人）名称及签章

出口商（受益人）名称及签章通常位于单据的右下方。

2.缮制出口商证明的注意事项

①出口商证明/受益人证明只是一种统称,在实际业务中,单据的名称可能因所证明事项不同而略异,但无论如何,单据名称应合适、恰当。

②单据一般应在规定的时间内做出,出具日期符合情理和业务实际情况。

③正文部分通常以“THIS IS TO CERTIFY”（或 DECLARE,STATE,EVIDENCE 等）或“WE HEREBY CERTIFY”等开始。

④正文部分一般的行文规则是以合同/信用证所提要求为准直接照搬照抄,但有时也应作必要的修改。例如信用证规定“BENEFICIARY'S CERTIFICATE EVIDENCING THAT TWO COPIES OF NON-NEGOTIABLE B/L WILL BE DESPATCHED TO APPLICANT WITHIN TWO DAYS AFTER SHIPMENT”,在具体制作单据时应将要求里的“WILL BE DESPATCHED”改为“HAVE BEEN DESPATCHED”。再比如对“BENEFICIARY'S CERTIFICATE STATING THAT CERTIFICATE OF MANUFACTURING PROCESS AND OF INGREDIENTS ISSUED BY ABC CO. SHOULD BE SENT TO SUMITOMO CORP.”的要求,“SHOULD BE SENT”最好改为“HAD/HAS BEEN SENT”。

⑤出口商/受益人证明一般不分正副本。若合同/信用证要求正本,可在单据名称正下方打上"ORIGINAL"字样。

⑥因属于证明性质,按有关规定证明人必须签章才能生效。如果该证明打印在带有出口商/受益人抬头的信笺上,那么签章与抬头显示的名称必须一致。

任务二 出口商证明的缮制与操作

一、寄单、寄样证明的缮制与操作

出口商证明(受益人证明)中最多见的是寄单、寄样证明。出口商/受益人根据合同/信用证要求,在货物装运前后的一定期限内,向合同/信用证规定的收受人寄送单据、船样、码样、样卡等物品,并提供相应的证明。

1.寄单证明

合同/信用证要求在货物装运前后一定时期内,邮寄/传真/快递给规定的收受人全套或部分副本单据,并将证明随其他单据交给银行。

例1:信用证规定:"BENEFICIARY'S CERTIFICATE EVIDENCING THAT TWO COPIES OF NON-NEGOTIABLE B/L WILL BE SENT TO APPLICANT BY COURIER SERVICE WITHIN TWO DAYS AFTER SHIPMENT."

对此,受益人应该按照信用证要求在货物装运后两日内,将两份提单副本通过快递寄送给开证申请人,出具如下证明,并将该寄单证明作为信用证项下议付货款的单据之一。

BENEFICIARY'S CERTIFICATE

_____(日期)

TO WHOM IT MAY CONCERN,

L/C NO. _____(信用证号)

WE HEREBY CERTIFY THAT TWO COPIES OF NON-NEGOTIABLE B/L HAVE BEEN SENT TO APPLICANT BY COURIER SERVICE WITHIN TWO DAYS AFTER SHIPMENT.

_____(签章)

例2:信用证规定:"BENEFICIARY'S CERTIFICATE CERTIFYING THAT BENEFICIARY HAS FAXED THE SHIPPING DOCUMENTS (B/L, INVOICE, PACKING LIST, PHYTOSANITARY CERTIFICATE) WITHIN TWO WORKING DAYS AFTER SHIPMENT DATE TO APPLICANT."

对此,受益人应该按照信用证要求在货物装运日后两个工作日内,将海运提单、发票、装箱单和植物检疫证明传真给开证申请人,出具如下证明,并将该证明作为信用证项下议付货款的单据之一。

```
                    BENEFICIARY'S CERTIFICATE
                                              _____（日期）
TO WHOM IT MAY CONCERN,
L/C NO. _____（信用证号）
THIS IS TO CERTIFY THAT WE HAVE FAXED THE SHIPPING DOCS. （B/L, INVOICE, PACKING LIST,
PHYTOSANITARY CERTIFICATE） WITHIN TWO WORKING DAYS AFTER SHIPMENT DATE TO APPLI-
CANT.
                                              _____（签章）
```

例 3：信用证规定："BENEFICARY'S DECLARATION CERTIFYING THAT THE COPY OF EXPORT LICENCE HAS BEEN SENT TO THE APPLICANT BY EXPRESS COURIER BEFORE CERTIFICATE OF QUALITY ISSUED BY CCIB/CCIC IN DUPLICATE."

对此，受益人应该按照信用证要求在商检机构出具的质量证明书日期之前，将出口许可证复印件快递给开证申请人，按信用证要求的名称出具如下证明，并将该证明作为信用证项下议付货款的单据之一。

```
                    BENEFICIARY'S CERTIFICATE
                                              _____（日期）
TO WHOM IT MAY CONCERN,
L/C NO. _____（信用证号）
THIS IS TO CERTIFY THAT THE COPY OF EXPORT LICENCE HAS BEEN SENT TO THE APPLICANT BY
EXPRESS COURIER BEFORE THE CERTIFICATE OF QUALITY DATE.
                                              _____（签章）
```

2. 寄样证明

合同/信用证要求在货物装运前后一定时期内，邮寄/快递给规定的收受人船样、码样、样卡等物品，并将证明随其他单据交给银行议付。

例 1：信用证规定："BENEFICIARY'S CERTIFICATE TO SHOW THAT THE REQUIRED SHIPPING SAMPLES HAVE BEEN SENT BY DHL TO THE APPLICANT ON JULY 10, 2021."

对此，受益人应该按照信用证要求在 2021 年 7 月 10 日，将所要求的船样通过指定的敦豪快递寄送给开证申请人，出具如下证明，并将该寄样证明作为信用证项下议付货款的单据之一。

```
                    BENEFICIARY'S CERTIFICATE
                                              _____（日期）
TO WHOM IT MAY CONCERN,
L/C NO. _____（信用证号）
THIS IS TO CERTIFY THAT THE REQUIRED SHIPPING SAMPLES HAVE BEEN SENT BY DHL TO THE AP-
PLICANT ON JULY 10, 2021.
                                              _____（签章）
```

例2：信用证规定："TWO SETS OF SHIPPING SAMPLES AND ONE SET OF NON-NEGOTI-ABLE SHIPPING DOCUMENTS MUST BE SENT TO APPLICANT BY SPEED POST/COURIER SERVICE WITHIN FIVE DAYS FROM THE DATE OF BILL OF LADING AND A CERTIFICATE TO THIS EFFECT FROM BENEFICIARY TOGETHER WITH RELATIVE SPEED POST/COURIER RECEIPT MUST ACCOMPANY THE DOCUMENTS."

对此，受益人应该按照信用证要求在提单日后5日内，通过邮政快件或快递公司将两套船样和一套不可议付的货运单据寄给开证申请人，出具如下证明，证明上述事实，并将该证明和相应的邮政快件或快递收据一起作为信用证项下议付货款的单据之一。

BENEFICIARY'S CERTIFICATE

_____（日期）

TO WHOM IT MAY CONCERN,

L/C NO. _____（信用证号）

WE CERTIFY THAT TWO SETS OF SHIPPING SAMPLES AND ONE SET OF NON-NEGOTIABLE SHIPPING DOCUMENTS HAVE BEEN SENT TO APPLICANT BY SPEED POST/COURIER SERVICE WITHIN FIVE DAYS FROM THE DATE OF BILL OF LADING.

_____（签章）

二、货物补充说明的缮制与操作

有的合同/信用证规定出口商/受益人需要提供一些补充说明，证明货物品质、包装、标签、检验、产地等信息。

1.标签证明

例：信用证规定："A CERTIFICATE FROM THE BENEFICIARY TO THE EFFECT THAT ONE SET OF INVOICE AND PACKING LIST HAS BEEN PLACED ON THE INNER SIDE OF THE DOOR OF EACH CONTAINER IN CASE OF FCL CARGO OR ATTACHED TO THE GOODS OR PACKAGES AT AN OBVIOUS PLACE IN CASE OF LCL CARGO."

对此，受益人应该按照信用证要求在装运整箱货物时，把一套发票和装箱单贴在每一个集装箱箱门内侧，出具如下证明，并将该证明作为信用证项下议付货款的单据之一。

BENEFICIARY'S CERTIFICATE

_____（日期）

TO WHOM IT MAY CONCERN,

L/C NO. _____（信用证号）

WE CERTIFY THAT ONE SET OF INVOICE AND PACKING LIST HAS BEEN PLACED ON THE INNER SIDE OF THE DOOR OF EACH CONTAINER.

_____（签章）

在装运拼箱货物时，把一套发票和装箱单贴在货物包装显眼的位置，出具如下证明，并将该证明作为信用证项下议付货款的单据之一。

```
BENEFICIARY'S CERTIFICATE
                                                    _____（日期）
TO WHOM IT MAY CONCERN,
L/C NO. _____（信用证号）
WE CERTIFY THAT ONE SET OF INVOICE AND PACKING LIST HAS BEEN ATTACHED TO THE GOODS OR
PACKAGES AT AN OBVIOUS PLACE.
                                                    _____（签章）
```

2. 包装证明

例1：因进口国规定进口货物不能使用木质包装，所以合同要求制造商出具非木质包装证明，以使进口货物顺利清关。

合同规定："A DECLARATION OF NO-WOOD PACKING MATERIAL STATING THE SHIPMENT DOES NOT CONTAIN WOOD PACKING MATERIALS. "

对此，制造商应该按照合同要求选用非木质包装，以合同规定的名称出具下列证明，并将该证明与合同项下其他单据一起以符合合同的方式交给进口商。

```
DECLARATION OF NO-WOOD PACKING MATERIAL
                                                    _____（日期）
TO WHOM IT MAY CONCERN,
L/C NO. _____（合同/发票号）
WE CERTIFY THAT THE SHIPMENT DOES NOT CONTAIN WOOD PACKING MATERIALS.
                                                    _____（签章）
```

例2：信用证规定："A STATEMENT FROM THE BENEFICARY EVIDENCING THAT PACKING EFFECTED IN 25KGS CTN. "

对此，受益人应该按照信用证要求包装货物，将货物用纸箱包装且每箱重量为 25 kg，出具如下证明，并将该证明作为信用证项下议付货款的单据之一。

```
BENEFICIARY'S CERTIFICATE
                                                    _____（日期）
TO WHOM IT MAY CONCERN,
L/C NO. _____（信用证号）
WE HEREBY CERTIFY THAT PACKING EFFECTED IN 25KGS CTN.
                                                    _____（签章）
```

例3：信用证规定："BENEFICIARY CERTIFICATE IN TRIPLICATE STATING THE SHIPMENT DOES NOT INCLUDE NON-MANUFACTURED WOOD DUNNAGE, PALLETS, CRATING OR OTHER PACKAGING MATERIALS, THE SHIPMENT IS COMPLETELY FREE OF WOOD BARK, VISIBLE PESTS AND SIGNS OF LIVING PESTS. "

对此，受益人应该按照信用证要求包装货物，保证不使用非加工的木质衬垫、托盘、板条箱或其他包装物,无树皮、无肉眼可见的害虫、无活虫迹象,出具如下证明一式三份,并将该证明作为信用证项下议付货款的单据之一。

BENEFICIARY'S CERTIFICATE

_____（日期）

TO WHOM IT MAY CONCERN,

L/C NO. _____（信用证号）

WE CERTIFY THAT THE SHIPMENT DOES NOT INCLUDE NON-MANUFACTURED WOOD DUNNAGE, PALLETS, CRATING OR OTHER PACKAGING MATERIALS; THE SHIPMENT IS COMPLETELY FREE OF WOOD BARK, VISIBLE PESTS AND SIGNS OF LIVING PESTS.

_____（签章）

【实操训练】

根据项目十中实操训练中的信用证,制作受益人证明文件。

BENEFICIARY'S CERTIFICATE

_____（日期）

TO WHOM IT MAY CONCERN,

L/C NO. _____（信用证号）

WE CERTIFY THAT.

_____（签章）

项目十二　出口结汇单证缮制与操作

【项目目标】
知识目标
- 明确出口结汇单证的定义、种类和作用
- 掌握出口结汇单证的缮制依据、基本要求和缮制方法
能力目标
- 能够熟练缮制信用证和托收项下出口结汇单证
思政目标
- 通过对结汇单证基本知识的学习,培养学生认真负责、严谨细致和精益求精的职业素养
- 引导学生了解随着 ERP 单证管理系统和电子单据的广泛运用,高效、高品质的单证不但为外贸企业增强了竞争力,也会为企业树立良好形象、建立较高的信誉起到不可估量的作用,从而培养学生的创新意识和高度的社会责任感

【工作情景】

　　上海威尔进出口公司的业务员在安排货物出运取得海运提单后,单证员殷实开始缮制相关的全套结汇单证。

【工作任务】

任务一　结汇单证概述

一、结汇单证的定义和种类

1.结汇单证的定义

　　结汇单证是指在国际贸易中,为解决货币收付问题所使用的单据、证明和文件。出口业务中,国际结算所涉及的单据种类繁多,不同的收款方式、不同的地区、不同的商品,对结汇单证的单据要求会有所不同。近年来,结汇单证有逐步简化的趋向。

2.结汇单证的种类

（1）商业单证
商业单证主要有商业发票、包装单据、运输单据、保险单等。

（2）官方单证

官方单证主要有产地证明、检验证书、许可证等。

（3）金融单证

金融单证主要有汇票等。

（4）其他附属单证

其他附属单证主要包括出口商证明、运输机构出具的证明等。

二、结汇单证的作用

1. 付款依据

对进口商而言，根据出口商提供的结汇单证，可以了解并掌握出口商交付货物的品质、交货时间。通过单据说明出口商已按合同规定交货，进口商必须支付货款。在信用证方式下，结汇单证是开证银行付款的唯一依据。

2. 履约证明

在国际贸易中，无论采用哪种方式收取货款，出口商都要提供结汇单证，说明自己已经履行了合同中规定的义务，做到了及时交货、按质交货，并为进口商顺利提取货物、使用货物和转售货物提供了保障。

3. 物权凭证

国际贸易中的买卖双方相隔遥远，交货过程中，有关单据起到了物权凭证的作用，如提单就具有凭以提取货物的作用，持有提单就意味着控制或取得了货物。

三、结汇单证的交付

出口商在结汇单证制作和审核完毕后，需向有关方面递交，俗称"交单"。当收汇方式为汇付时，出口商直接将结汇单证寄交进口商。当收汇采用托收或信用证方式时，出口商必须向有关银行交单，由银行将结汇单证寄交代收行或开证行，再转进口商。银行向进口商转交单证是以进口商付款或承兑付款为条件的，也就是说，进口商若要取得单证就必须完成付款义务或承兑手续。

任务二　信用证项下结汇单证缮制与操作

一、结汇单证缮制依据和基本要求

缮制结汇单证有两个依据：一是买卖合同，二是信用证。如果采用的付款方式为托收，出口商就要按照进口商在合同中的要求或用其他方式发出的指示来制作单证。在信用证付款方式下,则更强调单据与信用证完全一致和单据与单据之间的完全一致。

出口结汇单证的缮制要求:单单一致、单证一致、单货一致、单同一致。

二、解读信用证的主要条款

以下列信用证为例见表12.1。

表12.1　信用证示例

ISSUE OF A DOCUMENTARY CREDIT		
ISSUING BANK	THE ROYAL BANK, TOKYO	(1)
SEQUENCE OF TOTAL	1 / 1	(2)
FORM OF DOC. CREDIT	IRREVOCABLE	(3)
DOC. CREDIT NUMBER	JST-AB12	(4)
DATE OF ISSUE	20210405	(5)
EXPIRY	DATE 20210615 PLACE CHINA	(6)
APPLICANT	WAV GENEAL TRADING CO., LTD	(7)
	5-18 ISUKI-CHOHAKI, OSAKA, JAPAN	
BENEFICIARY	HONGDA TRADING CO., LTD	(8)
	224 JINLIN ROAD, NANJING, CHINA	
AMOUNT	CURRENCY USD AMOUNT 10300.00	(9)
AVAILABLE WITH/BY	BY ANY BANK OF CHINA	(10)
DRAFTS AT …	DRAFTS AT SIGHT FOR FULL INVOICE VALUE	(11)
DRAWEE	THE ROYAL BANK, TOKYO	(12)
PARTIAL SHIPMENT	ALLOWED	(13)
TRANSSHIPMENT	ALLOWED	(14)
LOADING IN CHARGE	NANJING PORT, CHINA	(15)
FOR TRANSPORT TO …	OSAKA PORT, JAPAN	(16)
LATEST DATE OF SHIP-MENT	20210531	(17)
GOODS DESCRIPTION	LADIES' GARMENTS AS PER S/C NO. SHL553	(18)
	PACKING:10 PCS/CTN	
	ART NO.　　　　　QUANTITY　　　UNIT PRICE	
	STYLE NO. ROCOCO　1000 PCS　　USD 5.50	
	STYLE NO. ROMANTICO 1000 PCS　USD 4.80	
	CIF OSAKA	
	SHIPPING MARK:ITOCHU/OSAKA/NO.1-200	

续表

DOCS. REQUIRED(19)	* 3/3 SET OF ORIGINAL CLEAN ON BOARD OCEAN BILLS OF LADING MADE OUT TO ORDER OF SHIPPER AND BLANK ENDORSED AND MARKED "FREIGHT PREPAID" NOTIFY APPLICANT (WITH FULL NAME AND ADDRESS). (20) * ORIGINAL SIGNED COMMERCIAL INVOICE IN 5 FOLD. (21) * INSURANCE POLICY OR CERTIFICATE IN 2 FOLD ENDORSED IN BLANK, FOR 110PCT OF THE INVOICE VALUE COVERING THE INSTITUTE CARGO CLAUSES (A), THE INSTITUTE WAR CLAUSES, INSURANCE CLAIMS TO BE PAYABLE IN JAPAN IN THE CURRENCY OF THE DRAFTS. (22) CERTIFICATE OF ORIGIN GSP FORM A IN 1 ORIGINAL AND 1 COPY. (23) * PACKING LIST IN 5 FOLD. (24) * CERTIFICATE STAMPED AND SIGNED BY BENEFICIARY STATING THAT THE ORIGIAL INVOICE AND PACKING LIST HAVE BEEN DISPATCHED TO THE APPLICANT BY COURIER SERVISE 2 DAYS BEFORE SHIPMENT. (25)

ADDITIONAL CONDITIONS (26)	1. T. T. REIMBURSEMENT IS PROHIBITED
	 2. THE GOODS TO BE PACKED IN EXPORT STRONG COLORED CARTONS.
	 3. SHIPPING MARKS：
	       ITOCHU
	       OSAKA
	       NO. 1-200

DETAILS OF CHARGES (27)	ALL BANKING CHARGES OUTSIDE JAPAN INCLUDING REIMBURSEMENT COMMISSION, ARE FOR ACCOUNT OF BENEFICIARY.
PRESENTATION PERIOD (28)	DOCUMENTS TO BE PRESENTED WITHIN 10 DAYS AFTER THE DATE OF SHIPMENT, BUT WITHIN THE VALIDITY OF THE CREDIT.
CONFIRMATION (29)	WITHOUT
INSTRUCTIONS (30)	THE NEGOTIATION BANK MUST FORWARD THE DRAFTS AND ALL DOCUMENTS BY REGISTERED AIRMAIL DIRECT TO U. S. IN TWO CONSECUTIVE LOTS, UPON RECEIPT OF THE DRAFTS AND DOCUMENTS IN ORDER, WE WILL REMIT THE PROCEEDS AS INSTRUCTED BY THE NEGOTIATING BANK.

（1）ISSUING BANK

一般为进口地银行,也是出口人开具汇票的受票人。

（2）SEQUENCE OF TOTAL

信用证的页码。

（3）FORM OF DOC. CREDIT

"IRREVOCABLE"表示为不可撤销的。

（4）DOC. CREDIT NUMBER

"JST-AB12"表示信用证的编号。

（5）DATE OF ISSUE

汇票中一般要填写开证日期。

（6）EXPIRY

指信用证的有效期和到期地点，即受益人须在有效期或之前将所要求的单证在指定的到期地点交给银行。

（7）APPLICANT

一般为进口人，发票要以其为抬头。

（8）BENEFICIARY

一般为出口人。

（9）AMOUNT

即信用金额，也是受益人能够通过信用证从开证行获得的最大金额。信用证是按照合同开立的，一般情况下，信用证金额与合同一致。如合同中有溢短装条款，信用证金额就应有允许相应幅度的增减，否则，如果受益人多装货物，不但拿不到多装的那部分货物的货款，而且单证也有不符点。

（10）AVAILABLE WITH/BY

一般为通知行。如本条款为"BY ANY BANK OF CHINA"，受益人可将单证提交给任何一家自己选定的银行。

（11）DRAFTS AT…

该条款之后一般跟"SIGHT"或"×××DAYS SIGHT"，表示需开具即期或远期汇票。

（12）DRAWEE

信用证付款方式下该条款之后一般跟"ISSUING BANK FOR FULL INVOICE VALUE"，表示汇票受票人为开证银行，金额为发票金额。

（13）PARTIAL SHTPMENT

表示是否允许分批装运。

（14）TRANSSHIPMENT

表示是否允许转船。

（15）LOADING IN CHARGE

表示出口货物起运港名称。

（16）FOR TRANSPORT TO

表示货物运往之后所示的目的港。

（17）LATEST DATE OF SHIPMENT

表示货物装船的最后期限，提单签发日期不能迟于该日期。

（18）GOODS DESCRIPTION

表示所有单证中的货物名称都要这样写。

(19) DOCS. REQUIRED

表示受益人所需要向议付银行提交的单证如下。

(20) 3/3 SET OF ORIGINAL CLEAN ON BOARD OCEAN BILLS OF LADING

表示受益人需提交全套正本已装船清洁海运提单，即 3 份正本提单，且提单上需注明"ON BOARD"字样，没有任何说明货物或包装有什么问题的文字批注。包括以下条款。

①MADE OUT TO ORDER OF SHIPPER(凭发货人的指示)：表示提单收货人(CONSIGNEE)栏目里填写"TO ORDER OF SHIPPER"这几个英文单词，意味着提单控制在出口人手中，由出口人"BLANK ENDORSED"空白背书才能转让。

②FREIGHT PREPAID：表示提单上要注明"FREIGHT PREPAID"字样，意指海运费已交船公司。这要与单价条款中所用贸易术语相一致，即 CFR/CIF 时才这样写。

③FREIGHT COLLECT：表示提单上要注明"FREIGHT COLLECT"字样，意指海运费等货到目的港时才付，即由进口人支付，只有在 FOB 条件下才这样写。

④NOTIFY PARTY：表示提单的被通知人栏目如何填写，一般为 APPLICANT 开证申请人。

(21) ORIGINAL SIGNED COMMERCIAL INVOICE IN 5 FOLD.

正本签名的商业发票一式五份。

(22) INSURANCE POLICY OR CERTIFICATE IN 2 FOLD…

表示保险单或保险证书一式二份。"ENDORSED IN BLANK"表示空白背书。"FOR 110PCT OF THE INVOICE VALUE COVERING THE INSTITUTE CARGO CLAUSES (A), THE INSTITUTE WAR CLAUSES"表示按照发票金额的 110% 投保英国伦敦保险协会 A 险和战争险。"INSURANCE CLAIMS TO BE PAYABLE IN JAPAN IN THE CURRENCY OF THE DRAFTS."表示赔款地点在日本，赔款货币名称与汇票一致。

(23) CERTIFICATE OF ORIGIN GSP FORM A IN 1 ORIGINAL AND 1 COPY.

表示原产地普惠制证书一份正本和一份副本。

(24) PACKING LIST IN 5 FOLD.

表示装箱单一式五份。

(25) CERTIFICATE STAMPED AND SIGNED BY BENEFICIARY STATING THAT THE ORIGIAL INVOICE AND PACKING LIST HAVE BEEN DISPATCHED TO THE APPLICANT BY COURIER SERVISE 2 DAYS BEFORE SHIPMENT.

表示受益人盖章和签字的证书，证明一份正本发票和装箱单已经在装船前 2 天内用快递寄给了开证申请人。

(26) ADDITIONAL CONDITIONS

附加条款。

(27) DETAILS OF CHARGES

银行费用额分摊细节。

①PAYING BANK：具有付款义务的银行，一般为开证银行。

②REIMBURSING BANK：即为实际付款银行。

（28）PRESENTATION PERIOD

提交单据的日期。

（29）CONFIRMATION

是否保兑。

CONFIRMING BANK：一般为出口地的通知行，当它对信用证加保后即成为保兑行。

（30）INSTRUCTIONS

NEGOTIATING BANK：出口地银行，即受益人向其提交单证的银行。

ADVISING BANK：出口地银行，也有可能成为将来的议付行。

三、外贸单证员殷实缮制结汇单证

以上述信用证为样例和下述补充资料为依据缮制结汇单证。

（1）商品资料

①包装：10 PCS PER CARTON。

②单位毛重：15.40 KGS/CTN。

③单位净重：13.00 KGS/CTN。

④单位尺码：60 CM×40 CM×50 CM/CTN。

（2）其他资料

①发票号码：SH25586，汇票号同发票号。

②发票日期：2021 年 4 月 20 日。

③船名：DAFENG V3336。

④提单号码：SH223545。

⑤提单日期：2021 年 5 月 15 日。

⑥汇票出票日期：2021 年 5 月 20 日。

⑦产地证日期地点：NANJING，JIANGSU，APR. 20，2021。

1. 结汇单证种类

该信用证项下单证员殷实缮制的结汇单证种类如下。

①商业发票。

②装箱单。

③海运提单。

④保险单。

⑤原产地证。

⑥汇票。

⑦受益人证明。

2. 外贸单证员殷实缮制的结汇单证

（1）商业发票（表12.2）

表12.2　商业发票

宏达国际贸易有限公司

HONGDA TRADING CO., LTD.

224 JINLIN ROAD, NANJING, CHINA

TEL：025-4715004 025-4715619 **FAX**：4691619

COMMERCIAL INVOICE

To:	WAV GENEAL TRADING CO., LTD	Invoice No.:	SH25586
	5-18 ISUKI-CHOHAKI, OSAKA, JAPAN	Invoice Date:	2021-4-20
From:	NANJING PORT, CHINA	S/C No.:	SHL553
Letter of Credit No.:	JST-AB12	To: OSAKA PORT, JAPAN	

Marks and Numbers	Number and Kind of Package Description of Goods	Quantity	Unit Price	Amount
				CIF OSAKA PORT, JAPAN
ITOCHU OSAKA NO. 1-200	LADIES' GARMENTS STYLE NO. ROCOCO STYLE NO. ROMANTI-CO	1000 PCS 1000 PCS	USD5.50 USD4.80	USD5500.00 USD4800.00
	TOTAL:	2000 PCS		USD10300.00

SAY TOTAL: USD TEN THOUSAND AND THREE HUNDRED ONLY.

HONGDA TRADING CO., LTD.

殷实

（2）装箱单（表12.3）

表12.3　装箱单

宏达国际贸易有限公司

HONGDA TRADING CO., LTD.

224 JINLIN ROAD, NANJING, P. R. CHINA

TEL：025-4715004 025-4715619 FAX：4691619

PACKING LIST

To：WAV GENEAL TRADING CO., LTD	Invoice No.:	SH25586
5-18 ISUKI-CHOHAKI, OSAKA, JAPAN	Invoice Date:	2021-4-20
	S/C No.:	SHL553
From：NANJING PORT, CHINA	To：OSAKA PORT, JAPAN	
Letter of Credit No.: JST-AB12	Date of Shipment：2021-05-15	

续表

Marks and Numbers	Number and Kind of Package Description of Goods	Quantity	Package	G. W	N. W	Meas.
ITOCHU OSAKA NO. 1-200	LADIES' GARMENTS STYLE NO. ROCOCO STYLE NO. ROMANTICO	1000 PCS 1000 PCS	100 CTNS 100 CTNS	15.40 KGS/CTN 15.40 KGS/CTN	13.00 KGS/CTN 13.00 KGS/CTN	0.12 CBM/CTN 0.12 CBM/CTN

TOTAL：2000 PCS 200 CTNS   3080 KGS   2600.00 KGS   24.00 CBM

SAY TOTAL：   TWO HUNDRED CARTONS ONLY.

HONGDA TRADING CO. , LTD.
殷实

（3）海运提单（表 12.4）

表 12.4 海运提单

1. Shipper Insert Name, Address and Phone HONGDA TRADING CO. , LTD 224 JINLIN ROAD, NANJING, CHINA	**B/L No.** SH223545
2. Consignee Insert Name, Address and Phone TO ORDER OF SHIPPER	中远集装箱运输有限公司 **COSCO CONTAINER LINES** TLX：33057 COSCO CN FAX：+86(021) 6545 8984 ORIGINAL Port-to-Port or Combined Transport **BILL OF LADING**
3. Notify Party Insert Name, Address and Phone （It is agreed that no responsibility shall attach to the Carrier or his agents for failure to notify） WAV GENEAL TRADING CO. , LTD 5-18 ISUKI-CHOHAKI, OSAKA, JAPAN	RECEIVED in external apparent good order and condition except as otherwise noted. The total number of packages or units stuffed in the container, the description of the goods and the weights shown in this Bill of Lading are furnished by the Merchants, and which the carrier has no reasonable means of checking and is not a part of this Bill of Lading contract. The carrier has issued the number of Bills of Lading stated below, all of this tenor and date, one of the original Bills of Lading must be surrendered and endorsed or signed against the delivery of the shipment and whereupon any other original Bills of Lading shall be void. The Merchants agree to be bound by the terms and conditions of this Bill of Lading as if each had personally signed this Bill of Lading.

4. Combined Transport * Pre-carriage by	5. Combined Transport * Place of Receipt
6. Ocean Vessel Voy. No. DAFENG V3336	7. Port of Loading NANJING PORT, CHINA
8. Port of Discharge OSAKA PORT, JAPAN	9. Combined Transport * Place of Delivery

SEE clause 4 on the back of this Bill of Lading（Terms continued on the back hereof, please read carefully）.

* Applicable Only When Document Used as a Combined Transport Bill of Lading.

续表

Marks & Nos. Container / Seal No.	No. of Containers or Packages	Description of Goods（If Dangerous Goods, See Clause 20）	Gross Weight Kgs	Measure-ment
ITOCHU OSAKA NO. 1-200	200 CTNS	200 CTNS OF LADIES' GARMENTS CLEAN ON BOARD ON MAY 15, 2021 FREIGHT PREPAID	3080.00 KGS	24.00 M³
		Description of Contents for Shipper's Use Only（Not part of This B/L Contract）		

10. Total Number of Containers and/or Packages（in words） Subject to Clause 7 Limitation TWO HUNDRED CARTONS ONLY.					
11. Freight & Charges Declared Value Charge	Revenue Tons	Rate	Per	Prepaid	Collect
Ex. Rate	Prepaid at		Payable at	Place and Date of Issue NANJING PORT MAY 15, 2021	
	Total Prepaid		No. of Original B(s)/L 3/3	Signed for the Carrier, COSCO CON-TAINER LINES	

（4）保险单（表12.5）

表12.5　保险单

中保财产保险有限公司
The People's Insurance（Property）Company of China, Ltd

发票号码
Invoice No.　SH25586

保险单号次
Policy No.

海 洋 货 物 运 输 保 险 单
MARINE CARGO TRANSPORTATION INSURANCE POLICY

被保险人：
Insured：　HONGDA TRADING CO., LTD

　　中保财产保险有限公司（以下简称本公司）根据被保险人的要求，及其所缴付约定的保险费，按照本保险单承担险别和背面所载条款与下列特别条款承保下列货物运输保险，特签发本保险单。

　　This Policy of Insurance witnesses that the People's Insurance (Property) Company of China, Ltd. (hereinafter called "The Company"), at the request of the Insured and in consideration of the agreed premium paid by the Insured, undertakes to insure the undermentioned goods in transportation subject to conditions of the Policy as per the Clauses printed overleaf and other special clauses attached hereon.

保险货物项目 (Descriptions of Goods)	包装 (Packing)	单位 (Unit)	数量 (Quantity)	保险金额 (Amount Insured)
LADIES' GARMENTS		200 CTNS		USD11330.00

承保险别

Conditions:＿＿＿＿＿＿＿＿＿＿＿＿＿＿＿＿＿＿＿

COVERING THE INSTITUTE CARGO CLAUSES (A),

THE INSTITUTE WAR CLAUSES

货物标记

Marks of Goods:＿＿＿＿＿＿＿＿＿＿＿＿

AS PER INVOICE NO. SH25586

总保险金额

Total Amount Insured:U.S. DOLLARS ELEVEN THOUSAND THREE HUNDRED AND THIRTY ONLY.＿＿＿

保费　　　　　　　　　　装载运输工具　　　　　　　　开航日期

Premium:As arranged＿＿＿＿　Per conveyance S.S: DAFENG V3336　Slg. on or abt:MAY 15, 2021＿

起运港　　　　　　　　　　目的港

From:NANJING＿＿＿＿＿＿　To:OSAKA＿＿＿＿＿＿

所保货物,如发生本保险单项下可能引起索赔的损失或损坏,应立即通知本公司下述代理人查勘。如有索赔,应向本公司提交保险单正本(本保险单共有＿＿＿＿份正本)及有关文件。如一份正本已用于索赔,其余正本则自动失效。

In the event of loss or damage which may result in a claim under this Policy, immediate notice must be given to the Company's Agent as mentioned here under. Claims, if any, one of the Original Policy which has been issued in original (s) together with the relevant documents shall be surrendered to the Company. If one of the Original Policy has been accomplished, the others to be void.

赔款偿付地点

Claim payable at: ＿OSAKA＿＿

日期　　　　　　　　　　在

Date:MAY 10, 2021＿＿＿　at:NANJING＿＿＿＿＿＿

地址

Address:318 TIANSHI ROAD NANJING, CHINA＿＿＿＿

(5)原产地证(表12.6)

表 12.6　原产地证

ORIGINAL

1. Goods consigned from (Exporter's business name, address, country) HONGDA TRADING CO., LTD 224 JINLIN ROAD, NANJING, CHINA	Reference No. GENERALIZED SYSTEM OF PREFERENCES CERTIFICATE OF ORIGIN (Combined declaration and certificate)
2. Goods consigned to (Consignee's name, address, country) WAV GENEAL TRADING CO., LTD 5-18 ISUKI-CHOHAKI, OSAKA, JAPAN	**FORM A** THE PEOPLE'S REPUBLIC OF CHINA Issued in _____ (country) See Notes overleaf
3. Means of transport and route (as far as known) FROM NANJING PORT, CHINA TO OSAKA PORT, JAPAN BY VESSEL	4. For official use

5. Item number	6. Marks and numbers of packages	7. Number and kind of packages; description of goods	8. Origin criterion (see Notes overleaf)	9. Gross weight or other quantity	10. Number and date of invoices
1	ITOCHU OSAKA NO. 1-200	TWO HUNDRED (200) CTNS OF LADIES' GARMENTS * * * * * * * * * * * * * *	"P"	2000 PCS	SH25586 APR. 20,2021

11. Certification It is hereby certified, on the basis of control carried out, that the declaration by the exporter is correct.	12. Declaration by the exporter The undersigned hereby declares that the above details and statements are correct, that all the goods were produced in ___**CHINA**___ (country) and that they comply with the origin requirements specified for those goods in the Generalized System of Preferences for goods exported to **JAPAN** ---
NANJING, JIANGSU APR. 20, 2021 --- Place and date, signature and stamp of certifying authority	NANJING, JIANGSU APR. 20, 2021 --- Place and date, signature and stamp of authorized signatory

(6)受益人证明(表 12.7)

表 12.7 受益人证明

HONGDA TRADING CO. , LTD
224 JINLIN ROAD, NANJING, CHINA
CERTIFICATE

To: WAV GENEAL TRADING CO. , LTD
5-18 ISUKI-CHOHAKI, OSAKA, JAPAN

Invoice No. ： SH25586
Date： 2021- 4-20

WE CERTIFY THAT THE ORIGIAL INVOICE AND PACKING LIST HAVE BEEN DISPATCHED TO THE APPLICANT BY COURIER SERVICE 2 DAYS BEFORE SHIPMENT.

(7)汇票(表 12.8)

表 12.8 汇票

BILL OF EXCHANGE

| 凭 Drawn under | THE ROYAL BANK, TOKYO | 不可撤销信用证 Irrevocable L/C No. | JST-AB12 |

日期 Date　APRIL 5, 2021

号码 No.　SH25586　汇票金额 Exchange for　USD10300.00

支取 Payable with interest@　%　按　息　付款

南京 Nanjing　MAY 20, 2021

见票　******　at　sight of this FIRST of exchange (Second of exchange

日后(本汇票之副本未付)付交

Being unpaid) Pay to the order of　BANK OF CHINA, NANJING BRANCH

金额 the sum of　U.S. DOLLARS TEN THOUSAND AND THREE HUNDRED ONLY.

此致 To　THE ROYAL BANK, TOKYO

HONGDA TRADING CO., LTD
殷实
(Authorized Signature)

【实操训练】

1.阅读信用证,回答相关问题。

```
2021 OCT  01 09:18:11  LOGICAL TERMINAL  E102
MT S700   ISSUE OF A DOCUMENTARY CREDIT  PAGE  00001
FUNC  MSG700  UMR21881051
MSGACK DWS765I AUTH OK, KEY B202181689580FC5 , BKCHCNBJ RJHISARI RECORO
```

续表

BASIC HEADER	F 01	BKCHCNBJA940 0588 550628
APPLICATION HEADER	0 700	1057 071001 MIDLGB22B××× 7277 977367 071001 1557 N
		* MIDLAND BANK PLC
		* ITALY
USER HEADER	SERVICE CODE 103	
BANK. PRIORITY	113:	
MSG USER REF.	108:	
INFO. FROM CI	115:	
SEQUENCE OF TOTAL	* 27	1 / 1
FORM OF DOC. CREDIT	* 40A	IRREVOCABLE
DOC. CREDIT NUMBER*	20	MLC9067
DATE OF ISSUE	31C	211001
APPLICABLE RULE	* 40E	UCP LATEST VERSION
DATE/PLACE EXP.	* 31D	DATE 211115 PLACE CHINA
APPLICANT	* 50	UNIWORLD S. R. L
		VIAARZAGA 2820185
		MILANO, ITALY
BENEFICIARY	* 59	SUZHOU YONGDA TRADING CO. , LTD.
		15 DONGFANG ROAD, SUZHOU, JIANGSU, CHINA
AMOUNT	* 32B	CURRENCY USD AMOUNT 24000.00
AVAILABLE WITH/BY	* 41D	ANY BANK IN CHINA, BY NEGOTIATION
DRAFTS AT ...	42C	90 DAYS AFTER SIGHT
DRAWEE	42D	ISSUING BANK
PARTIAL SHIPMTS	43P	NOT ALLOWED
TRANSSHIPMENT	43T	ALLOWED
PORT OF LOADING	44E	SHANGHAI, CHINA
PORT OF DISCHARGE	44F	MILANO, ITALY
LATEST SHIPMENT	44C	211030
GOODS DESCRIPT.	45A	

40MT OF MANGANESE SULPHATE（硫酸锰）SPECIFICATION: ASSAY 96 PERCENT MINIMUM $MnSO_4.H_2O$ 96 PERCENT MINIMUM AT PRICE OF USD600.00/MTCIF MILANO, ITALY PACKED IN BAGS OF 1 MT EACH.

DOCUMENTS REQUIRED: 46A

+ ORIGINAL COMMERCIAL INVOICE IN QUADRUPLICATE.

+ FULL SET (3/3) OF CLEAN ON BOARD OCEAN BILLS OF LADING (BEARING CONTAINER NUMBERS) CONSIGNED TO ORDER, ENDORSED IN BLANK, MARKED 'FREIGHT PREPAID' EVIDENCING UNIWORLD S. R. L VIAARZAGA 28 20185 MILANO ITALY AS NOTIFY PARTY.

+ PACKING LIST IN QUADRUPLICATE.

+ MARINE INSURANCE POLICY OR CERTIFICATE FOR FULL INVOICE VALUE PLUS 10% COVERING ALL RISKS AND WAR RISKS FROM WAREHOUSE TO WAREHOUSE UP TO MILANO ITALY INCLUDING SRCC CLAUSE AS PER PICC 1/1/1981.

+ CERTIFICATE OF ORIGIN ISSUED BY THE CHINA COUNCIL FOR THE PROMOTION OF INTERNATIONAL TRADE.

+ INSPECTION CERTIFICATE OF QUALITY ISSUED BY CCIB.

+ ORIGINAL BENEFICIARY'S CERTIFICATE STATING THAT ONE FULL SET OF ALL COPY DOCUMENTS HAVE BEEN SENT TO UNIWORLD S. R. L. BY COURIER WITHIN 2 DAYS AFTER SHIPMENT.

+ SHIPPING ADVICE SHOWING THE NAME OF CARRYING VESSEL, DATE OF SHIPMENT, MARKS, QUANTITY, NET WEIGHT /GROSS WEIGHT AND MEASUREMENT OF THE SHIPMENT TO THE APPLICANT.

ADDITIONAL CONDITION： 47A

+ ALL DOCUMENTS MUST BEAR THIS CREDIT NO. DATE AND THE NAME OF ISSUING BANK.

+ A DISCREPANCY FEE OF USD50. 00 WILL BE IMPOSED ON EACH SET OF DOCUMENTS PRESENTED FOR NEGOTIATION UNDER THIS L/C WITH DISCREPANCY. THE FEE WILL BE DEDUCTED FROM THE BILL AMOUNT.

CHARGES   71B

ALL BANKING CHARGES ARE FOR THE ACCOUNT OF BENEFICIARY

CONFIRMAT INSTR   *49   WITHOUT

INS PAYING BANK   78

UPON RECEIPT OF DOCUMENTS PRESENTED IN ACCORDANCE WITH THE DOCUMENTARY CREDIT TERMS AND CONDITIONS WE WILL REMIT PROCEEDS AT MATURITY IN ACCORDANCE WITH YOUR INSTRUCTIONS. REIMBURSEMENT IS SUBJECT TO ICC URR 525

SEND REC INFO   72

DOCUMENTS TO BE DESPATCHED IN ONE LOT BY COURIER. To：MIDLAND BANK PLC, TRADE SERVICES, MILANO, INTERNATIONAL BRANCH, PO BOX 585, 4TH FLOOR, 6 ARTHUR STREET, MILANO ITALY

(1)信用证的号码是(   )。

(2)信用证的开证日期是(   )。

(3)40E APPLICABLE RULE(适用的惯例):UCP LATEST VERSION,理解为本信用证适用的惯例是(   )。

(4)信用证的开证申请人和受益人是(   )。

(5)信用证金额是(   )。

(6)信用证的有效期和到期地点是(   )。

(7)信用证汇票付款期限是(   )。

(8)信用证的付款行是(   )。

(9)信用证的最迟装运期是(   )。

(10)信用证对提单的要求是(   )。

(11)信用证未规定交单期,按《UCP600》理解为交单期是(   )。

(12)信用证规定原产地证书由谁签发? (   )

(13)信用证关于费用负担的规定是否合理? 为什么? (   )

2. 根据上述信用证及下面相关资料制作海运出口货物代运委托书、装船通知和受益人证明。

相关资料：
①INVOICE NO.：YD210068
②S/C NO.：YD20210910
③B/L NO.：CP00615429
④GROSS WEIGHT：42000.00 KGS
⑤MEASUREMENT：86.522 CBM
⑥OCEAN VESSEL：KANGKE V.36
⑦MARKS：N/M
⑧S/C NO.：YD20210910
⑨装船日期：2021 年 10 月 20 日
⑩委托日期：2021 年 10 月 6 日
⑪授权签字人：张浩
（1）托运单。

海运出口货物代运委托书

委托编号（Entrusting Serial）	提单号（B/L No.）	合同号（Contract No.）	委托日期（Entrusting Date）
发货人名称地址（Shipper's Full Name and Address）			
收货人名称地址（Consignee's Full Name and Address）			
通知方名称地址（Notify Party's Full Name and Address）			

装货港（Port of Loading）	目的港（Port of Destination）		船名（Vessel） 航次（Voy.）
唛头标记 （Marks & No.）	包装件数及种类 （No. & Kind of Packages）	货物说明 （Description of Goods）	重量 （Weight in KGS）	体积 （Measurement in CBM）
装船日期（Loading Date）	可否转船（Transshipment）		可否分批（Partial Shipment）
结汇日期（L/C Expiry Date）	提单份数（Copies of B/L）	正本（Original）	副本（Copy）
运费及支付地点（Freight Payable at）			
备注（Remarks）：			

续表

委托人签字(Entrusting Party Signature): 张三 地址(Address): 苏州市东方路 15 号 电话(Telephone): 0512-86712345	代理人签字(Agent Signature):CHINA NATIONAL FOREIGN TRADE TRANSPORTATION CORP. JIANGSU BRANCH 地址(Address):NO.56 SHUANGLAN ROAD SUZHOU,CHINA 电话(Telephone):0512-86732761

（2）装船通知。

装 船 通 知
SHIPPING ADVICE

1. 出口商 Exporter	4. 发票号 Invoice No.	
	5. 合同号 Contract No.	6. 信用证号 L/C No.
2. 进口商 Importer	7. 运输单证号 Transport document No.	
	8. 价值 Value	
3. 运输事项 Transport details	9. 装运口岸和日期 Port and date of shipment	
10. 运输标志和集装箱号码 Shipping marks；Container No.	11. 包装类型及件数；商品名称或编码；商品描述 Number and kind of packages；Commodity No.；Commodity description	
	12. 出口商签章 Exporter stamp and signature	

（3）受益人证明。

苏州永达贸易有限公司
SUZHOU YONGDA TRADING CO., LTD.
15 DONGFANG ROAD, SUZHOU, JIANGSU, CHINA

BENEFICIARY'S CERTIFICATE

SUZHOU YONGDA TRADING CO., LTD.

张浩

3. 根据所给资料审核并修改已填制错误的发票、产地证。

信用证范例。

27：1/1
40A：IRREVOCABLE
20：01CR3122/4039141
31C：210913
40E：UCP LATEST VERSION
31D：211016 CHINA
50：S. O. C. C.   S. P. A.
CORSO EUROPA 29-LOC ZINGONIA
260840 VERDELLINO BG
ITALY
59：JIANGSU WANDA   IMPORT AND EXPORT   CO. LTD.
255 YUNNAN ROAD
NANJING   CHINA
32B：USD151078. 50
39B：NOT EXCEEDING
41A：BCITITMMI40
BY PAYMENT
43P：NOT ALLOWED
43T：NOT ALLOWED
44E：SHANGHAI PORT CHINA
44F：GENOVA PORT ITALY
44C：210925
45A：2 SETS OF ESCALATORS(自动扶梯) A2T-30CC-10-10070
AS PER CONTRACT NO. 444280 DATED 08/19/2021 (TYPE D, 130-131)
TOTAL AMOUNT USD 151070. 00 MAX. EX WORK NANJING CHINA
46A：1) COMMERCIAL INVOICE IN 1 ORIGINAL AND TWO COPIES DULY SIGNED
    2) FULL SET CLEAN ON BOARD ORIGINAL OCEAN BILL OF LADING ISSUED TO ORDER, BLANK ENDORSED, NOTIFY APPLICANT
    3) CERTIFICATE OF ORIGIN ISSUED BY CHAMBER OF COMMERCE IN CHINA, PROVING CHINESE ORIGIN OF THE GOODS.
47A：ALL DOC SHOWING L/C NO.
71B：ALL COMMISSIONS AND CHARGES OUTSIDE ITALY ARE FOR BENEFICIARY'S ACCOUNT
48：WITHIN 21 DAYS AFTER SHIPMENT DATE BUT WITHIN VALIDITY OF THE CREDIT
49：WITHOUT
78：1) IN REIMBURSEMENT：UPON RECEIPT OF DOCUMENTS AT OUR COUNTERS IN CONFORMITY WITH ALL CREDIT TERMS AND CONDITIONS WE SHALL CREDIT YOU AS PER YOUR INSTRUCTIONS.
    2) DOCS MUST BE SENT TO OUR FOLLOWING ADDRESS BY COURIER SERVICE：INTESA SANPAOLO SPA-PIAZZA CAMERONI NR. 2 -24047 TREVIGLIO (BG) ITALY
相关资料：
发票号：55667
装船日期：2021 年 5 月 15 日
开船日期：2021 年 5 月 15 日

G. W：5850 KGS
N. W：5680 KGS
MEASUREMENT：23.43 CBM
NO. OF PACKAGES：200 CARTONS
船名、航次号：CIM67 V.123S
提单号码：CIM8800654
集装箱号/封号：YMU259654/56789
运输标记：N/M
授权签字人：张久
TOTAL PACKED IN 200 CARTON
G. W：5850 KGS
N. W：5680 KGS
MEASUREMENT：23.43 CBM

发 票
JIANGSU WANDA I/E CO. LTD
NANJING, CHINA
INVOICE

To：	TO ORDER			

		Invoice No.：	55667
		Invoice Date：	20210807
		S/C No.：	444280
		S/C Date：	20210819

From： SHANGHAI PORT

To： GENOVA PORT

Letter of Credit No.： 01CR312214039141

Issued By：INTESA SANPAOLO SPA

Marks and Numbers	Number and Kind of Package Description of Goods	Quantity	Unit Price	Amount
	ESCALATORS MOD. "ANLEV" COD. A2T-30CC-10-10070 FOB NANJING CHINA	1 SET	USD151070.00	USD151070.00
			TOTAL：	USD151070.00

SAY TOTAL：U.S. DOLLARS ONE HUNDRED AND FIFTY ONE THOUSAND AND SEVENTY ONLY

产地证

1. Exporter WANDA IMPORT AND EXPORT CO. LTD. 255 YUNNAN ROAD NANJING, JIANGSU CHINA	Certificate No. 1234567
	CERTIFICATE OF ORIGIN **OF** **THE PEOPLE'S REPUBLIC OF CHINA**
2. Consignee TO ORDER	
3. Means of transport and route FROM SHANGHAI PORT CHINA TO GENOVA PORT ITALY BY SEA	5. For certifying authority use only
4. Country / region of destination CHINA	

6. Marks and numbers	7. Number and kind of packages; description of goods	8. H. S. Code	9. Quantity	10. Number and date of invoices
NON-APPLICABLE	200 CARTONS OF ANLEV' COD	851000000	200	CIM8800654

SAY TOTAL TWO HUNDRED CARTONS ONLY	05- 07- 2021

| 11. Declaration by the exporter
The undersigned hereby declares that the above details and statements are correct, that all the goods were produced in China and that they comply with the Rules of Origin of the People's Republic of China.

JIANGSU ENTRY-EXIT INSPECTION AND QUARANTINE BUREAU
THE PEOPLE'S REPUBLIC OF CHINA

20210508, NANJING

Place and date, signature and stamp of authorized signatory | 12. Certification
It is hereby certified that the declaration by the exporter is correct.

JIANGSU WANDA IMPORT AND EXPORT CO. LTD.

20210518, NANJING

Place and date, signature and stamp of certifying authority |

附　录

1. 代理报关委托书

代　理　报　关　委　托　书

编号：00128617703

我单位现 　　　（A 逐票、B 长期）委托贵公司代理 　　　等通关事宜。(A、填单申报 B、辅助查验 C、垫缴税款 D、办理海关证明联 E、审批手册 F、核销手册 G、申办减免税手续 H、其他) 详见《委托报关协议》。

我单位保证遵守《海关法》和国家有关法规，保证所提供的情况真实、完整、单货相符，否则，愿承担相关法律责任。

本委托书有效期自签字之日起至 　　年　月　日止。

委托方（盖章）：

法定代表人或其授权签署《代理报关委托书》的人（签字）

委　托　报　关　协　议

为明确委托报关具体事项和各自责任，双方经平等协商签定协议如下：

委托方		被委托方		
主要货物名称		*报关单编码	No.	
HS 编码	☐☐☐☐☐☐☐☐☐☐	收到单证日期	年 月 日	
货物总价		收到单证情况	合同☐	发票☐
进出口日期	年　月　日		装箱清单☐	提（运）单☐
提单号			加工贸易手册☐	许可证件☐
贸易方式			其他	
原产地/货源地		报关收费	人民币	元
其他要求：		承诺说明：		

背面所列通用条款是本协议不可分割的一部分，对本协议的签署构成了对背面通用条款的同意。	背面所列通用条款是本协议不可分割的一部分，对本协议的签署构成了对背面通用条款的同意。
委托方业务签章：	被委托方业务签章：
经办人签章： 联系电话：	经办报关员签章： 联系电话： 年 月 日

中国报关协会监制

（白联：海关留存、黄联：被委托方留存、红联：委托方留存）

CCBA

2. 出口许可证网上申请表

您当前的操作：查看　　　　出口许可证申请表

申请表状态	已打印	审核日期	20100104

审核意见　2020年01月04日初审通过；2020年01月04日复审通过；

2010　配额年度许可证

出口商代码	340073303593X	申请表号	10340073303693X600000
发货人代码	340073303593X >>	出口许可证有效截止日期	20100208 ...
贸易方式	一般贸易	进口国（地区）	HK >>
合同号	***	付款方式	汇付
报关口岸	5300 >>	运输方式	海运、陆运
商品代码	0102900090 >>	名称	非改良种用其他牛

规格、等级	数量 头	单价 币别	总价
		港元	
	18	6000	108000
合计	18		108000

备注：最多32汉字

非一批一证	是否一批一证　○是　◉否

发证机构	商务部驻深圳特办	最终用户证明书编号	
联系人	黄超	部门代码 00	申请人 ALGJ
联系电话	13602564813	申请日期 20100104	份数 1
批复单号			

如果商品是监控化学品、易制毒化学品、臭氧层物质三种商品时，该项必须录入
附加说明信息

商穗特配调C字【2009】095号

关　闭

3. 出口许可证

<table>
<tr><td colspan="2" rowspan="2">中华人民共和国出口许可证
EXPORT LICENCE OF THE PEOPLE'S REPUBLIC OF CHINA</td><td colspan="3">No.8514299</td></tr>
<tr></tr>
<tr>
<td colspan="2">1. 出口商：
Exporter　　　3400678943053
安徽安粮实业发展有限公司</td>
<td colspan="3">3. 出口许可证号：
Export licence No.

11-AD-700401</td>
</tr>
<tr>
<td colspan="2">2. 发货人：
Consignor　　　3400678943053
安徽安粮实业发展有限公司</td>
<td colspan="3">4. 出口许可证有效截止日期：
Export licence expiry date

2021年12月15日</td>
</tr>
<tr>
<td colspan="2">5. 贸易方式：
Terms of trade　　　一般贸易</td>
<td colspan="3">8. 进口国（地区）：巴林
Country/Region of purchase</td>
</tr>
<tr>
<td colspan="2">6. 合同号：
Contract No.　　AFHX2011-080</td>
<td colspan="3">9. 付款方式：
Payment　　　　　托收</td>
</tr>
<tr>
<td colspan="2">7. 报关口岸：
Place of clearance　　大连海关</td>
<td colspan="3">10. 运输方式：
Mode of transport　　海上运输</td>
</tr>
<tr>
<td colspan="2">11. 商品名称：
Description of goods　冻的不带骨鸡块(包括鸡胸脯、鸡大腿等)</td>
<td colspan="3">商品编码：
Code of goods　0207141900</td>
</tr>
<tr>
<td>12. 规格、等级
Specification</td>
<td>13. 单位
Unit</td>
<td>14. 数量
Quantity</td>
<td>15. 单价（USD）
Unit price</td>
<td>16. 总值（USD）
Amount</td>
<td>17. 总值折美元
Amount in USD</td>
</tr>
<tr><td></td><td>千克</td><td>*400,000.0</td><td>*2.6300</td><td>*1,052,000</td><td>$1,052,000</td></tr>
<tr><td></td><td></td><td></td><td></td><td></td><td></td></tr>
<tr><td></td><td></td><td></td><td></td><td></td><td></td></tr>
<tr>
<td>18. 总　计
Total</td>
<td>千克</td>
<td>*400,000.0</td>
<td></td>
<td>*1,052,000</td>
<td>$1,052,000</td>
</tr>
<tr>
<td colspan="3">19. 备　注
Supplementary details

非一批一证</td>
<td colspan="3">20. 发证机关签章
Issuing authority's stamp & signature</td>
</tr>
</table>

4. 自动进口网上申请表

您当前的操作：浏览申请表　　　　　　　自动进口许可证申请表

状态	待复审	审核日期	20100226

审核意见 2010年02月25日初审通过。

2010 年度许可证

申请进口单位	340073303693X	申请表号	10340073303693X600135
	安徽安粮国际发展有限公司	进口商	340073303593X
进口用户			安徽安粮国际发展有限公司
进口用户名称	安徽安粮国际发展有限公司		
贸易方式	一般贸易	外汇来源	银行购汇
贸易国（地区）1	US 美国	贸易国（地区）2	
原产地国（地区）1	US 美国	原产地国（地区）2	
原产地国（地区）3		原产地国（地区）4	
报关口岸1	5200	拟关口岸	
有效截止日期	20100824	预计到晚日期	20100302
商品用途	内销		
商品代码1	0404100000	名称1	乳清及改性乳清，不论是否浓缩、加糖或其他物质
商品代码2		名称2	
商品代码3		名称3	
商品代码4		名称4	

规格、型号	数量 千克	单价 币别 美元	总价
	100000	1.05	105000
合计	100000		105000

备注（最多32个汉字）

是否国营贸易

是否统一证 ●是 ○否
是否保税仓库货物 ○是 ●否

是否异地领证 ○是 ●否　　异地出证机构
注意：异地出证机构即是签打证机构，不能和发证（审核）机构相同

发证机构	安徽省商务厅	份数	1
申请日期	20100224	部门代码	00	申请人	ALGJ

与本次申请有关的其他资料

联系人	张旋	今年已进口报关数量（吨）	914.90
联系电话	2831027	上年进口数量（吨）	8325.80
缮证时间	20100113	进口合同号	AU100642

附加说明信息

英 阳

5. 自动进口许可证

中华人民共和国自动进口许可证
AUTOMATIC IMPORT LICENCE OF THE PEOPLE'S REPUBLIC OF CHINA No. 1697010

1. 进口商: Importer	340073303593X	3. 自动进口许可证号: Automatic import licence No.		
安徽安粮国际发展股份有限公司		09-12-W31955		
2. 进口用户: Consignee	340073303593X	4. 自动进口许可证有效截止日期: Automatic import licence expiry date		
安徽安粮国际发展股份有限公司		2009年12月31日		
5. 贸易方式: Terms of trade	一般贸易	8. 贸易国（地区）: Country/Region of exportation	美国	
6. 外汇来源: Terms of foreign exchange	银行购汇	9. 原产地国（地区）: Country/Region of origin	美国	
7. 报关口岸: Place of clearance	上海海关	10. 商品用途: Use of goods	内销	

11. 商品名称: Description of goods		商品编码: Code of goods 0207141100		商品状态: Status of goods
冻的带骨鸡块(包括鸡胸脯、鸡大腿等)				

12. 规格、型号 Specification	13. 单位 Unit	14. 数量 Quantity	15. 单价（ ） Unit Price USD	16. 总值（ ） Amount USD	17. 总值折美元 Amount in USD
	千克	*24,500.0	*1.3000	*31,850	$31,850
18. 总 计 Total	千克	*24,500.0		*31,850	$31,850

19. 备 注: Supplementary details	20. 发证机关签章: Issuing authority's stamp
	（自动进口许可专用章 安徽）
	21. 发证日期: Licence date 2009年12月12日

第二联 （存本） 银行付汇凭证

6. 装货单

深圳港口国际集装箱运输标准单（新版）

D/R No. （编号）	SZCD3B 1639073
CWNSSZ100594	

Shipper （发货人）
安徽安粮国际发展股份有限公司

装货单
SHIPPING ORDER

第一联

Consignee （收货人）
POWERCASE ENNTERPRISE CO TLD

9323015
AA485W
E800121336
E00000A8ND8E0001

船代载单日期:2010-01-23 17:00
海关截关日期:2010-01-23 17:00
船代公司: 深圳市俊路国际船舶代理有限公司
报关公司: 深圳市锦裕报关有限公司
报关操作员 :LUCY1
联系人:王瑜 联系电话:075526690002

Notify Party （通知人）
SAME AS CONSIGNEE

Pre-carriage by （前程运输） Place of Receipt （收货地点）

Ocean Vessel（船名） Voy.No（航次） Port of Loading（装货港）
HS BACII AA4B5W MCT

Port of Discharge（卸货港） Place of Delivery （交货地点）
SANTOS

Final Destination for the Merchants Reference （目的地）
巴西

Container No. （集装号）	Seal No.（封志号） Marks & Nos. （标记与号码）	No.of containers or Pkgs （箱数或件数）	Kind of Packages; Description of Goods（包装种类与货名）	Gross Weight 毛重（公斤）	Measurement 尺码（立方米）
CCLU7002856/40购 01月21日		806 纸箱	音箱	8480KGS	

9323015

AA485W

EB00121336

TOTAL NUMBER OF CONTAINERS OR PACKAGES (IN WORDS) 集装箱数或件数合计（大写）	1x40HQ

FREIGHT & CHARGES （运费与附加费）	Revenue Tons（运费吨）	Rate（运费率）	Per（每）	Prepaid（运费预付）	Collect （到付）

Ex&ale. （见条款） Prepaid at（预付地点）	Payable al（到付地点）	Place of issue（签发地点）
Total Prepaid（预付总额）	No.of Original B(s)'L （正本提单份数）	

Service Type on Receiving ☐-CY,☐-CFS,☐-DOOR	Service Type on Delivery ☐-CY,☐-CFS,☐-DOOR	Reefer Temperature Required（冷藏温度）	°F
TYPE OF GOODS 种类	☐ Ordinary. （普通） ☐ Reefer. （冷藏） ☐ Dangerous. （危险品） ☐ Auto. （裸装专辑）	危险品	Class; Property; IMDG Code page. UN No.
	☐ Liquid （液体） ☐ Live Animal （活动物） ☐ Bulk （散物）		

可否转船 :	装船期 :	船舶代理人	海关
可否分批 :	结汇期 :		
FOB 金额 :		锦裕	
制单日期 :			

NK

本单由深圳船舶代理学会统一格式印制，翻版必究

7. 提单

8. 提货单

CHINA OCEAN SHIPPING AGENCY, SHANGHAI

进口集装箱货物提货单

DELIVERY ORDER

标记与集装箱号	货 名	集装箱数或件数	重量(KGS)	体积(M³)

9. 保险单

中国人民财产保险股份有限公司货物运输保险单

PICC PROPERTY AND CASUALTY COMPANY LIMITED CARGO TRANSPORTATION INSURANCE POLICY

总公司设于北京
Head Office Beijing

一九四九年创立
Established in 1949

AEYIEE2008Z01
印刷号 (Printed Number) 3400 1100002413
34001100002413

保险单号 (Policy No.) PYIE2011340193000001208

合同号 (Contract NO.)
发票号 (Invoice NO.) ALS15D11046
信用证号 (L/C NO.)
被保险人 (Insured): AHCOF INDUSTRIAL DEVELOPMENT CO., LTD.

中国人民财产保险股份有限公司 (以下简称本公司) 根据被保险人要求,以被保险人向本公司缴付约定的保险费为对价,按照本保
险单所列条款承保下述货物运输保险,特订立本保险单。
THIS POLICY OF INSURANCE WITNESSES THAT PICC PROPERTY AND CASUALTY COMPANY LIMITED(HEREINAFTER CALLED
"THE COMPANY")AT THE REQUEST OF THE INSURED AND IN CONSIDERATION OF THE AGREED PREMIUM PAID TO THE
COMPANY BY THE INSURED, UNDERTAKES TO INSURE THE UNDERMENTIONED GOODS IN TRANSPORTATION SUBJECT TO
THE CONDITIONS OF THIS POLICY AS PER THE CLAUSES PRINTED BELOW.

标记 MARKS&NOS.	包装及数量 QUANTITY	保险货物项目 GOODS	保险金额 AMOUNT INSURED
AS PER INVOICE NO. ALS15D11046	3520 BAGS	CHINESE LONG SHAPE WHITE KIDNEY BEANS	USD94,380.00

总保险金额:
Total Amount Insured : US DOLLARS NINETY FOUR THOUSAND THREE HUNDRED AND EIGHTY ONLY
AS ARRANGED

保费 (Premium) : HUI HONG 802 V.B531S
装载运输工具 (Per Conveyance) :

启运日期 (Date of Commencement) : May. 31, 2021

自
From HUANGPU CHINA

经
Via

到
To VALENCIA SPAIN

承保险别 (Conditions) :
COVERING ALL RISKS AS PER OCEAN MARINE CARGO CLAUSES (2009) OF THE
PICC PROPERTY AND CASUALTY COMPANY LIMITED.

10. 信用证通知书和信用证

安徽省分行
BANK OF CHINA ANHUI BRANCH

信 用 证 通 知 书

致： AHCOF INTERNATIONAL
DEVELOPMENT CO,LTD

通知编号： AD0886911001493

日期： 2021-04-28

送启者：

我行收到如下信用证一份：

开证行： Credit Industriel Et Commercial

开证日： 2011-04-27

信用证号： 00181011110808

金额： USD 34,793.55

现随附通知。贵司交单时，请将本通知书及正本信用证一并提示。其他注意事项如下：

本信用证之通知系遵循国际商会《跟单信用证统一惯例》第600号出版物。

如有任何问题及疑虑，请与中国银行股份有限公司联络。

电话： 传真

附言：

中国银行 安徽省分行
BANK OF CHINA ANHUI BRANCH

Eximbills Enterpriste Incoming Swift
===================================

Message Type:MT700
Send Bank:CMCIFRPPXXX

Recv Bank:BKCHCNBJ780

User Name:ah101042
Print Times:1
Print Date:2011-04-28 MTR:110427CMCIFRPPAXXX3319741070
===================================

:27:[Sequence of Total]
1/1
:40A:[Form of Documentary Credit]
IRREVOCABLE TRANSFERABLE
:20:[Documentary Credit Number]
00181011110808
:31C:[Date of Issue]
110427
:40E:[Applicable Rules]
UCP LATEST VERSION
:31D:[Date and Place of Expiry]
110601 CHINA
:50:[Applicant]

:59:[Beneficiary]
/00000187201151355
AHCOF INTERNATIONAL DEVELOPMENT
CO., LTD
13F, SUNON PLAZA NR 389-399 JINZHAI
RD, HEFEI ANHUI CHINA
:32B:[Currency Code, Amount]
USD34793,55
:39B:[Maximum Credit Amount]
NOT EXCEEDING
:41A:[Available With...By...]
BKCHCNBJ780
BY NEGOTIATION
:42C:[Drafts at...]
AT SIGHT
:42A:[Drawee]
CMCIFRPPXXX
:43P:[Partial Shipments]
PROHIBITED
:43T:[Transshipment]
ALLOWED
:44E:[Port of Loading/Airport of Departure]
NINGBO PORT IN CHINA

ADDRESS: 313 CHANGJIANG MIDDLE ROAD, HEFEI, ANHUI, CHINA
SWIFT CODE: BKCHCNBJ780

BANK OF CHINA ANHUI BRANCH

:44F:[Port of Discharge/Airport of Destination]
LE HAVRE PORT IN FRANCE
:44C:[Latest Date of Shipment]
110520
:45A:[Description of Goods and/or Services]
+ SHOES
+ DETAILS AS PER PROFORMA INVOICE NR 29110303 DATED 03MAR11
FOR LATEST SHIPMENT DATE ON THE 20MAY2011 TO BE SENT IN ONE LOT
.ORDER 133702 CAD CODE 6 003 081 1200 PRS AT USD 3.95/PR
.ORDER 134599 CAD CODE 9 002 011 1400 PRS AT USD 6.05/PR
.ORDER 134601 CAD CODE 9 002 012 2200 PRS AT USD 6.05/PR
.ORDER 136204 CAD CODE 9 003 005 1500 PRS AT USD 5.75/PR
(MENTION TO APPEAR ON COMMERCIAL INVOICE)
F O B NINGBO PORT IN CHINA
AS PER INCOTERMS 2010 OF ICC PARIS
:46A:[Documents Required]
+ ORIGINAL AND 4 COPIES OF DATED AND SIGNED COMMERCIAL INVOICE
BEARING THE MENTION 'DETAILS AS PER PROFORMA INVOICE
29110303 DATED 03MAR2011' AND EVIDENCING DEDUCTION OF ONE PER
CENT DISCOUNT AND THE INCOTERM FOB NINGBO
+ ORIGINAL AND 4 COPIES OF PACKING LIST (ONE PACKING LIST PER
CONTAINER IN CASE OF FULL CONTAINER LOADING), INDICATING
IMPERATIVELY THE TYPE OF CONTAINER(S) USED, CONTAINER NUMBER(S),
DETAILS PER PACKAGE (EXACT NET AND GROSS WEIGHTS IN KILOS PER
PACKAGE, EXACT VOLUME PER PACKAGE AS WELL AS TOTAL VOLUME AND
TOTAL WEIGHTS IN KILOS, AND MENTIONING ORDER AND CODE NUMBER
+ FULL SET OF ON BOARD ORIGINAL OCEAN BILLS OF LADING, MADE OUT
TO ORDER AND BLANK ENDORSED, ISSUED BY _____ _____
CO. LTD (AS CARRIER OR AS AGENT FOR A NAMED CARRIER),
NOTIFY ___ __ ___ __ __, __ _ _____, ___ _ __ __ __
_____ ____, FRANCE, ALSO NOTIFY ___ __ __ __ _ ____, _ ___ __
____ _____ ____ ____ _____ __ _____ _____ AND MARKED
FREIGHT COLLECT. ANY ADDED ON BOARD NOTATION MUST BE SIGNED BY
THE CARRIER, THE CAPTAIN OR THE AGENT
+ ORIGINAL AND ONE COPY OF DOCUMENT ENTITLED 'CERTIFICATE OF
CONFORMITY' ISSUED AND SIGNED BY THE BENEFICIARY, CONFIRMING THAT
HE ACCEPTS THE TERMS OF THE DOCUMENT REGARDING THE REACH
REGULATION THAT HE RECEIVED FROM ___ _____
.HE MUST CERTIFY THAT HE DID NOT USE SUBSTANCES AND DYEING STUFFS
MENTIONED ON PAGE 1 AND 2 OF THE DOCUMENT IN ANY OF THE ARTICLE
MENTIONED ABOVE.
.HE MUST IMPLICATE HIS RESPONSIBILITY IN CASE OF NON-RESPECT OF
COMMUNITY USANCES AND ENGAGE HIMSELF TO FREE ___ FROM ANY
JUDICIARY ACTION, FROM ANY SENTENCE CONCERNING CONSUMER HEALTH
OR/AND ADMINISTRATION (CUSTOMS AND ANY OTHER AUTHORITIES
CONCERNED)
+ ORIGINAL AND ONE COPY OF BENEFICIARY'S ATTESTATION CERTIFYING
THAT EVERY ARTICLE BEARS A LABEL INDICATING THE PICTOGRAM OF
COMPOSITION AND THE CONVENTIONAL IDENTIFICATION NUMBER 1335
+ ORIGINAL AND ONE COPY OF CERTIFICATE ISSUED AND SIGNED BY THE
MANUFACTURER INDICATING THE COUNTRY OF ORIGIN OF ALL THE RAW
MATERIALS UTILIZED FOR THE PRODUCTION OF EVERY ARTICLE AND
INDICATING THE PLACE OF ASSEMBLING FOR EVERY ARTICLE

ADDRESS: 313 CHANGJIANG MIDDLE ROAD, HEFEI, ANHUI, CHINA
SWIFT CODE: BKCHCNBJ780

中国银行 安徽省分行
BANK OF CHINA ANHUI BRANCH

+ ORIGINAL AND ONE COPY OF CERTIFICATE SIGNED BY BENEFICIARY
CONFIRMING THAT ONE COPY OF ALL DOCUMENTS HAVE BEEN SENT BY
SPEED MAIL DIRECTLY TO ? ___ ___ ? WITHIN 10 DAYS AFTER
SHIPMENT DATE. (AND SPEED MAIL RECEIPT DULY DATED MUST BE JOINED)
:47A:[Additional Conditions]
+ THE FULL ADRESS OF ? ___ ___D, NINGBO BRANCH IS:
RM ___ ___ ___ ___ ___ ___ ___ ___
___ ___ ___ ___ ___
CONTACT: CARRIE ___ CARRIE. ___ ? AT ? ___ ___.CN
+ INSURANCE COVERED BY THE BUYERS
+ ALL DOCUMENTS TO BE SENT TO US IN ONE LOT
+ THE BANK OF CHINA IS ALLOWED TO TRANSFER THIS L/C AND MUST
ADVISE US BY AUTHENTICATED SWIFT MESSAGE FOR EACH TRANSFER
EFFECTED MENTIONING BENEFICIARY'S NAME AND ADDRESS
+ ALL DOCUMENTS TO BE ISSUED IN ENGLISH
+FOR EACH SET OF DOCUMENTS, BENEFICIARY'S CERTIFICATE CONFIRMING
THEIR ACCEPTANCE AND/OR NON-ACCEPTANCE OF ALL THE AMENDMENTS MADE
UNDER THIS CREDIT QUOTING THE RELEVANT AMENDMENT NUMBER IS
REQUIRED. IF THIS CREDIT HAS NOT BEEN AMENDED, SUCH CERTIFICATE
IS NOT REQUIRED
+ IF DISCREPANCIES ON DOCUMENTS CHARGES FOR EUR 100 OR
EQUIVALENT ARE FOR BENEFICIARY S ACCOUNT AND WILL BE
DEDUCTED FROM SETTLEMENT
+ DOCUMENTS MUST BE SENT TO US PER DHL OR ANY OTHER RAPID
COURIER SERVICE TO CIC BANQUES, SERVICE CREDITS
DOCUMENTAIRES, 33 AVENUE LE CORBUSIER, 59000 LILLE, FRANCE
+ AN EXTRA PHOTOCOPY OF ALL DOCUMENTS IS REQUIRED FOR
ISSUING BANK. EUR 10 WILL BE DEDUCTED FROM OUR PAYMENT
IF THIS CONDITION IS NOT RESPECTED.
+ THE AMOUNT OF ANY PRESENTATION UNDER THIS CREDIT MUST BE
ENDORSED BY PRESENTING BANK ON THE ORIGINAL L/C ADVICE. THE
PRESENTING BANK SIGNIFIES THAT THE ENDORSEMENT HAS BEEN MADE BY
MAKING A PRESENTATION.
:71B:[Charges]
ALL ABROAD BANKING CHARGES AND OUR
CABLE CHARGES ARE FOR BENEFICIARY
ACCOUNT. IF ANY NON UTILIZATION OR
CANCELLATION ART 37C UCP 600 NOT
APPLICABLE
:48:[Period for Presentation]
12 DAYS
:49:[Confirmation Instructions]
WITHOUT
:78:[Instructions to the Paying/Accepting/Negotiating Bank]
FOR REIMBURSEMENT AT RECEIPT OF CONFORMABLE DOCUMENTS AT OUR
COUNTERS WE SHALL COVER THE PRESENTING BANK THROUGH THEIR USD
CORRESPONDENT.
:57D:["Advise through" Bank]
BANK OF CHINA
155, CHANGJIANG ROAD
HEFEI
CHINA

ADDRESS: 313 CHANGJIANG MIDDLE ROAD. HEFEI, ANHUI, CHINA
SWIFT CODE: BKCHCNBJ780

参考文献

［1］全国国际商务单证专业培训考试办公室.国际商务单证理论与实务［M］.北京：
中国商务出版社,2022.